Wedding I
Signal Box Café

Annette Hannah is a Liver Bird who relocated to leafy Hertfordshire in the 80s and now lives near a river with her husband, two of their three grown up children and a crazy black cocker spaniel. She writes romantic comedies in settings inspired by the beautiful countryside around her and always with a nod to her hometown.

She worked in marketing for many years as a qualified marketeer which she loved as it tapped into her creative side.

As an avid reader, she began to review the books she read, became a book blogger and eventually plucked up the courage to fulfil her life-long dream of writing a book.

For four years she was a member of the Romantic Novelists' Association's new writers' scheme, during which time she wrote a book a year. After signing a two-book deal with Orion Dash in 2020 she graduated to full member of the organisation and is also their Press Officer.

She loves long walks along the river, travelling to far flung places and spending time with her friends and family.

You can follow her on
twitter @annettehannah
www.sincerelybookangels.blogspot.com
www.annettehannah.com

Also by Annette Hannah

The Cosy Little Cupcake Van

Wedding Bells at the Signal Box Café

Annette Hannah

This edition first published in Great Britain in 2021 by Orion Dash,
an imprint of The Orion Publishing Group Ltd.,
Carmelite House, 50 Victoria Embankment
London EC4Y 0DZ

An Hachette UK Company

A CIP catalogue record for this book is
available from the British Library.

ISBN (Paperback) 978 1 3987 0813 6
ISBN (eBook) 978 1 3987 0087 1

www.orionbooks.co.uk

This book is dedicated to my Guardian Angels: my beloved mum Irene, and my Nana and Grandad, Peggy and Danny Young. I wish you were all here to share my special moment, but you will live on forever in my heart.

Prologue

Perfectly timed cherry blossom petals fell softly from the branches overhead like pale pink snowflakes. Delicately dancing on a light breeze, they performed their swansong, flitting and swirling before settling like nature's confetti in the bride and groom's hair.

The air was filled with a chorus of songbirds, chirping cheerily, each species with their own individual tune. It was joyful, the sound of happiness and calm.

The photographer danced around the couple, her camera clicking and whirring as it captured every beautiful detail.

'And now can we please have one of the groom kissing the bride?' she requested, squinting as her perfectionist's eye scrutinised the images on the screen at the back of the camera. The bride blushed profusely; her cheeks as flushed as the wild pink roses entwined in her golden curls. But the groom, whose handsome face looked serious throughout the photos, perked up. His steely grey eyes opened wider as he gazed at the bride's beautiful pink glossed lips.

'This is the last one,' he said before sliding his hand up into her hair at the side of her neck and pressing his lips against hers. His thumb gently stroked her perfectly contoured cheek. After a second or two the bride melted into his kiss and the photographer captured the money shot. The kiss that continued long after she had finished clicking was perfect. The cheeky pageboy sticking his tongue out and the big shaggy dog biting the groom's trouser leg and growling with all his might as if to say, 'get off my mummy,' added an extra charm to some of the shots.

When the pageboy noticed what they were doing he couldn't contain his disgust and uttered a loud 'Ew,' the groom abruptly stopped kissing the bride and faced the photographer.

'That's it, sis, we're quits now. No more favours and definitely no more fake wedding shoots.' And loosening his tie whilst licking his lips, he stalked off to his open-topped convertible, which was parked just yards away, but not before handing the bride a folded piece of paper that he retrieved from inside his jacket pocket.

'Here's the cleaning bill for my car – thankfully the stains did come out, but it was touch and go.'

The bride was still reeling from the kiss, her fingers pressed against her lips, which felt swollen still from his touch. She looked at her fingertips, at the spots of rose lip gloss. She had noticed as he walked away that his lips also shone with evidence of what had just taken place between them. She didn't particularly like this man, but that kiss had turned her insides upside down. She breathed in deeply; she could still smell his aftershave on her, a tantalising mix of citrus and cedar wood. Her heart wasn't just racing; it felt like it was taking part in a full-on sports day and was currently doing hurdles. She had never been kissed like that before but boy did that man make her mad.

Chapter 1

Two months earlier

After a four-hour drive that should only have taken two, Lucy's whole body sighed with relief when she saw the sign for the quaint little market town. The beeping of the level crossing combined with the red flashing lights and barriers brought memories flooding back. Having spent many happy summers with Nana and Grandad as a child she was eager for her son Jackson to experience the joys of Bramblewood for himself.

The hailstorm wasn't quite the welcome she'd hoped for. Her ancient red Mini, already groaning with the weight of their entire collection of belongings and a large shaggy dog of indeterminate breed, was now being pelted by a barrage of frozen rain. Jackson stared open-mouthed at the downpour. Lucy closed her eyes and took a calming breath. She hoped this wasn't a bad sign as having given up her flat, her job and enrolled Jackson into the local school she had a lot riding on this move.

Lucy hadn't hesitated when her parents suggested she stay at her grandad's house whilst he recuperated in a nursing home. The timing had been perfect as she and Jackson needed a fresh start and if it hadn't been here it would have been somewhere else. At least this way they could see her grandad and Jackson could get to know him better.

Whilst sheltering in the car Lucy checked her phone messages; there was just one from an unknown number. She popped her earphones in and pressed play. Listening to it she yelped involuntarily, and clasped her hand over her mouth. 'Oh my gosh!' she muttered through her fingers.

'What is it, Mummy?' Jackson wrestled one of his dinosaurs out of Baxter's mouth.

Lucy smiled. 'That was a lady called Joy and she has asked me to plan her wedding in just a month. She's my first official client for my new business and what an exciting challenge that will be.' She looked at the background picture of her home screen: she in graduation cap and gown, cuddling a smiling Jackson.

Studying online for her Event Management Degree whilst working full time in the hotel and bringing up her son had been no mean feat. But now she had both experience and qualifications, she was bubbling with excitement to start her dream business. A shiver of apprehension ran down her spine to bring her back down to earth. It wouldn't all be plain sailing. She no longer had a regular source of income and with only a month's worth of savings in the bank, she needed to start earning straight away. Thankfully, her grandad insisted on her staying there rent-free, which would make things a lot easier.

As soon as the hail stopped, Lucy got out of the car and stretched her legs. The familiar structure that once housed the signal box towered in front of Grandad's house and the railway track. She helped Jackson out and showed him the neglected building, paint flaking off the rotten wooden fascia boards, windows all boarded up.

'See up there.' She directed Jackson's gaze to the top floor of the building. He blinked as a huge raindrop bypassed his glasses and splashed into his eye. 'That's where Grandad used to work – he was the signal box controller. So, if a train was coming, he would be responsible for dropping the barriers and raising them again.'

'Wow' said Jackson as he looked up to the building and pushed his little round glasses further up his nose. 'Grandad must be strong to lift those. Is he a superhero?'

Lucy laughed at the vision his eight-year-old imagination had created; she could just see her grandad with a mask and flowing cape. 'Well he'll always be a superhero to me, but he didn't actually lift them with his bare hands – he would get a signal and then use the controls to do it. When I was little and came here to visit, my grandad would often let me help him to lift and lower the barriers. I had such happy times here.'

'Will Great-Grandad let me do that?' he asked, cuddling Baxter as the dog had an exploratory sniff around his new environment.

'I'm afraid not – sorry, Jacks, it's all automated now so it's done by computer.'

'Where is Great-Grandad now?'

'He's had to go into a nursing home for a little while as he was poorly, so he just needs looking after until he's better. That's why we're here, isn't it? We're going to look after his house and visit him lots.'

'Which one is his house?' He turned to the row of tiny cottages.

'Do you see the one with the sign that says Railway Cottage?'

'Yes.' He punched the air. 'I was hoping it was that one. When I grow up, I'm going to live in a house called Astronaut's Cottage and it's going to have a sign just like that one and a picture of the moon next to it.' His blue eyes sparkled behind his glasses.

Lucy laughed. 'I'm sure you will, and I bet it'll be in outer space too won't it?'

He nodded and she ruffled his soft blond hair.

The rain thrashed down hard again in thick stripes rather than drops, the angry sky so dark it gave the impression of being much later in the day than it was.

'Oh, quick let's get inside before we get drenched.'

She searched for the keys in her bag and pulled Jackson by the hand. He in turn pulled Baxter by the lead.

Steadying Jackson as his trainers failed to grip the slippery slate stepping-stones that led to Railway Cottage, Lucy was quite taken aback at how small the place appeared compared to how she remembered it. Her nana would stand at this door to greet her cheerfully every time she came to visit. The delicious aroma of cakes baking would wrap around her and pull her into the warmth and comfort of Nana's house. Then all too soon she would wave her off tearfully when it was time to say goodbye at the end of the holidays.

The shiny black front door creaked open to welcome them into a small hallway with a staircase, underneath which was a tiny cupboard.

'Oh, look, Jackson, here's your bedroom.' Lucy smiled. 'You can be just like Harry Potter.' He giggled and opened a wooden door that led to the living/dining room, which ran the short length of the cottage. At the far end of the room a door led to a small kitchen. Old-fashioned units painted cream stood firmly on terracotta-tiled flooring. The top half of the back door consisted of a thick mottled glass window. She stood on tiptoe to reach the heavy bolt at the top of the door. which opened onto a tiny garden with a wooden swing in it.

'Jackson, look out here. I loved playing on this. It's a bit ancient now but my grandad made it for my dad when he was younger.' He ran straight out and threw himself on to the soaking wet seat.

'Look, Mummy, I'm going to swing right up as high as the bar.' He shouted as the familiar squeak of the swing echoed round the garden and reminded Lucy of happy days. They had lived in a tiny shoebox of a flat in Brumstoke so having a garden of their own would be a huge novelty.

'No, Jackson, come in, it's soaking out there.'

'Okay just two more swings.' She could hear the squeaking getting faster as the rusty swing remembered its purpose with gusto after such a long time of inactivity and flew Jackson higher into the air.

'No, come in now and be careful,' she shouted, her heart leaping into her mouth as he jumped off the swing from quite a height. She remembered doing the same thing; she must have given Nana and Grandad quite a few scares over the years.

Her eyes scanned the garden to see what else was out there; a wrought-iron café table with two chairs looked cosy although at the moment they had water pouring off them, which sloshed noisily onto the patio. She would look forward to sitting out there when the weather changed for the better.

Grandad had pre-arranged for the central heating to come on for her so stepping into the warmth of the cosy cottage was as welcoming as a hug. She felt a real sense of belonging, like she had come home.

First things first, Lucy put the kettle on, then unpacked Baxter's box of tricks. She poured water and food into his bowls and opened the back door again to let him out. He'd been eyeing up one of Grandad's pot plants in the living room and that would not be a good start.

She left most of the luggage in the car until tomorrow and brought in what they would need for one night. Jackson hauled his bag up the stairs, eager to get unpacking.

Lucy had Grandad's room with the double bed, large double wardrobe and Nana's highly polished mahogany dressing table with her vintage perfume atomisers arranged as they always were. Lucy had loved playing with those as a child. She picked up an elegant black one with feathers around the bulb and squeezed it. The kiss of cool spray tickled behind her ears and she remembered giggling when her nana sprayed it for her. The fresh soapy smell of gardenia had not dulled over the years and Lucy closed her eyes; her skin tingled as she felt swathed in her nana's love.

Jackson had the spare room, which contained a foldaway single bed, bedside cabinet, wardrobe and a table with a train set on it. A small window overlooked the backyard. Lucy turned the light on for him and he dropped to his knees at the little table, playing happily with the trains and tiny figures. She delighted in watching as he entered his own little world and she marvelled at his vivid imagination.

After fiddling with the cooker for a few minutes she grilled some cheese and onion toasted sandwiches. Grandad had told her to help herself to anything in the cupboards, so she opened a Victoria sponge cake and cut some slices for them.

She carried everything in on a tray and rested it on the extended side of the drop-leaf walnut table. She remembered helping her nana to polish this table when she was younger. Her beaming face would reflect in the shine when she'd finished. Nana always said it took lots of elbow grease to get a shine like that.

'Jackson, dinner's ready.' She shouted up the stairs. Baxter howled as he always did when she raised her voice. She swore this dog thought he was human and tried to repeat what she was saying.

The sound of eight-year-old boy thundering down the stairs preceded the living room door bursting open and Jackson joined his mum at the table. He tucked into his food as though he hadn't eaten for a month. He was eager to get back to his train set but that didn't stop him from having two slices of cake.

Lucy cleared away and washed up by hand. She then went upstairs to the small bathroom, which featured old-fashioned avocado-coloured units, and she ran a bubbly bath for Jackson. He was reluctant to come away from the trains, but with the promise of an extra hour's play before bed, hewas soon gleaming clean in his pyjamas, his wet blond hair brushed over to the side.

Curled up on the couch back in the cosy living room she could now relax. She poured herself a glass of red and listened to the hail pinging against the window. She leant her head back on the sofa cushion and breathed out a sigh of contentment.

On the wobbly chess table next to her she found a little note from Grandad with useful addresses and telephone numbers on it, including the address of Sycamore Lodge, the nursing home he was in. He was normally very independent, but his recent diabetes diagnosis combined with a broken arm he'd sustained in a fall had knocked his confidence. She smiled at the thought of seeing him tomorrow. Being back at Railway Cottage and all the memories it held reminded her how much she missed him.

Her eyes settled on the framed photo of her nana and grandad, which stood proudly on the mantelpiece. They looked so happy together. A love like theirs was something she dreamt of having one day.

The *Bramblewood Echo*, the local paper, had been lying on the floor in the hall when she arrived. Out of interest she flicked through it and saw an article about Sycamore Lodge.

Firefighters were called to Sycamore Lodge to free a Bramblewood pensioner from a tree. Mr Joseph Elderwood, 83, was trying to impress his lady friend by retrieving her scarf, which had blown into the famous sycamore tree that the nursing home was named after. Upon reaching twenty feet, his fear of heights kicked in and he remained paralysed up there until the fire brigade were able to get him down safely. When asked if it was something he would do again for love he replied, "No I bloody wouldn't – no sooner was I up there than bloody Eric Pilkington waltzed off with her."

Both Mr Pilkington and the lady in question, who wishes to remain anonymous, declined to comment.

The article was accompanied by a photograph of the old man's face peeking out of the tree, looking really rather miserable and cold. Lucy chuckled; poor Mr Elderwood. She'd have to ask her grandad about that tomorrow.

Heavy eyelids were losing the fight to stay open, so she took her wine upstairs to drink in the bath. Baxter was snoring loudly, no doubt relieved to be in his bed at last. She turned out the light and locked up the front door. As she ran her bath, she checked on Jackson and found him asleep with his head on the table, still clutching the train he'd been playing with. She gathered him up in her arms and noticed the train track had left an imprint on his cheek. She planted a kiss on his apple shampooed head and laid him comfortably in his bed, covering him up with his astronaut quilt, which he soon snuggled into. She folded his glasses and put them on the small bedside cabinet and plugged his nightlight in.

Her heart burst with love for this little boy. He was her everything and she was determined that no one was ever going to change that or burst their little bubble ever. They didn't need anybody else.

Chapter 2

The next morning Lucy woke bright and early thanks to the rumble of the trains being so close to the house. From her childhood memories she knew it was simply a case of getting used to them and after a few days she would hardly hear them. Feeling well rested she looked out of the window at the old signal box building. Her mind flashed back to when she was younger. She and Nana would look out of this window and Grandad would wave from his workplace. One time she came for the whole summer and even at the end of the six weeks she still didn't want to go home. How she'd loved those carefree days.

By the time Jackson woke up she had unpacked the rest of their things and had taken Baxter for a quick walk to do his business.

After breakfast they headed out and walked along the river to the nursing home. The gravel crunched beneath their feet as they walked along the towpath. Jackson's face lit up as he fed his leftover toast crusts to Canada geese almost as tall as he was. Tentatively at first, wary of their tongues wriggling like little worms in their beaks, he quickly learned to throw the bread away from him, causing them to squabble noisily with each other and leave him alone. He wiped the crumbs on his trousers and skipped along in front of his mum.

Further along the river they reached a boat called *Serendipity*, a pretty café boat covered with multi-coloured flowers in vibrant painted pots. The smell emanating from the boat led Jackson to it like it was the pied piper. The rain had stopped but the sky was still overcast.

'Oh, Mum, can we go in there? I'm starving.' Lucy didn't bother reminding him he'd only just had breakfast as the smell of warm scones drew her in. She bought some lunch for later and they were soon on their way to visit Grandad.

Sycamore Lodge was an imposing building that had been a mansion house in its day. The outer walls were painted lemon and surrounded by spacious communal areas with benches and flowerbeds bursting with colour. Wooden tables and chairs overlooked the river. A wooden fence surrounded the gardens and the gate required a code for access. Grandad had given her the code in the notes he had left her. She reeled the numbers off to Jackson and held him up so he could reach the keypad. He said the numbers out loud as he carefully pressed each one.

The inside was grandiose and apart from a strong disinfectant smell it could have been a luxurious hotel. A care assistant in a white overall took them to Grandad's room. From the doorway Lucy saw him sitting in an overstuffed wing-backed chair reading a newspaper with his glasses perched on the end of his nose. He looked up and removed his glasses, putting them down on the table before he tried to get up. He looked slightly frailer, slightly greyer, and his once piercing blue eyes were a little more faded but that didn't stop them twinkling with delight on seeing who his visitors were. The joy spread across his face and shone out of him as brightly as the sun after a particularly dark cloud has passed it by. He beamed a welcoming smile.

Lucy ran over to him, tears springing to her eyes. She felt like a little girl again. She glanced around the room.

13

Having expected a starched hospital environment she was pleasantly surprised to see that it was more like a hotel room, tastefully decorated in muted shades of cream with white cornices, dado rails and a thick beige carpet. Grandad was provided with a wardrobe and a desk, two comfortable armchairs, a bedside table with a lamp and a bookshelf. It looked remarkably homely.

'Grandad, how are you?' she asked as she hugged him, tentatively so as not to knock his arm that was in plaster.

'I'm all the better for seeing you, my darling, and look at Jackson here – what a fine-looking young man you've grown into. Do you remember me?'

Jackson looked up at his great-grandad and, pushing his glasses further up his nose, he nodded.

'Yes, we all went to the caravan when I was little, and you helped me to build sandcastles.'

'That's right we did, and we caught some crabs, didn't we?' Dougie Woods hugged the boy; his pale blue eyes glassy, his emotions running high at seeing the two people he loved more than life itself.

'We got you a present, Grandad,' said Jackson, thrusting the paper bags from Serendipity into his hands.

'Rosie from Serendipity sent them for you when she heard you were ill; she sends her love and wishes you a speedy recovery,' added Lucy.

'Mmm something smells good in here,' he said opening them and finding a still-warm sausage roll and the freshly baked giant scone with cream and jam. 'I'm going to enjoy those later. How did she know you were my grandson?' He placed them on his bedside table.

'Jackson told her our life story.' Lucy laughed.

'No, I didn't, I just told her that we were staying in Railway Cottage and she said she knew you and that you

14

were her best customer.' He pulled an empty paper bag out of his pocket and held it up. 'She gave me a cookie for free and said that we must go back there one day when we've got more time. She was really nice – I liked her.' He threw the paper bag across the room and it landed in the bin.

'Jackson,' shouted Lucy. 'Stop that.'

He grinned his cheeky missing-toothed grin. 'What? I got it in, didn't I?'

His grandad chuckled and winked at Lucy. 'You have to admit it was a good shot.' He turned to Jackson. 'Well when you do see her, can you tell her thank you from me?'

'Will do.' Jackson ran to the window. 'You can see the river from here, Mummy, and there's Rosie's boat just a bit further along.

'I got your note.' Lucy nodded to her grandad and sneaked him a bag containing two bottles of whisky.

'Thanks, love, my fellow inmates will be pleased with that.' He winked at her and hid the bag in his wardrobe. 'Right so who wants to play a game of three-armed table tennis?'

'What's that?' Jackson screwed his face up in confusion.

Grandad lifted his plastered arm up. 'Well I've only got one and you've got two, so that makes three altogether.' He held out his good arm to his great grandson and Jackson clutched it tightly.

After a general tour of the building and a couple of bouts of ping-pong with Grandad emerging the champion despite trying his hardest to let Jackson win, they sat in one of the dining rooms for coffee and cakes.

'It's not that bad here actually,' he said. Lucy poured the coffees and Jackson busied himself with a jigsaw puzzle he'd found in the entertainment drawer. 'I've made lots of friends already. There's quite a few restrictions but I've discovered ways around them, a sort of underground movement.' He tapped the side of his nose.

Lucy laughed. 'I take it that's what the *you know what* was for.'

'Yes and believe me when you have Nurse Ratched watching your every move you've always got to be one step ahead.' He gestured to the manager standing by the door who could either be smiling or sucking on a particularly bitter lemon judging by the look on her face. Lucy laughed.

'Anyhow, Lucy, I just wanted to say thank you. I'm not sure how long I'll be in here and it's lovely to see you both but I would never expect you to uproot your life just to look after the house. Your mum and dad were talking about cancelling their cruise and they've had that planned for ages so I wouldn't let them.'

'Its fine, Grandad, honestly – I've been in a bit of a rut to be truthful and this has provided me with an ideal opportunity to start again.' Lucy put her hand on his and squeezed it. She pointed to the swallow tattoo between his thumb and forefinger. 'Do you remember when Jackson was little, and he got a baby wipe and tried to wash this off?'

'Yes, and what about the time when you drew one on your hand because you wanted to be like me?'

Her hand clapped to her mouth as she laughed out loud. 'Do you remember what I used though?'

'I do.' He laughed. 'Your nana's permanent laundry marker. She was so worried. I remember her trying to scrub it off.'

'So do I – it really hurt.' She smiled at the memory and rubbed at her hand where it had been. 'And then because I had to go back to school a couple of days later, she wrapped my hand in a bandage and told me to tell the teachers I'd

16

sprained it.' They laughed together. 'I really miss Nana; it was hard for me to come to see you at first after she'd gone and then when Jackson came along, I didn't have a minute to myself.'

'I understand, sweetheart, children are hard work. I remember your dad would get himself into all sorts of scrapes; a complete livewire he was. Jackson is the image of him. Cherish these moments as they go far too fast and then before you know it you're a silly old man stuck in a place like this.'

'You're not silly or old and you just say the word and you can move back in any time; we'll break you out whenever you want us to.'

'I might just hold you to that one day.' He smiled.

'Talking of silly old men, I saw an article in the paper about an old man stuck in the tree. I hope he's okay now. He looked heartbroken in the picture.'

'Ah you mean Stan Elderwood, he's an absolute hoot,' he pointed to a couple sitting at the far end of the room. 'There he is over there, he used to be a sailor and is often climbing up that tree, he thinks it's a mast. Normally they can get him back down again but he was sulking because his lady friend went off with old Eric.'

'Is that her?' asked Lucy, referring to the woman he was sitting with.

'Oh no love, this one he refers to as *new blood*, she only moved in two days ago and he moved in on her about an hour later.'

'Good for them.' Lucy smiled at the term 'new blood' especially as the lady was wearing a birthday badge with number ninety-two on it.

'What about you Grandad, do you have any lady friends?

'Don't be daft,' he replied, 'Who'd want an ugly old bugger like me?'

'Hey, you could give that Stan Elderwood a run for his money.' Lucy laughed, thinking how cute it was that he was blushing a little.

'So, come on then, tell me what you've been up to. You can talk while I get stuck into this cake.' He said, changing the subject.

'Well having worked in the hotel pretty much since I left college, I'm sure you can imagine that I got to know the place inside out. I've worked in every department. My worst job being in the laundry room—' she screwed her nose up '—but the job I enjoyed most was helping with organising the weddings. I worked with so many wedding planners over the last couple of years and it just clicked one day that that's what I wanted to do. It looked like such a fun and fulfilling job. To be able to create such wonderful scenes and make the most important day in two people's lives so spectacular is a wonderful feeling.' She spoke quickly, swept along by her passion for the subject. 'So, I got my head down to study events management and now that I've graduated, the next logical step for me is to start a business as a wedding planner. And thanks to you, I've already got my first customer.'

'Ah so my friend's granddaughter got in touch then? Well done you,' he said, pride shining in his eyes. 'I remember you playing weddings with Nana when you were little. She made you a little wedding dress and veil and you'd grab a bunch of flowers and we'd have to sing "Here comes the bride" over and over again and throw petals at you. It's all you wanted to do. Your nana would be so happy and proud of you.'

'Ah what a little nightmare I must have been.' She laughed. 'I'm proud of myself too. I couldn't have done it whilst working, studying, and looking after Jackson so moving into your place means I don't have to pay rent for a while – that is if you're still happy about that.' Her eyes met his.

'Of course I'm happy. I should be paying you for house-sitting.'

'No, you shouldn't but it does give me a little bit of breathing space money wise. Basically it was now or never and I'm grateful to you for the opportunity. Also, getting Jackson enrolled in the local school is the cherry on the top. He didn't really have any friends in the old one so I think a fresh start will do us both good.'

'I've finished,' yelled Jackson as he put the final piece into the jigsaw, before breaking it apart again and throwing it back in the box. 'Can we go back to your room and watch telly now, Grandad?'

'Yes, we can, son; now do you remember the way?'

'I think so.' Jackson grabbed his grandad's hand and led the way.

They left when Grandad's eyes started to droop. He'd admitted to getting tired quicker these days due to the medication he was on and Lucy didn't want to wear him out; she knew he would have tried to keep up with Jackson if he could.

'It's something about this place that makes me sleepy.' He yawned. 'Anyway, I hate to ask, Lucy, as I know you've already got a lot on your plate but I was wondering what you thought about looking after Maud for me?' As he spoke a little old lady walked into his room looking lost. Grandad smiled at her, said, 'Hi, love,' then carried on talking. 'So, as I was saying, she's only tiny and as good as gold. She won't be any trouble.' The old lady was now sitting in one of the comfy chairs and looked as though she were about to drift off to sleep.

Lucy scratched at a non-existent itch at her temple. She looked at the old lady and then back to Grandad. He was looking at her expectantly.

'Erm, when you say look after her, what do you mean exactly?'

'Oh, you know usual things: feed her, let her out when necessary and basically let her live out her years in the comfort of Railway Cottage.'

'Oh, I see.' Lucy was hesitant simply because she didn't quite know what to say. 'But where would she sleep?'

'She'll be fine in the living room; they will give her bed back when you collect her. She's fretting you see and that makes me sad.'

'Well I suppose it will be a bit of a squeeze but if it's what you want, Grandad, then I'm sure we can work something out. The only trouble is I'm not around much in the daytime.'

'Well that's absolutely fine – she's very self-sufficient,' he assured her.

She couldn't quite get to grips with what she could be letting herself in for. The woman seemed nice enough, but Lucy didn't have any experience of caring for the elderly.

'So, when exactly were you thinking of this arrangement starting?' she asked, dreading the answer.

'I'm sure they'll let you take her now if that's okay?'

Grandad appeared so relieved she couldn't possibly say no. She stood up to go. She and Jackson cuddled Grandad and promised to come back and see him tomorrow. Then she made her way over to the old lady and patted her on the arm to wake her.

'Are you ready, Maud?' she said loudly as if speaking to a child.

Grandad scratched his ear, as if struggling to comprehend what was happening.

'Erm, Lucy, what are you doing?' He gave her a sidelong glance. She was helping the old lady out of her seat but stopped to look at her grandad.

'I thought you wanted me to take Maud.'

Grandad could hardly speak. Laughter burst out of him like machine gun fire. Lucy had never heard him laugh so heartily. Every time he tried to speak he pointed at Lucy and then at the old lady with whom she was now holding hands and the laughter stole his words.

'I can't tell which of you looks more bewildered,' he eventually managed to say. 'This is Elsie.' He guffawed again. 'Maud—' he spluttered '—is my cat.' He was bent over double now, laughing until his face was a deep red.

Lucy was now laughing too and helped the poor woman back into her seat, relieved that she wouldn't be her house guest for the foreseeable future.

'I'm so sorry for the mix-up,' said Grandad, still laughing. 'Poor Elsie likes to have a wander around the rooms and always falls asleep in someone else's chair. She can't hear very well and doesn't speak but she seems content to do what she does.'

Despite aching feet and sleepy eyes when they got home, they fed Baxter and took him for a little walk along the towpath in the opposite direction to this morning. Large mock Tudor houses and apartments overlooked the river and a green space encompassed a small enclosed children's play area at the far end. Baxter, having been released from the shackles of his lead, chased after his ball. Divots of mud and grass flew into the air as he galloped around the green like a Grand National winner about to make his owner a lot of money. His tail wagged frantically each time he dropped the ball at Jackson's feet.

Eventually, panting heavily, he slowed down. Lucy reattached his lead to his collar and began the short walk home. She watched her boy and his best friend walk along together, with Jackson pointing things of interest out to the dog. Her heart warmed, and she knew she could be truly happy here.

The next day they went to collect the real Maud from a place called Kitty's Kattery. Grandad had given her the address when he'd finally managed to stop laughing. Remembering the misunderstanding set Lucy off laughing again. Her grandad had looked completely flummoxed when he saw her trying to help the poor old lady out of the chair. She was still chuckling to herself when a pretty lady called Carrie opened the door.

'Ah yes our lovely little Maud,' she said when Lucy asked for her. 'She's been fretting for your grandad and for her own home; she's okay but hasn't eaten much since she's been here. We've had the vet check her over and she said she'll be absolutely fine when she gets home again.

Carrie soon brought Maud out in a carrier and handed Jackson the bed in a plastic bag. Lucy was relieved that the bed was so tiny and not the single bed she thought was going in the living room to accommodate the old lady. Laughter once again bubbled up inside her.

'Here we go, if there are any problems then do let me know. Here's my card. You can usually find me here or in Kitty's Abode, the B&B in Market Square.

'Ah lovely, thank you,' said Lucy, peering into the carrier as she went to the car.

The cat was beautiful – black with tan and white markings; one eye blue and the other a yellowy green. She had a burgundy collar with dainty silver studs along it. Lucy kept her fingers crossed that Maud and Baxter would get on well. The little bell on her collar jingled all the way home. Jackson had begged to have the carrier on his knee for the short car journey and he was speaking very gently to Maud, explaining what was going to happen when they got home. Lucy could see by the soppy look on his face that he'd already fallen in love.

Maud hissed a little at Baxter on their first introduction while she was still in the carrier. Baxter had run away and was now shaking in his bed. As she strutted out of the box, there was no denying who was the boss. She stealthily made her way to the kitchen and drank some of Baxter's water before drinking her own; wolfed down three packets of the cat food that Lucy had bought her, then curled up in her bed, which was the other side of the armchair to Baxter, for a long and leisurely sleep. As long as Baxter maintained a wary distance from her at all times the relationship worked well.

Chapter 3

The day had come for Jackson to start at his new school and an acrobat was rehearsing for the show of his life in Lucy's stomach – at least that's what it felt like.

She wiped away a rogue tear when she saw her little boy looking all smart in his navy jumper with red school emblem, black trousers, light blue shirt and navy and light blue stripy tie. He had a new astronaut lunchbox and a school bag with a train on it, along with matching pencil case and pencil sharpener. Her heart melted when she pointed her phone at him to take a photo and asked him to smile. His two top teeth had come through much bigger than the baby teeth surrounding them and the bottom two were missing. She loved that crooked smile and the cute little freckles across his nose.

Nestled amongst a patchwork quilt of fields, one of which ran alongside the footpath and contained reddish brown shire horses with black manes, the school was a twenty-minute walk from Railway Cottage and much smaller than the one in Brumstoke where he'd been unhappy.

When she collected him later, he was buzzing with excitement. His teacher told her he'd settled in well. The children vied for his attention, all wanting to be friends with the new boy, especially when he told them that he lived in Railway Cottage and that his grandad used to be the signalman. Jackson took great pride in telling everybody that. Lucy couldn't believe the transformation in her son and suspected this had been the best move she had ever made. Coming to stay at her grandad's house was just the sort of fresh start that she and Jackson both needed, and she wouldn't have to look over her shoulder anymore.

With Jackson settled in at school Lucy was looking forward to some time for herself. First on the agenda was meeting up with her childhood friend who lived in Bramblewood. Abbie Cavendish and Lucy were inseparable on those visits to her grandparents. They first met when they were only six years old and had become pen pals, sharing their secrets, hopes and dreams. The letters had drifted off as the years went by and life became too busy, but they still sent Christmas and birthday cards. When Lucy had told Abbie of her plans to return, she was delighted and couldn't wait for her friend to come back.

Flowerpots – the local garden centre – was the perfect place to meet for coffee. The café was packed just like it used to be. Lucy found the familiarity of crockery clattering and voices chattering soothing and reminiscent of working at the hotel. She'd been happy working there, but the time was right to move on. She had that sense of belonging again that she'd felt at Railway Cottage. She came here often with her grandparents many years ago, but it had changed a lot since then. The café had been a wooden construction way back then, like a large garden room, but the company had expanded over the years and it was now part of a huge extension on the main building and a reason in itself to visit the garden centre.

Whilst waiting for Abbie, she looked around the large room. It was popular with the oldies but quite a few tables had groups of new mums at them. She overheard them, swapping tips and techniques on how to raise a happy healthy baby. Most of them rocked as they talked with a baby either over their shoulder, on the hip or at the breast. A boundary made of pushchairs had sectioned them off into their own exclusive little club. She noted that they were all about her age, mid to late twenties. She was nineteen when she had Jackson, so young yet at the time she thought she was so grown up.

She took a deep breath as a pang of longing took her by surprise. She hadn't had the chance to meet with other mums when Jackson was a baby as they were all much older than her and she lacked the confidence to meet new people. She had been happy hanging out with her mum during the day and didn't go to many places alone for the first year or so. Although looking around at this group of friends, she reflected that it might have been quite nice to get involved with other mums, the only trouble being that awkward questions were asked, questions that she did not want to answer.

Her thoughts were interrupted by an excited squeal as Abbie joined her. Lucy jumped up and they hugged each other tightly.

'It's so good to see you again, Lucy. I hope you're moving here for good; I couldn't believe it when I got your message. How's Jackson? Have you got any pictures of him? I can't wait to meet him.' She laughed and flicked her long dark hair off her shoulder. 'Sorry, now it's your turn to talk.'

Abbie's excitement was contagious. 'I'm good thank you – you're looking as gorgeous as ever, I see.' Lucy happily took out her phone and showed her pictures of Jackson.

'Oh, he looks so cute,' Abbie gushed. 'And just like you but with shorter hair – and I recognise that uniform; that's my old school.'

'Yes, I remembered you always loved going to that school and it's so handy for Railway Cottage.'

The conversation flowed easily as they caught up with each other's news. The waitress had already been over twice to ask them what they wanted. On her third visit they forced themselves to look at the menu so they didn't have to ask her for five more minutes. 'I'm so sorry,' said Abbie, 'we haven't seen each other for years.'

'That's okay,' replied the waitress. 'I'm used to it.'

They ordered coffees and cake. Lucy's eyes lit up as the mountainous slice of Limoncello cake was placed in front of her and Abbie tucked into a slice of coffee and walnut.

'So,' Abbie said between mouthfuls of bliss. 'Tell me all about this wedding planner business of yours. It sounds exciting and perfect for you. I'm sure you were the only seven-year-old with your own Filofax!'

Lucy laughed out loud. 'I can't believe you remember that – it was my dad's old one that he'd never used. I never went anywhere without it. I guess I've always been organised.'

'I imagine you'd have to be with a young boy around.'

'Funnily enough, he was the one thing that I hadn't organised, and my life has been pretty chaotic with him in it, but I wouldn't change a thing. Business wise though I'm still Mrs Filofax.'

'He sounds adorable.' She smiled as another memory surfaced. 'Talking of young boys, remember when I fancied Harry Stephenson and you gave him some sweets to marry me?'

'Yes, I do.' She chuckled. 'And didn't he wet himself because the ceremony went on too long?'

'He did but he was only five, and Dom told us off because they were his sweets that we'd found in his secret hiding place. Oh, we had such fun, didn't we?'

Lucy's stomach fluttered at the mention of his name. 'How is your brother? He was always so mean to me.'

'He was, wasn't he? He was never like that with my other friends. I think he fancied you; they always say that boys are mean to girls they like. Anyway, Dom's just Dom, the golden boy. I'm the flighty one who wanted to travel the world whilst he did everything properly and became this hotshot lawyer. He's all right though, I suppose, as brothers go.'

Lucy blushed and hoped Abbie didn't notice. She'd never confessed her childhood crush.

'You'll never guess what though . . . He is actually getting married and guess who's doing the photography.' She pointed her thumbs to herself.

'Who Dom?' she asked too loudly. Her heart fluttered.

'Noooo, Dom get married again – ha that'll be the day. I meant Harry Stephenson.'

'Oh, that's fantastic, well done – let's hope he doesn't have a repeat performance.' She laughed.

Abbie continued. 'Anyway, sorry I interrupted you. So you're going to be a wedding planner?'

'Yes, I really envied the wedding planners who came into the hotel where I worked and after gaining the experience in every aspect of hospitality, I found that area the most rewarding. Seeing the looks of joy on the faces of brides, grooms, and their guests, ooh it just gives me shivers down my spine. In a good way,' she added.

'I can understand that. I've been doing travel photography for the last few years but I'm really keen to get into weddings. I got a distinction on my wedding photography module and I won an award with my portraiture.' She popped the last piece of cake in her mouth and licked her lips.

'That sounds fantastic. I've been researching various wedding facilities and services available in the area and have created a couple of huge files. One online and a physical one that I can show to potential clients. I've also worked at lots of wedding fairs that were held in the hotel. People are constantly looking for something unique and I'm always on the lookout for potential places.'

'You must have passed the bug on to me at some point because in my spare time I've been making little personalised bridal favours. I can do all sorts of designs including little boxes with pictures of the bride and groom on, usually taken from their engagement photo shoot. I've also done Harry's wedding stationery. You should come round to see my portfolio and maybe we could work together some time.'

'I would love that; it would be fantastic to join forces. We could be like Charlie's Angels except with just two of us.'

'The great thing is it wouldn't involve much in the way of costs up front and it would be a great side-line for me to help while I'm setting my photography business up. Just think we could call it Wedding Bells with Lucy and Abbie.

'What about just calling it Wedding Belles, as in Belle from *Beauty and the Beast*.'

'Fantastic, I love it.' Abbie clapped her hands.

Lucy checked her watch and put her coat on. 'Well that's settled then, Wedding Belles, Planning and Photography Services. It sounds perfect. I can't believe how quickly the time has gone. I must go as I need to pick up Jackson, but it's been so lovely getting together again.' She kissed Abbie on both cheeks.

'It's been a joy and I can't wait to see you again. I'll call you.'

Chapter 4

Every day Lucy visited her grandad and sometimes took him out for walks. One particular Sunday she brought him to Railway Cottage to spend some time with Maud, who never left his side the whole time he was there. She meowed loudly at him as if complaining to him. Grandad stroked and talked to her as if he was having a two-way conversation with her. 'I'm sorry you think Baxter's a useless mutt, Maud. No, I didn't want to leave you, but I had a fall. You should be glad I didn't land on you. You're lucky to be here because Lucy thought you were a real old lady and nearly moved her in.' Grandad chuckled heartily and Jackson laughed until his belly hurt and tears streamed down his face.

Lucy wanted her grandad to feel special on his visit home so had cooked him a roast beef lunch with all the trimmings. Jackson had been looking forward to his visit and was thrilled when Grandad fetched a brass key that hung on a hook in the pantry and unlocked the door to the garage, which was attached to their back garden. Inside was the most amazing miniature railway that his grandad had been collecting and making for twenty years. There were mountains and villages and signal boxes galore. The detail was unbelievable.

'Did you really make these, Grandad?' asked Jackson as he pushed his glasses up, completely in awe.

'Yes, I did and when my arm is better, I'm going to teach you how to make them too.'

Jackson's face broke into a huge smile as he and his grandad played with the train set.

Lucy had left them to it and was busy making an apple crumble in the kitchen. Baxter was getting under her feet; he was torn between spending time with her or Jackson and kept flitting from one to the other.

When she called them into dinner she had to smile as they both came in wearing Station Master's hats. Excitement shone from their eyes and Lucy realised they were quickly becoming best buddies. Grandad was telling Jackson about the special paint that he used to give the trains a metallic look even though they were made from wood. Lucy was pleased to see her grandad was much more animated than when they first saw him in his room.

When they walked him back to Sycamore Lodge, Lucy pointed to the old signal box building and told her grandad of the special memories it held for her.

'I loved that job, you know.' He sighed. 'It was never quite the same after they automated the system. That was almost fifteen years ago now and then that building became defunct. Do you remember I used to wave to you through the window?'

Lucy laughed. 'I used to think you were famous whenever I saw you up there. I loved coming in to help you with the barriers. What a shame the railway hasn't done anything with the building. I mean the shape of it almost looks train-like if you can imagine a double decker train. It would make a brilliant café or something – imagine all the commuters coming back from London and being able to pick a hot meal up, either to eat in or take away.'

'Ooh yes,' agreed Grandad, 'or lovely bacon rolls and coffee in the morning – imagine that.'

Lucy could almost taste them. 'You know my friend went to a café once and they had little miniature trains bringing the drinks to the table.'

Jackson's ears pricked up. 'That would be so cool; Grandad, we could make them.'

Grandad nodded. 'That's a brilliant idea, Jackson my boy – we could easily do that.' He ruffled the boy's hair then turned to Lucy. 'You know, Lucy, the railway doesn't own that building. There was a furore at the time and the plans had been cocked up. That building is on my land and the railway signed it over to me many years ago. Next time I come round I'll dig out the paperwork.'

'What? Wait, do you mean this is something we could actually do?'

Her grandad nodded, his eyes smiling at the enthusiasm in her voice.

'There's no reason why not. I think it would be a brilliant idea.'

A tremor of excitement at the thought of a new business ran through Lucy's veins and ideas buzzed around her head like busy little bees. She was constantly trying to think of unique places for weddings; what could be more unique than this beloved old signal box, which held such happy memories for their family? But they would need money and probably lots of it to pull off something this big.

Grandad wanted to draw up some plans so needed to stop off at the paper shop on the way back and he bought himself a notebook and some pencils and pens. Lucy got herself a notepad and pen and Jackson a colouring book and felt tips. They would all be busy tonight. Lucy didn't feel as sad leaving Grandad at Sycamore Lodge this time

32

as he looked much perkier. On the way in they heard a lady shout, 'Douglas.' They turned and saw an extremely attractive lady in her seventies give him a flirty wave.

'Hello, Violet, how are you today?' He said it, matter-of-factly but Lucy couldn't help noticing a little light flick on in his eyes.

Chapter 5

Lucy couldn't wait to talk to Grandad the next day and he was equally excited. After she'd dropped Jackson off to school, she met up with him over breakfast at Sycamore Lodge. Once they'd finished eating a tasty full English, Lucy walked over to the far side of the dining room to put their trays on the trolley rack whilst Grandad spread his papers on the starched white tablecloth. Lucy returned with two cups of strong tea and placed one in front of each of them. She watched her grandad thoughtfully as he pointed to various parts of his drawings and described them. He was like a different man. He held himself straighter and excitement danced in his eyes. Lucy tried to put her finger on what the difference was and then realised he'd regained his sense of pride. He wasn't just withering away in an old people's home he had a new sense of purpose; she could hear it in his voice as he spoke.

'As you suggested we could decorate the downstairs, which used to be offices, to look like the inside of a railway carriage, maybe something quite posh like the Orient express with little lamps on the tables and upstairs could be a function room so that we could have evening receptions there too.'

He had drawn up what sort of work he thought needed doing and made some sketches. He still knew people in the rail industry and knew he could buy train seats from disused carriages.

'Wow, Grandad, I'm impressed. You have been so busy, you must have been up late last night,' she said.

'I hardly slept a wink, but I haven't been this motivated in years.' He shuffled the papers and showed her another drawing. 'I could make those trains to take the drinks to the table you know, Lucy. This would be a brilliant project for me,' he said with a new twinkle in his eye. 'It's just what I've needed, something to keep me busy. I've been so bloody bored; especially these last ten years without your nana. I still miss her terribly.'

Lucy thought of her sweet nana and of how much she missed her too and her heart ached for her grandad.

'You know, Grandad, I'd like to get a quote for this building work and maybe I could try and get a bank loan.'

'Well I've got a bit put by, love, so I think it would be very sensible to draw up what we need and get some quotes in. Then we can do some serious number crunching.

They divided up a list of jobs and arranged to meet the next day to organise some quotes. That night they both slept fitfully.

Two of the quotes had come back astronomically high, which completely threw their plans out of the window and Lucy's mood dipped. It would have been such a good project to work on but now it was scuppered before they'd even started. Lucy crossed her fingers that the third quote wouldn't be so bad.

Finn Calahan had taken over his father's business after the older man had become too weak to take on the manual work and was known around the town as a trustworthy and hardworking man. He was impressed with their plans and thought it was just what the village needed. Lucy flushed on seeing him as he was extremely handsome but the gold ring on his third finger had dashed any hope of him being available – not that she was looking for a relationship anyway, she reminded herself.

Finn was qualified in all aspects of building and engineering so there wasn't a single job involved in this project that he couldn't do. This prevented the need for drafting in other tradesmen and cut the costs down hugely. He gave them a ballpark figure but said he would be more specific when he had worked everything out. Lucy and her grandad looked at each other with glee as it came to just within their budget.

Lucy paced up and down outside the building, eager to take a look inside. Grandad had the key but Finn had insisted they waited for him so he could give them safety helmets, just in case there was any falling debris. The remnants of the signal controls were still up there on the top floor and she hoped they could be rescued and maybe they could be displayed somewhere. Finn had assured them that structurally the building wasn't as bad as it appeared. He estimated that the renovations would take about a month from beginning to end. He could recommend decorators too should they need them.

'I was thinking that over here—' Lucy kicked her way through some rubble on the floor and gestured to the windowless wall at the back of the room, her arms outstretched '—we could have TV screens made to look like windows playing a film of an actual train journey so that the customers could almost believe they are on a train.'

'Now that is a brilliant idea,' said Finn, chewing on a pencil, his mind already starting to create a plan of action. This was a project he would be able to sink his teeth into and it was completely different to anything else he'd worked on before.

'I'm very impressed and it will certainly give you the unique edge you're looking for. You could have the train seats upstairs along the windows as well and then movable versions for the rest of the room so it can be a dance floor.'

'That's what we were hoping for,' agreed Lucy.

'So, what is this amazing venue going to be called?' he asked them.

Lucy and Grandad looked at each other. 'The Signal Box Café?' she suggested shrugging her shoulders.

'Perfect,' agreed Grandad, his face breaking into a wide smile.

'Brilliant,' added Finn as he measured up.

Chapter 6

Lucy sat holding her head in her hands after receiving the rejection from the bank. It was a massive setback and she desperately didn't want to have to tell her grandad the bad news. Her brain was aching from overthinking as she tried to come up with ideas. She could start by selling off things they didn't need anymore. There was a regular car boot sale just ten minutes away that took place early every Sunday. It was worth a try, but she'd had a sort-out already before they moved and donated most of her and Jackson's old clothes to charity.

She looked out of the living room window and eyed her car up but shook her head again. She wouldn't get that much for it and it was an absolute necessity, especially now she had her own business. Considering she'd only had one month's notice, the wedding she had planned for Joy, her first customer, had gone swimmingly and she was awaiting quite a substantial amount of money from that. From the beautiful mermaid-style dress to the white doves that were released after the reception, everything had been perfect. Joy was now happily living in Abu Dhabi with her partner as his job had moved out there.

Part of the reason why she'd been rejected for the loan was because the bank said she hadn't done enough market research but also because the Wedding Planning business wasn't bringing in that much money yet. It was a rookie mistake and she had an idea to rectify that immediately. She had a brainstorm and wrote down everything she could think of. She grabbed a couple of highlighters and coloured the things she could do now in yellow and those that would need more time in pink.

First on her yellow list was to call Finn and ask him what they could do to reduce the costs. He promised to look into his suppliers to see if there was anything that could be done. He also suggested that they could pay his labour costs over six months in instalments. Unfortunately materials would have to be paid for up front. Lucy thanked him for his huge generosity. They'd factored in a couple of thousand pounds for decorators so Lucy struck that from the figures; she and Grandad could do that. First things first she popped to the wholesalers to buy bacon and bread rolls, napkins and red and brown sauce. She quickly put together a questionnaire and printed off fifty of them.

At five forty-five the next morning Lucy groaned and switched her alarm off then proceeded to grill and fry bacon and buttered the bread rolls. The smell and the sound of sizzling was mouth-watering. As each bacon roll was assembled, she wrapped it in a napkin and piled them all onto her nana's hostess trolley. She put the sauces on the shelf and sellotaped a poster she'd hastily made to the front and made her way across the railway track where the platform was bustling with commuters. 'Free bacon rolls for answering a few questions,' she shouted.

'What's the Signal Box Café?' asked one man after reading the poster.

'See that building over there,' she said. The man nodded. 'Well that's going to be the Signal Box Café and I need to be able to show the bank that there's a demand for it.'

'I'll have one,' shouted a young city type who looked a bit worse for wear. 'Me too,' shouted another. Within two minutes all twenty-five had gone and she was being asked for more. She went backwards and forwards three more times until she'd given out a hundred rolls and even more leaflets. She'd asked everyone to post the leaflets through the letterbox.

Later that day she called the council to do a health and safety check on Railway Cottage. Luckily, they had a cancellation and within days her kitchen was approved for making the rolls. Every day she traipsed across the railway track to give out her leaflets and sell her bacon rolls. She eventually added fruit juices, chocolate bars and crisps to her repertoire, which accumulated to over a thousand pounds per week. By eight o clock she had time to sort Jackson out and take him to school. Which left the rest of the day for her wedding planning work.

Grandad called a meeting with Finn and Lucy. They met at the signal box after Lucy had dropped off Jackson and picked up Grandad.

'You're looking a little bit tired, love – are you okay?'

'I'm fine thanks, Grandad. I'm getting up earlier but also going to bed earlier now as well, pretty much just after Jackson.' She laughed. 'The thing is, Grandad, I'd completely underestimated the demand for breakfast in the morning. I actually can't keep up with it. I've made thousands of pounds in just a couple of weeks. If I carry on doing this for let's say six months and by then my wedding planner business starts becoming viable, I can try again for a smaller loan and they might approve my application. I've even considered putting the wedding business on hold and applying for other jobs just to bring the money in.'

'No way – I would not want you to give up on your dream.'

'But the Signal Box Café is our dream, Grandad – yours and mine. I've got plenty of time to fulfil mine but . . .' She stopped as she realised what she was saying.

'You're absolutely right – if I don't do it now I never will.'

'Oh, Grandad, you know what I mean.' She laughed. 'I've got a few casual lunchtime shifts at the pub along the high street. Jackson and I are also walking the neighbours' dogs as he really wanted to help.'

'Ah bless him,' said Grandad. 'He's got a good work ethic like his mum. But that's what I wanted to talk to you about. I was as devastated as you were when your loan got rejected but it's been so heartening seeing your actions since then. Some people would have given up but not you. You've shown such determination and I can see how much you really want this Signal Box Café to work. So . . .'

Lucy had no idea what to expect and held her breath.

Grandad continued. 'Your nana had set aside some money that I was to give to you when you were looking to buy a property. But unfortunately, property prices have shot up way beyond what we would ever have imagined. I mean it would be enough for a reasonable-sized deposit but then you'd need to pay a mortgage too. Anyway, what I'm suggesting is that you take it now and if you wanted to you could put it towards our dream.'

Lucy burst out crying. 'I couldn't possibly take that,' she said. 'It belongs to you.'

'No, it doesn't, I promise. It's in an account in your name and I asked your nana what she thought last night when I prayed and all I could see was her beautiful face smiling.'

Lucy hugged him and both of them shed a tear.

When Finn arrived, Grandad was able to tell him that his contact from the railway had located a stack of reclaimed railway sleepers that could be used for flooring and the staircase for next to nothing. They jiggled around the numbers again and Lucy went home to fill in a new loan application form with the revised figures on it, including projected figures for one of her brainstorming ideas. Children's parties were real money-spinners and the Signal Box Café would be perfect for them.

While she waited for the answer, she continued with her commuter breakfasts, which she enjoyed doing. It reminded her of working in the hotel. She had lots of banter with her customers and some of them had requested jacket potatoes for the end of the day. Her little empire was growing stronger by the day.

That is until one morning when the area manager for the railway turned up and told her that for health and safety reasons, she was no longer allowed on the platform to sell. Tears of humiliation stung her eyes as the man spoke to her as if she were nothing. He was quickly booed by her regulars who helped her move to the pavement outside the station. Within a week, the much smaller loan was approved by the bank, the building work had begun, and the Signal Box Café was not just a dream anymore; but there was still a long way to go and there was a lot of red tape to get through first . . .

Chapter 7

It was all systems go now that the council had finally approved the change of use of the building. Lucy had been on a food hygiene course and passed with flying colours and Finn and his crew had started working on the building, which was now covered in scaffolding.

She had also taken on the planning of lots of weddings and had applied for a licence so that weddings could be performed in the building. She and Abbie had split the cost of a wedding magazine advert and Lucy's phone was ringing constantly. She was starting to believe in herself again. She was a problem solver, a wedding fixer. From locating errant grooms at two o'clock in the morning the night before the wedding – he was cling-filmed naked to a lamppost – to arranging hen weekends in foreign climes, including sourcing the Where's Wally outfits or whatever the theme happened to be. She loved every single minute of it and there was nothing she couldn't handle.

Her grandad was in his element. He'd had the cast taken off his arm now and his blood sugars were all under control so there was no real need for him to be at Sycamore Lodge. But he didn't have the heart to tell Lucy he wanted to come home in case it made her uncomfortable.

He and Violet had become quite friendly. He liked her very much; she wasn't like the others who only wanted to go to sleep or play dominoes. She was full of energy; she loved to play poker for money, drink whisky and go out dancing. She had a wicked sense of humour and could be accused of leading Dougie astray.

Lucy didn't quite know what to make of it when she received the first phone call from Sycamore Lodge. She was asked to come to a meeting with the manageress, a stern-sounding lady who wouldn't give anything away over the phone other than to tell her that her grandfather was perfectly healthy. Lucy raced up to the home and left Jackson playing by the entrance with Baxter. Jackson had insisted on wearing his new Cowboy outfit that he was obsessed with since grandad had introduced him to John Wayne movies..

Jackson was throwing the ball and Baxter fetching; the game was going quite well up until the ball landed in the river and with a huge splosh Baxter jumped in after it. After a pleasant swim he eventually got back out again and, dripping with mud, he dropped the ball at Jackson's feet. Jackson didn't have a good feeling about this. He picked the ball up and was about to throw it when he saw Baxter was about to jump up at him and get him filthy. In order to save himself he threw the ball as hard as he could behind him, thinking this diversionary manoeuvre would confuse Baxter and stop him in his tracks. Baxter, however, had other ideas. He chased after the ball and dived into the open-topped Aston Martin that was parked in the car park. Jackson's heart was racing; this could get them in big trouble. He ran to the previously spotless car.
    'No, Baxter, no. Mummy's going to be mad at you,' he shouted. Baxter looked up from trying to get the ball

from under the seat and shook his huge body. Muddy water flew everywhere, all over the cream upholstery, the inside of the windscreen and all over Jackson too. The timing couldn't have been worse as a man came out of Sycamore Lodge, very smart in his snappy suit, chatting on the phone and aiming his remote at the car. On seeing the sight before him his jaw dropped open in disbelief. Baxter jumped out of the car and straight up at him. His muddy paws left imprints on his freshly laundered shirt. Jackson called the dog and they ran as fast as their legs and paws could carry them.

Dominic Cavendish was not happy; his face twisted in a mix of horror and disbelief; he could not take in what had just happened. Not only had he been summoned up to Sycamore Lodge to be told that his gran was running some sort of illegal gambling den with a man called Dougie Woods and that they operated a three strikes and you're out policy. But now his brand-new Aston Martin had been ruined by a crazy dog and the Milkybar Kid. He felt like he was going to explode. His blood coursed through the vein in his neck like an express train. His heart was either missing a beat or adding an extra one back in – he couldn't quite work out which – and he wondered if this was what having high blood pressure was like. He stormed back into Sycamore Lodge and demanded to know who the dog and the kid belonged to; however, nobody owned up to it.

Lucy, oblivious to the drama outside, was sitting in Grandad's room laughing with him over the whisky incident. When the manageress had accused him of illegal gambling and having contraband alcohol in the home, he had acted dumb as if he didn't know what she was talking about. He simply pretended he had lost his memory. In the end the manageress gave up interrogating him and reminded him of the three strikes rule. He apologised but swore he couldn't remember the incident whatsoever. He maintained his innocence even when his room had been searched and they had found a quarter of the bottle of whisky left. He had looked surprised and insisted that someone must have planted it there. Lucy made him promise to be more careful, but her heart went out to him because he was being so restricted.

As she came out, she received a text from Jackson saying that Baxter had jumped in the river, so he'd taken him home. She dreaded what she would find when she got there but was quite surprised to find he'd used the garden hose and a bowl of soapy water and had cleaned him up really well. He was such a good boy.

Chapter 8

Lucy carried a tray of dark orange teas thick enough to stand a spoon in, as well as biscuits and a sugar bowl for Finn and his team. Despondency overwhelmed her as she had a look around the building. Rotten, splintered wood hung down from the rafters, plaster was crumbling off, windows were smashed behind the boards, the floor was uneven, and the dust was inches thick. As if that wasn't bad enough, sinister-looking huge black cobwebs darkened each corner, the ceiling and the walls. She imagined that if she had a stick and swirled it around the place, she could soon make a gigantic dirty black Halloween candyfloss. She dreaded to think how big the monsters that made them must have been. Lines appeared across her forehead as she found it hard to imagine how it would eventually look. Finn noticed her expression and reassured her as much as he could.

'This looks a lot worse than it is I promise you,' he said. 'This is as bad as it gets and it's all uphill from here, honestly.' He smiled at her and blew his floppy black fringe out of his eyes as he took one of the mugs of tea.

She smiled weakly, dispersing the frown lines, and nodded. 'I'm sure you're right – it just seems so bleak like this.'

'You need to remember that image you have in your mind of what you want it to look like. My wife is an artist

47

with a great vision, and she has a picture of this place as it looked before we started the renovations. You should pop into her art gallery and take a look. He dug into his jeans pocket for a business card and handed it to her. Lucy accepted it gratefully; it had a tiny watercolour of the gallery, which was called Davinci's. She smiled with recognition.

'Ah, I've seen this place along the river but have never been in as I've always had Baxter with me. I'll pop along there later – thanks for that.'

'No problem,' said Finn as he put his hard hat back on again and went back to tackle the rubble. 'Thanks for the tea.'

Lucy couldn't wait to get to the art gallery and so decided now was as good a time as any. The walk along the river always managed to bring a smile to her face and relax her. Flocks of geese and ducks swam alongside her for a little while, hoping that she had some treats for them. They quickly lost interest when it became apparent that she didn't, quacking and honking their disgust loudly.

Davinci's was a striking building, a beautiful converted lock house with a side extension that housed the art gallery. She studied some of the stunning portraits and landscapes in the large picture windows before she went inside. The masterpieces were hung on plain white walls fitted with spotlights that shone on them, showcasing the talent of Gracie and another artist called Dolly Davinci. A separate area was dedicated to local artists and a notice board showed details of the winner of the Dolly Davinci bursary.

As she walked into another showroom towards the back of the building, she saw a lady with dark hair tied in a ponytail carefully hanging a new painting of a wedding at the old church in the village. The detail was amazing.

48

She jumped as she turned around and saw Lucy standing there. She recovered quickly and laughed. Her hands covered her mouth.

'I'm so sorry, I really need to put a bell on that door. I often get carried away in my own little world here.' She held out her hand to Lucy. 'Hi, my name's Gracie. How can I help you?'

Lucy returned the handshake. Her eyes moved from Gracie's friendly face to the huge bump under her top, which couldn't go unnoticed.

'I'm Lucy – oh congratulations. When are you due?'

'In a couple of months – the trouble is I keep forgetting this bump is there and end up knocking into things.' They both laughed. 'Have you got any children?'

Lucy's heart lit up as she spoke. 'Yes, I've got my little man Jackson. He's eight years old and I love him to bits.' She took out her phone and showed her a picture of him cuddling Baxter the dog.

'Aw he's gorgeous; I'm so excited and can't wait for mine to be born.'

'Is this your first?'

'Yes, although I do have a stepdaughter from a previous relationship who's all grown up now. I was just going to get myself a drink. Would you like a glass of wine?'

Lucy instinctively looked at her watch. It was past twelve, though only just, but this lady appeared very friendly and a chance for a little chat and a chill-out moment was so tempting.

'Oh, go on then, yes please,' she answered. 'Do you know what you're having?'

Gracie went behind the small bar and poured a prosecco for Lucy and a glass of sparkling elderflower water for herself; she put some crisps and nuts on the bar top and rested the drinks on small coasters, which had the same wonderful watercolour of Davinci's on them.

'No, I was desperate to know but Finn, my husband, wants a surprise. And I must admit the not knowing does add to the excitement.'

'Yes, it was Finn who told me about this place as he's doing some work for me at the moment and he said you had a painting of the old signal box.'

'Ah so you're the lady who's opening it as a café. I think that's an amazing idea and Finn is well impressed. Here come and see this.' They picked up their drinks and Gracie led the way to the back of the gallery; the spotlights highlighted the amazing detail in each painting. First Gracie showed her the painting of the signal box, which she had done about a year ago, and one that had been painted by her mentor and great friend, the late Dolly Davinci.

Lucy gasped out loud when she saw it. Gracie continued, 'As you can see by the date Dolly painted this one thirty-five years ago. This is the building in its original form as a working signal box. Look, you can even see the little man in there.'

'It's beautiful and believe it or not that little man is my grandad. We are going into partnership together with this venture.' She felt as though she would burst with pride and was desperate to tell her grandad. 'Is this picture for sale? My grandad would love it.'

Gracie shook her head. 'I'm afraid not – we can't part with any of Dolly's originals, but we do offer limited edition prints so that there will never be more than one hundred copies. I'll show you what else we can do. She popped behind the bar again and opened a door. Lucy could see it led to a small office. Gracie reached under the desk and brought out a box full of tablemats and coasters displaying various paintings that hung on the wall.

Lucy could picture the paintings of the signal box of past, present and future on these placemats, coasters, leaflets and aprons. Maybe even on wedding stationery if she could pull it off as a successful wedding venue. She spent the rest of the afternoon with Gracie and had another prosecco and then a coffee. Gracie showed her a painting she had done of Davinci's just from imagination as the place was derelict when she'd painted it. Lucy commissioned her to do one of the Signal Box Café as she needed to start advertising it now and stirring up some interest.

Gracie pulled a notepad and pen from a drawer behind the bar and made some notes of what Lucy's vision of the future signal box would be like. She assured her that she would check out the details with Finn to ensure they were realistic. Lucy could tell that she and Gracie were going to be great friends.

Lucy had ordered a large framed print of each of the signal box paintings that Gracie had but decided she wouldn't tell Grandad yet as that would be a lovely surprise for him. She would wait for Gracie's final picture to be done before ordering the placemats.

Jackson was home from school and bored so asked if he could take Baxter for a walk. Lucy was busy making dinner and agreed but ran through all the rules he had to follow when out alone. He repeated them parrot fashion as he counted them off on his fingers.

'No talking to strangers; no playing by the water; don't go near any roads and no playing on the train track and make sure I have my phone and keep Baxter on the lead and make sure I pick up his poop in a poop bag.' He patted his pocket, which crinkled to let her know he had the poop bags in there.

'And one more,' said Lucy holding a finger up to him for emphasis.

'Oh yes, always make sure I can still see the signal box,' he added.

'Good boy,' said Lucy kissing him on the top of the head. She could never have let him out alone where they used to live but Bramblewood was so much safer and the children had a bit more freedom, plus he had a basic phone so she could keep a check on him.

Twenty minutes later as she was dishing up his favourite meatballs and spaghetti and putting her home-made sticky toffee pudding in the oven, she heard a hammering on the door. Her heart pounding, she ran to open it only to find a breathless Jackson covered top to toe in mud all down his front whilst a wet-faced Baxter, who was clean apart from his paws, was munching on a very large slithery fish.

'What on earth's happened?' she asked, pointing to his shoes so he would take them off. Jackson kicked off his shoes without untying them and left them in the hallway. Lucy chased the dog into the garden with his disgusting slimy feast and scooted Jackson upstairs for an immediate shower. She took his muddy glasses off and rinsed them under the water as Jackson caught his breath and explained.

'There were some fishermen along the river with their green tents up and little camping chairs and one man was talking to another when Baxter dived into his net and stole the biggest fish. The man shouted at him and called him a big hairy hound and Baxter was scared so he ran off. I tripped and fell in the muddy bit along the river and Baxter pulled me along for a bit but then the man picked me up and I ran off.' He shivered but then laughed. 'The man's face was so funny, Mummy. He wasn't happy about losing his fish, but his friend was laughing at him.'

'Oh, my goodness, you poor thing,' she said wrapping him in a warm towel and kissing his head. 'Thank goodness you're not hurt, but what on earth were you doing along the river? You know you're not supposed to go that far.'

'I'm sorry, Mummy but Baxter wanted to see Rosie. It was only a little way down the river, and I could still see the top of the signal box just about peeping through the trees.'

'Well I hope you've learnt your lesson now,' she scolded gently as he pulled his pyjama top over his head. 'Now come on, dinner is ready.'

Dominic Cavendish was in the pub later listening to his friend tell the others about the fish that got away, his face serious as usual but he had to join in the laughter as his mates took the mick out of him. He shook his head as he remembered panicking when he saw the boy being dragged through the mud. This kid and his dog were intent on terrorising him. He was tempted to shove the cleaning bill for his car into the kid's hand when he picked him off the ground but he was too concerned that he was hurt. He hadn't seemed hurt when he flew like the wind after that crazy dog. His eyes crinkled at the sides as he laughed again. It had been like a comedy sketch.

He bantered back with the lads, telling them it was definitely a prize-winning catch and yes it was the one that got away. It was a funny situation but slightly worrying too. He couldn't help feeling relieved that one, he had never had kids and two, he had never had a dog.

Chapter 9

Abbie had been trying to persuade Lucy to come out for a drink for ages, but she couldn't go because she hadn't got a babysitter for Jackson. So, when he had gone on a school trip for a couple of days, she decided that now was the time to have a night on the town. Or at least to the local pub. The Flamingo's Leg was situated on the corner of Market Square and had a pleasant beer garden overlooking the river. It was late spring, and the trees were still heavily laden with frothy pink blossom, which had spilt onto the grass around them. Moored long boats bobbed up and down on the river and some were moving along, their owners waving as they passed by.

They had chosen to sit outside until it started getting dark; Abbie plonked an ice bucket on the wooden table with the bottle of Pinot Grigio in it and two glasses. Lucy had received a text from Jackson saying he'd arrived safely and was having a wicked time, so she was able to relax at last.

She had been pretty worked up about him going away with the school as he had never stayed anywhere overnight before apart from at her mum and dad's but that didn't count. Her worries were somewhat lessened by the excitement he'd expressed on being able to go on the trip and she knew she couldn't stop him – much as she might want to. He was growing up now and getting to be a big boy.

She felt like a big girl now, all grown up and out with another adult. She even had make-up on. She cracked open the bottle and filled both glasses.

'So, how're the signal box plans going?' asked Abbie.

'Really well, thank you, but it still doesn't feel real yet. Not like Wedding Belles where we can immediately see how things are going.' She smiled and took a sip of wine. 'Oh that tastes so good.' She smacked her lips together noisily. 'I think it tastes even better when you don't have to get up to an eight-year-old ball of energy the next morning. We might need a bigger bottle.'

Abbie laughed. 'There's plenty more where that came from – don't you worry about that, missy.'

'Back to business though, I think we're doing okay. The bookings are coming in slowly but surely. We could do with a few more but I'm sure they'll come. I had a really weird one the other day: this man asked me if I could arrange a wedding for him and his ferret.'

'Are you serious?' screeched Abbie. 'Ew, those weird little things make my skin crawl.' She shivered.

'And men who want to marry them make my skin crawl too.' Lucy laughed. 'We really need some advertising but that costs money, which we haven't got.'

'Well it's only a couple of weeks until our wedding at the Majestic hotel. I still can't believe you managed to get in there at such short notice, so I'm sure we'll get some recommendations from that, although I still can't believe the groom asked for shotguns on the invitations.' Abbie chuckled.

'I know, strange sense of humour. Thank God the bride put her foot down. Ah it's quite sweet really, a surprise baby.'

'Very sweet but a headache for the dressmaker I imagine. Anyway, talking of advertising, I noticed a competition in one of my photography magazines for the most unusual wedding venue. I thought it would be ideal publicity for you and the Signal Box Café – what do you say?' she asked, reaching into her bag and handing Lucy the clipping.

Lucy loved the idea but was hesitant. 'But the closing date is too soon. We won't be able to take a proper picture of the venue,' she complained.

'But that's where I come in,' said Abbie nudging Lucy in the ribs for encouragement. 'I can edit the picture, so as soon as the lady from the art gallery completes her painting, I can use it as the background.'

'Are you serious? That would be amazing.' Lucy gulped down some more wine in celebration before continuing. 'Wait, on the background of what?'

'On the background of our fake wedding photo of course. We just need a bride and a groom.'

'Sounds great but where are we going to get them from?'

'Well that's where you come in. I've got a mate from my course – Eddie; we always help each other out on shoots. He'll be the groom and you . . .' She wagged her finger in Lucy's face. 'You are going to be the bride.'

'Who me? No way, Abbie, there's no way I can do that. Can't you do it? I'd be far too embarrassed.'

'Well who would take the photos if I'm the bride?'

'Oh yes, I never thought of that. Can't we use a model or something?'

Abbie batted away her objections. 'Okay, do you have any idea how much models cost?'

'No.' She pouted.

'Well it's a lot, and do you know how much money we have?'

'Erm, let me think,' joked Lucy. 'That would be none, I believe.'

'Exaaaactly, zilch. So that means that you, Lucy, are going to have to be our blushing bride and it means that you are going to get to wear a wedding dress, which you can't deny has been your childhood dream. It'll be great, I promise.'

'I just have one question: what does Eddie look like?'

'He's absolutely gorgeous,' answered Abbie, giggling as Lucy waggled her eyebrows, 'and gay.'

'Oh damn,' chuckled Lucy. 'Just my luck.'

'So, we're on then?'

'I'm sure I'll regret it in the morning but yes we're on.' They chinked their glasses together and decided to go inside to order another bottle and some food. As they approached the door the sound of shouting distracted them. They glanced over to the river just in time to see the back of two bandana-wearing pensioners on a mobility scooter racing along the towpath, followed by a convoy of five or six more of the scooters all being chased by two breathless ladies in white overalls. Lucy and Abbie looked at each other and laughed hysterically until they were doubled over, wondering whether they had actually seen that or whether it was too much wine.

Once inside they ordered their food, found a seat and continued their chat. The pub was full and buzzed with a friendly atmosphere. One of the owners, Ray, stopped to introduce himself and asked how their food was. The ecstatic looks on their faces said it all. 'Aren't you the lady who's converting the signal box?' he asked Lucy.

'Yes, I am along with my grandad and I'm also offering a complete wedding planning service with my other Wedding Belle here.' She pointed to Abbie who smiled at him.

'I know Dougie well – please tell him Ray from the pub sends his regards?'

'Will do.'

'I don't suppose you have a card you can sneak to me whilst my better half is looking the other way? Only I've got an idea I'd like to discuss with you.' He put his finger to his lips and gestured to a handsome man serving behind the bar. Lucy took a business card out of her bag, which he took and quickly slipped into his back pocket. He made the shape of a phone with his thumb and little finger and motioned that he'd call her.

Abbie and Lucy looked at each other with wide eyes and huge smiles. 'I've only just had them printed too,' said Lucy.

Loud laughter came from the other side of the bar and Lucy saw a group of men chatting and drinking. She caught the eye of one in particular that she couldn't take her eyes off. Tall and broad with dark blond hair swept over to the side; he looked like a city type. His dark grey designer suit looked smart and edgy. He had an arrogance about him that intrigued her. His eyes were steely grey and when he laughed with his friends, crinkles appeared at the sides of them. His cheekbones were sharp and chiselled, his lips perfectly formed; he looked just like a model she thought.

'Who looks like a model?' asked Abbie, following Lucy's gaze.

'Oh, did I say that out loud?' She giggled, holding her fingers to her mouth as if to stop any other inappropriate words from coming out.

'Which one are you talking about?' She craned her neck to see over the crowd. 'Oh actually my brother is over there – maybe he can tell us who he is.' She stood up to gain his attention. 'Dom, Dom,' she shouted, beckoning him over.

Lucy nearly fainted when she realised it was the guy she had been ogling. He gestured to his friends that he would be back in a minute. Lucy imagined that she was having a menopausal hot flush as the heat rose from her toes to her hair roots.

'Don't you dare ask him and don't tell him it's me!' she growled at Abbie. She couldn't believe this was the guy who used to tease her mercilessly when they were younger. He would pull her pigtails and take toys from her and call her names. He used to do the same with Abbie too, but they clearly got on much better now as grown-ups.

Abbie smiled mischievously as realisation dawned on her.

He came over and hugged his little sis, then lifted his hand up to say hello to Lucy. She would never have recognised him, and he didn't seem to recognise her thankfully.

'Lucy, this is Dom,' said Abbie, grinning inanely after how Lucy had described him. She pulled kissy faces at her behind Dom's back.

Lucy was trying desperately hard to keep a straight face.

'It's nice to meet you, Lucy.' He appraised her and appeared to like what he saw but his eyes didn't linger for long. He stopped himself with a shake of the head. He seemed agitated as though eager to get back to his friends. 'How's the job going, Sis?'

'Erm, I'm not actually working there anymore.' Abbie looked sheepish.

His eyes narrowed. 'What did you do this time?'

'No, I didn't do anything. I gave my notice in; I wasn't sacked.'

'Abbie, I got that job for you in good faith. You said you were back from your travels for good now.'

'Dom, I am grateful to you for getting me the job, but it wasn't what I thought it would be. Ah don't roll your eyes at me. I wasn't getting to use my skills there. Look, you don't have to worry because Lucy and I have decided to go into business together. She's a wedding planner so we can help each other out with potential clients.'

'A wedding planner.' His lip curled into a cynical smile. 'I suppose I should be grateful that some people still believe in the sanctity of marriage. Keep up the good work, Lucy, as you're keeping me in a job.' He turned to walk away, his cheeks hollowed as if grinding his teeth with tension. He looked unbelievably sexy but had annoyed Lucy.

'Weddings are beautiful,' she said. 'And what do you do that's so important?'

'Weddings may be beautiful, but marriages certainly aren't. When the flowers have died and the cake has gone stale, then what are you left with?' He picked up a napkin and tore it into little pieces. 'Paper dreams that's what.' He threw the bits of napkin in the air like confetti over their heads. 'Wedding business, ha – I'll give it a month.' He smirked and stalked off.

Abbie helped Lucy pick the bits of tissue out of her blonde curls. 'I'm so sorry about that, Lucy; he got divorced two years ago and still feels bitter, as you can see.'

'Oh, right okay, perfectly understandable – I see his personality hasn't improved much over the years. So, what did you say he does again?'

'He's a divorce lawyer,' she answered.

That explains a lot,' Lucy replied. 'Well don't you worry, Abbie, we'll show him.'

Chapter 10

Early next morning, Lucy couldn't figure out what the noise was at first, she wasn't used to drinking much and her head was splitting. It didn't help that the sun was shining brightly. She eventually realised it was her phone and answered it under the covers.

'Good morning this is Mrs King from Sycamore Lodge. May I speak to Ms Wood please.' Lucy's head shot out from under the duvet. She hoped Grandad was all right.

'Yes, speaking. Is my grandad okay?'

'That's a matter of opinion, dear, health wise he's fine but behaviour wise is a different story. Could you please come in as soon as possible for an urgent meeting?'

'Oh, what now?' Lucy thought as she showered quickly and got dressed. She took some painkillers as the pain shot across her eyes every time she bent down. When she got downstairs, she realised she couldn't go anywhere without a coffee and poured some into a travel cup. She fed Baxter and Maud and quickly let them out into the garden.

As she passed the signal box, she could hear the machinery from the men working in there. It was a sound that made her smile; she knew that that sound was bringing her closer to achieving her dream. She took the shortcut down the high street to Sycamore Lodge as Mrs King did not sound like the sort of lady who liked to be kept waiting. She took a swig of her coffee feeling the need for caffeine to prepare her for whatever it was Nurse Ratched, as her grandad had nicknamed her, had to say. She didn't seem like the sort of lady who would call with any good news.

Once there she was asked to sit outside Mrs King's room until she was called. Her grandad was sitting on one of the chairs looking quite sheepish. It was like she was sitting outside the headmaster's office.

She kissed him on the cheek and couldn't help smiling at him.

'What have you been up to now, Grandad?' she asked in mock exasperation.

'We just wanted an Indian meal that's all,' he said. 'They never cook curry in here or anything with any flavour for that matter in case our sensitive stomachs can't handle it. We only wanted a bit of spice in our lives.'

As the door to Mrs King's office opened Lucy heard the tail end of a conversation with a man's voice promising that it wouldn't happen again. She jumped as she came face to face with Dom and the older lady who she recognised as Violet. She saw Violet wink at her grandad as they passed each other. Dom flashed a look of recognition but didn't acknowledge her as he answered his phone. He did not look happy.

Lucy braced herself for the worst as they entered the office. She was right to be prepared. Mrs King turned her computer screen to face Lucy and her grandad to show the local newspaper's online edition. It consisted of six mobility scooters racing along the river, with a total of eight pensioners riding on them. Two uniformed assistants were chasing after them. The picture was huge and the headline even bigger.

Lucy and her grandad both had to stifle a snigger as Mrs King in her plum-in-her-mouth accent read out the headline.

'Tandoori Nights and Support Tights for Bramblewood's Hot and Spicy Pensioners.'

She continued with the article after looking sternly over the top of her glasses at her visitors.

'Spice-loving pensioners from local retirement village, Sycamore Lodge, caused havoc in the sleepy town of Bramblewood as they forged a breakout. Six mobility scooters were stolen in the event and police have warned that further charges such as driving without due care and attention and mobility scooters taken without consent will be taken into consideration.

'The owner of the local Indian restaurant *Bramblewood Spice* has said they will not press charges for the non-payment of bills as long as the money is repaid.'

Lucy was almost bursting with mirth; this lady was taking it so seriously when the police and restaurant owner had seen it as funny. There was even a smaller picture of a policeman in uniform laughing at the scene. She covered her giggle with a cough and looked at her grandad with tears in her eyes.

'So, what do you have to say for yourself then, Grandad?' she asked, her voice shaking.

'What's that, love?' he replied, and she knew he'd turned his hearing aid off. She apologised to Mrs King on his behalf and promised he would be much better behaved in the future. She plucked up the courage to ask whether maybe the residents could be offered some spicier foods every now and then or whether the home could arrange regular trips to some of the restaurants in the town for those who were still lively enough to enjoy it.

Mrs King promised to look into it. Lucy knew she was true to her word because after her grandad had been in trouble over the gambling and whisky, Lucy had filled a slip in for the Sycamore Lodge suggestions box to request a drinks trolley, which could come round serving alcohol. Also, whether they could introduce events such as race nights, which she thought the residents would enjoy. Both of these had been implemented and had been a real hit. When they got back to Grandad's room, he switched his hearing aid back on again and they both laughed so heartily that Lucy's tummy ached.

'That's pensioner power for you, Lucy,' he said.

'Are you sure you want to stay here, Grandad?' she asked gently.

'I'm having the time of my life love,' he answered with a twinkle in his eye. 'There's a new guy who moved in last week and his name's old Bill, cos he's old and his name's Bill but guess what?'

'I don't know what? Has he got a wife called Gill? Bill and Gill.'

'No, he used to be a policeman, so he's old Bill and he's known as Old Bill. He cracks me up. His son got called up too by Nurse Ratched – he was the policeman laughing in the article. He's known as young Bill.'

Lucy chuckled along and couldn't help but be proud of her grandad even though he was a bit of a rebel.

She promised to collect him the next day to meet up with Finn so they could discuss the intricacies of the train tracks for the restaurant and the signal controls they were going to clean up and display. Grandad had been in touch with his contact from the railway and had organised the delivery of the reclaimed train seats in a couple of weeks. He had the use of a little workshop at Sycamore Lodge and had been carefully working on the trains that would be used to deliver the drinks. He had promised to let Jackson help him to paint them and they were both looking forward to that.

Chapter 11

Giggles popped out of her like bubbles being blown through a wand as she left Sycamore Lodge. The thought of Grandad leading a posse of pensioners along the river on mobility scooters with Violet riding pillion had her in tears. The sun shone down from a cloudless blue sky and her hangover had been laughed away. There were a few cars in the car park, including a very flashy open-topped Aston Martin. Dominic Cavendish was leaning against it; his shades covered his eyes. He called out to her as she walked past.

'So, Douglas Woods is your responsibility, is he?' he asked in not a particularly friendly fashion.

'He's my grandad. Why?' she replied, not bothering to stop walking even though the sight of him turned her legs to marshmallows.

'Can you please just tell him to leave my gran alone?'

She stopped abruptly and tried to look in his eyes but could only see her own reflection in his sunglasses. This made her feel self-conscious as her curls looked wild and her face was distorted in the lenses. She looked at his lips instead, but they looked so kissable she had to look away from them; maybe his ear would be safe. She spoke to the ear.

'Is Violet your gran? If so, don't you think that she is old enough to decide who she can be friends with?'

Dom seemed to think she was looking past him and turned behind to check there was nobody there.

'She's an old lady who wants some peace and quiet and your grandad is leading her astray. If he gets her into trouble again then she will be kicked out of Sycamore Lodge and there isn't anyone to look after her with Abbie and me working. This is serious business,' he snapped.

'Well I think that you are completely underestimating your gran and she seems to me like a very intelligent woman who is full of life. You shouldn't write people off just because they're old you know; they still have a lot to give. Besides, I think they're very fond of each other.'

'Well you would think that wouldn't you – everything's all hearts and flowers in your little romantic dream world. I mean I can't believe that you persuaded Abbie to give up her real job for a pipe dream. So, Little Miss Wedding Planner, welcome to the real world where actions have consequences and just tell your grandad to back off.'

Tears sprang to her eyes. She decided to not lower herself by answering, turned away from him and walked off.

What a horrible man, she thought, even if his lips are unbelievably kissable, she would not kiss them even if he was the last man on earth. She stomped off and heard his engine roar as he drove away.

Dominic Cavendish regretted that conversation as soon as it was over. She hadn't asked for that at all. He expected all women to be like his ex-wife who drove him crazy with her selfish, pampered money-grabbing ways. She had loved to row. And made it seem like a conversation wasn't normal unless it was shouted at least twenty decibels too high, and both parties were spitting venom. He'd almost forgotten how to talk to the opposite sex now; surrounding himself with laddish friends and girls who were up for just one night was about all he could cope with.

This Lucy was having a strange effect on him and she seemed to appear every which way he turned, including in his thoughts far too often for his liking. She was gorgeous and had he been looking for someone to spend time with, she would have been a perfect choice superficially. But he'd had it with relationships. His job certainly helped him stick to those convictions. He'd dealt with enough fallout from relationships that had started out as one day that cost more than some people's houses, only for it to fall to pieces and end up costing even more to split up. His married years had been a huge waste of time and money and there was no way he would ever go down that road again. He was working on a tricky case right now for a well-known actor who against his advice had not signed a prenup and it was a total headache.

The last thing he needed right now was his gran being all over the front page of the local newspaper. Not to mention possibly getting kicked out of this prestigious retirement home; after all he was a respected lawyer with an impeccable reputation. That Lucy had some gall trying to make out that his gran was to blame and not to mention the fact that she'd led his sister astray. He loved Abbie and her zest for life, but she was settling down now and his mate Phil had done him a huge favour giving her that job. The women in his family appeared to be hypnotised by Dougie and Lucy Woods.

His annoyance was somewhat abated by the flicker of fire he'd noticed in Lucy's eyes when she challenged him. He was glad he'd had his shades on, as he was sure those piercing, baby blues would have seen straight through him. She was gutsy and attractive. There was also a familiarity about her that he couldn't quite place. He was probably making himself look like a complete prat in front of her but weddings, and all that romance shit, just didn't do it for him.

Chapter 12

The coach full of waving children lumbered into the school playground to be greeted by a crowd of excited parents, all waiting to have their exhausted children back home again after the school trip. Black bin bags of dirty, soaked clothing were handed to parents and a box of filthy smelly lost property was tipped out onto the ground, most of it left unclaimed.

Jackson skipped the whole way home as he held Lucy's hand; she pulled his little trolley case along with the other, the black bin bag balanced on top of it. She could see he'd had a brilliant time; he was growing up far too quickly. That was his first residential school trip and he was already talking about the next one.

She told him that Grandad had said the trains were ready for painting now and he was allowed to help him in the workshop. Jackson yelled 'Yes!' and punched the air in delight. As a welcome-home treat, they popped down to Serendipity for dinner. It had quickly become Jackson's favourite place to be and Rosie had become his favourite person outside the family. She often treated him with little extras like comics and colouring books. He excitedly told her and his mum about some of the fun activities on his trip – he'd been canoeing and horse riding and abseiling. He looked happy, tired and like he could do with a good scrub.

Lucy thought back to when he was little and she'd spent every moment of his life with him. Now he was doing these exciting new things without her. Although she knew he needed to do that in order to grow and live in the real world as an independent person, part of her wished she could bundle him up in cotton wool to keep him safe and sound. However, that was impossible and she knew she would have to cherish the time that he wanted to spend with her because he would soon outgrow her and want to be with his friends. She thought fondly of Gracie – a new baby, what an amazing adventure she had to look forward to and with a lovely supportive husband by her side. They were lucky.

She could see Jackson's eyes starting to close so they gathered up their things and headed home. He needed a lovely bubbly bath, then story, then bed.

Grandad and Jackson worked hard all weekend on painting their trains; once they were done Lucy brought them both back to Railway Cottage for a lamb roast dinner. Grandad sniffed the air hungrily as he walked in. Lucy could tell that fond memories of coming home to his wife's roasts had resurfaced, bringing a tear to his eye. Maud meowed loudly and rubbed herself against his legs before curling up on his lap as soon as he sat down.

'I've missed this little place but have loved every minute of you and Jackson staying here. You know I haven't been this happy since your lovely nana was here.'

'And we've loved being here too, Grandad. It really feels like home.' Lucy poured herself a glass of red, Grandad a beer and poured a ginger beer for Jackson who felt ever so grown up and took a swig every time he saw Grandad take one.

'To family,' said Grandad raising his glass.

'To family,' repeated Lucy and Jackson.

After a delicious dinner, Grandad and Jackson played with the trains they'd worked so hard on. Grandad was revisiting skills he hadn't used for a long time and had put working engines in them. He had miles of spare tracks that he would be able to utilise for the restaurant but in the meantime he and Jackson had fun by sitting on the floor at either end of the lounge/diner and sent biscuits and coins to each other via the trains.

After lunch Lucy answered a call from a bride in floods of tears. It was the day before her wedding and the cellar where her champagne had been stored had flooded and the labels were ruined. She'd planned to give some as presents to their parents and best man, some for the table and each guest was to have a small bottle as a wedding favour.

'Don't worry,' Lucy had said, 'I can fix this.' She asked her for a photo of the couple and took the wedding details down. She called Abbie and asked her for help. Twenty minutes later Lucy was unloading crates of champagne from her mini and Abbie was unloading the rest from her car. She called Grandad and Jackson and they formed a human chain to get the crates into Railway Cottage. Whilst the boys scrubbed off what was left of the old labels with nailbrushes and soapy water. Abbie and Lucy worked on creating personalised labels for the different-sized bottles using the pictures and details of the wedding. Abbie added Wedding Belles contact details in small letters across the bottom. 'Genius,' said Lucy.

Whilst they got into the rhythm of sticking the labels on, Ray from the pub called. Lucy put the phone on speaker and he explained his idea. She and Abbie shared excited glances and her heart fluttered with anticipation of working on his plans.

As quickly as the labels were printing off, Lucy and Abbie were cutting them out and sticking them onto the bottles. The production line was working well until the printer made a loud screeching followed by a chugging sound and then began spewing out smudged black, screwed-up paper.

'No,' cried Lucy. 'Not now.'

'What's happened?' asked Abbie.

'It's bloody jammed. I thought it was too good to be true.' Lucy tried to reset it, pulled it, poked it, switched it on and off but all to no avail. She was about to hurl it to the floor when Abbie came up with a solution.

'Don't worry I'll call Dom. He's got a super-duper printer – he won't mind us using it.' Abbie called him and from the conversation that Lucy could hear he'd agreed to do it. 'Okay you just need to pop round and pick the printouts up. He lives just opposite the green at number 30.'

Lucy didn't relish the thought of going to see him but Abbie had a couple more of the personalised labels to create for the best man and ushers, so she had to.

She found the house easily and knocked on the door. She could feel her face flushing already in anticipation of seeing him.

'Hi,' he said, when he opened the door. He was wearing jeans and a sweatshirt and had a bottle of beer in his hand. She could hear the football on the telly in the background. He looked softer without the suit, more relaxed.

'Hi, I'm sorry to interrupt the game. My stupid printer packed up and it was an urgent last-minute job.'

'Don't worry,' he said, 'I'm used to Abbie having the odd crisis.'

Lucy searched his face for criticism but found none. He actually appeared normal. He led her upstairs to his office, which had a desk and a sofa in it. The printer was already noisily churning out reams of paper. He picked one of the printed sheets and studied it. 'That's a really clever idea. I knew you'd be able to sort it, but I never expected something this good.'

'Oh.' Lucy was taken aback. 'Do you know the couple?'

'Yes, the best man is a friend of mine.. Funny enough I handled his divorce for him not so long ago. He told me about their predicament, so I recommended you. I'm glad you pulled it off though.'

Lucy didn't think it was the least bit funny but decided not to bite on that subject. 'Wow, I didn't expect that but I'm grateful you did. Thank you and thanks for this.' She pointed to the pile of paper. 'I guess we need to invest in a more efficient printer.'

'It's no problem – it's quite nice to see you without having to worry about my gran getting booted out of her home.'

She was about to go on the defensive but noticed he was smiling; his smile changed his whole persona and was highly contagious. The corners of her mouth responded by curling upwards, totally without her permission, and her stomach was enjoying a ride on the waltzers. She knew she had to keep her guard up against him. Anyone who could make her feel like this could cause her a lot of damage in the long run. Having been hurt before, she didn't relish the thought of opening herself up again.

His phone beeped, breaking the awkward silence as Abbie sent more labels and he forwarded them wirelessly to the printer. When they'd finished, he handed the stack of papers to Lucy. She almost dropped them as a jolt of electricity swept through her when his hand brushed against hers. She wondered whether he'd felt it too as his eyes met hers just for a second before he looked away.

'You must let me pay for these or at least let me buy you more printer cartridges.' She held the stack of paper to her chest.

'I thought you were going to say you'd buy me a drink then.' He laughed.

'Well I can do that too if you like.' Her cheeks were on fire. 'I mean I can buy you some beer, to have at home, I mean, not to go on a . . .' She stopped herself before she sounded any more ridiculous than she did already.

'No, it's fine really – just keep our Abbie out of trouble. I have to say she seems to be taking this wedding stuff seriously for once in her life. I actually think you make a good team.'

He brought his beer bottle to his full lips and Lucy couldn't help wishing she could take its place. She stood open-mouthed watching him swig from the bottle and didn't notice that he was speaking.

'Are you all right?'

She realised that she was staring, and her toes curled with embarrassment. She shook her head and snapped herself back to reality. 'Yes, yes sorry I just remembered something else I have to be getting on with. Anyway, thank you for this – you're a lifesaver.'

She galloped down the stairs and ran back to Railway Cottage, her heart pounding all the way.

Once she and Abbie finished sticking the labels on, Lucy wrapped those intended as gifts in cellophane and Abbie tied them with bows to match the bridesmaids' dresses using ribbons from her box of tricks. Eventually they had transformed all 200 bottles and with an aching back and satisfied smile Lucy called the bride. Before they were collected Lucy took pictures of them as they would look great in her portfolio and added personalised bottles to their list of services.

'What a transformation. They look smashing, love,' said Grandad, his eyes filled with pride.

The groom and his best man collected them and twenty minutes later the bride called her, again in floods of tears, but this time happy ones as she was so delighted with the unique touch that Lucy and Abbie had provided.

After a while, Lucy could see Jackson's eyes start to droop and Grandad stifling a yawn, neither wanting the day to end, but Baxter was itching to go for a walk so they attached his lead and walked Grandad back to Sycamore Lodge.

Chapter 13

The day of the photo shoot for their joint venture had arrived and between them Abbie and Lucy had managed to beg, steal and borrow wedding outfits for Lucy and Jackson. The stolen items were wild roses they had found along the river, which they crafted into a small bouquet and a head-dress for Lucy. Abbie had carefully applied her make-up and Lucy could hardly recognise herself. Her curls had been tamed and entwined with the deep pink roses. The white dress had a sweetheart neckline, which sparkled with sequins and fitted all the way down with a fishtail bottom. It was a perfect fit and clung to her curves like a second skin.

Lucy was torn between feeling self-conscious and absolutely fabulous. She'd never worn a wedding dress before, and it seemed deceitful to be wearing one now just for a photo shoot. She wondered whether she would ever genuinely wear one or whether she was destined to be a spinster for the rest of her life.

Abbie had chosen the blossom trees that lined the beer garden of the Flamingo's Leg as the setting. It was perfectly picturesque and would be ideal for natural confetti too.

She began by taking pictures of Lucy and Jackson as bride and pageboy, before drafting in Baxter who wore a huge pink ribbon around his neck. She took some beautiful close-ups and a wonderful shot of Lucy sitting amongst the deep carpet of pink blossom petals.

'Okay, Lucy, now grab handfuls of the blossom and when I shout go, I want you to release them.' Lucy did as she was told – after all this is what she'd been born to do – and Abbie caught the shot as the pale pink petals swooped and swirled around Lucy. 'Now that takes me back, Lucy. You came in the Easter holidays one year and we took it in turns to be bride and bridesmaid. We spent hours throwing the blossom over each other.'

'Yes, we did and then I got my bucket and spade from Nana and Grandad's house and we filled it to the top and made perfume out of it.'

Abbie's phone pinged in her pocket and she looked down at the text and frowned.

'Is everything all right?' asked Lucy as she struggled to get back up again in the restraining dress. She held out her hands and Jackson giggled as he pulled her up.

'Yes, everything's fine,' she replied with an exaggerated brightness. 'Our groom is running a bit late, that's all. Why don't you have a little break for five minutes?'

Abbie walked away from Lucy nearer to the river to get a better phone signal and so she could think. She dialled her brother's number.

'Hi, Dom, I need you to help me out. Are you working from home today?'

'Yeeeeees, why?' His voice was laced with suspicion.

'Just wondering.' She glanced over at Lucy tickling a giggling Jackson. 'Dom, do you remember that time when I lied for you to get that strange girl off your back?'

'Oh God. Yes, what a nightmare that was; in fact I thought we both vowed never to mention that incident again.'

'Yes, we did but do you remember how you said you owed me big time?'

'Oh, I get it now; I might have known you weren't just ringing me to see how I was. What do you want?'

'Ah thanks, bruv, you're a life saver. I just need you to put on a snappy suit and help me out with a photo shoot as my friend Eddie has let me down at the last minute.' She heard him groan.

'Can't I just send you on an all-expenses paid holiday instead, or let you beat me up with a baseball bat?'

'Noooo, although the holiday idea does sound fantastic. Please, Dom, everything is all set up; we're literally just round the corner from you. Under the trees by the Flamingo's Leg – it's for a competition and it's urgent.'

'Oh, all right then, I've got an appointment with my accountant later so I won't be able to stay long. I'll be there in ten minutes.'

'Make that five,' she replied, her shoulders relaxed, and she hung up on him.

'Okay, Lucy, the groom is on his way so let's get you ready.' She brushed off a few errant cherry blossom petals, added a layer of gloss to Lucy's lips and arranged the veil over her face. She gave Jackson a once-over and pulled a couple of twigs out of his hair from where he'd been rolling on the grass with Baxter.

Seven minutes later Dom pulled up into the pub car park and made his way to the trees. He took one look at the scene in front of him and immediately turned and walked away. Abbie almost tripped over her own shoelace in her eagerness to catch him up. She ran in front of him and stopped him, her hands on his arms.

'Please, Dom, I really need to win this competition. I've only got two days left before the closing date and

I need to edit the pictures too. You're my last hope – please.'

'Okay but be as quick as you can.' He stood quite wooden at first, like a groom on a cake. She took a few shots, then asked him to pull the veil back.

'Oh, it's you,' he said as his eyes met Lucy's.

'Don't worry I wasn't expecting you either,' she said, trying to ignore the firework that had exploded inside her when their eyes met. This man had no manners whatsoever, but she decided to show him that she did. 'Thank you for helping us out – this will be an amazing way to advertise our wedding businesses.'

'Touché.' He smirked and she knew she had got him back politely but firmly.

Abbie admonished him. 'Dom, come on, this is meant to be the happiest day of your life. Can you please lose the poker face and make an effort to smile. Just think, the sooner I get my money shot the sooner you can go and then I'll owe you.'

Lucy started to get the giggles, which made him more miserable until he noticed how cute she looked when she laughed, her nose crinkled, and when her pale pink lips parted, he observed her perfectly shaped white teeth.

She had an amazing figure. The beautiful dress showed off every inch of her body. He could think of plenty of worse ways to spend the day so decided to try and enjoy himself and relax a bit. This woman was annoying but there could be no denying she was gorgeous too.

'Now I want you to look deep into each other's eyes,' Abbie instructed from behind the camera.

They did as she asked and he allowed himself to drift into the piercing light blue of her big innocent eyes. He watched as the pupils dilated and felt an attraction he hadn't experienced in a long time. Her nose was crinkling again. She blinked and giggled, apologising to Abbie. She was embarrassed. Her relief was almost tangible when he also blinked and released a pent-up laugh and then it clicked.

He remembered many years ago – he must have been about ten – when he and a friend had thrown down their bikes and climbed up this tree. They were swapping top trumps cards when he heard girls' voices down below. His friend started to talk to him, and Dom had shushed him, gesturing with his finger to his lips. When he looked down, he saw his sister Abbie, who was two years younger than him. Her friend from Railway Cottage was with her. Her white blonde hair flowed around her shoulders, kinked from the pigtails that usually restrained it. He watched as they laughed and giggled, grabbing handfuls of the pale pink blossom and throwing it over their heads as they walked below the branches, one behind the other.

He nodded to his friend. 'Watch this.' He bounced the branch up and down, releasing thousands of pastel pink petals around them. They laughed and swirled, arms outstretched. 'It's snowing,' Abbie had shouted. 'We're in a snow globe.' Lucy had laughed. Dom shook the branch so hard he almost lost his footing and kicked a twig, which fell to the ground. Lucy saw it and picked it up. A full-blossom flower was still attached to it. She inspected it closely then looked up, using her hand as a shield against the sun. He tried to hide but it was too late; she saw him. Their eyes locked for a couple of seconds, just long enough for him to notice how blue hers were.

She gave him a slight smile and then he roared loudly, which made her stop in her tracks. His friend joined in the roaring game, causing both girls to screech in a pitch high enough for a dog whistle and they ran off in the direction of Railway Cottage. 'Stupid girls,' muttered Dom. His friend had agreed, and they carried on with their game. His mind returned to the present to hear Abbie giving him directions.

'Now, Dom, you stand behind her. Lucy, you turn your head and gently touch his cheek with your right hand. Dom, you pretend you're moving in for a kiss.'

'Frigging hell, sis, this might be easier with a twister mat: put your left hand here and lips over there.' He laughed.

Lucy giggled again but they tried to hold the pose for as long as they could. It felt very intimate being this close to someone but then she supposed if you were getting married, you'd be allowed to be intimate. She simply wasn't used to it.

Jackson and Baxter had been playing behind a tree and soon skipped over to join the wedding party.

'Mum have we nearly finished?' he whined. 'I'm bored and want to go home. My friend's coming soon to play with the train set.'

Dom took one look at them, then looked at Lucy and back at Jackson and then his eyes turned into slits as he screwed them up to look at Baxter. He turned to Lucy.

'Are you kidding me – are these really yours?' he said pointing to the offending pair.

'Yes, this is my son Jackson and dog Baxter. Why?'

'Why? Because not only do I have to put up with your grandad running amok with my gran but I also have to put up with your son encouraging this hairy hound to jump soaking wet and filthy into my brand-new car and steal my bloody best fish. I've been waiting to find the parents of this one.'

81

'I didn't, Mum; it was an accident, honest!' cried Jackson, holding his hands out palms upwards.

Abbie had missed the whole of this conversation as she'd been replacing the batteries in her camera so hadn't picked up on the vibes and continued as before.

'And now can I have one of the groom kissing the bride please?'

Lucy squirmed as Dom looked at the ground, shook his head and then went in for the kill. 'This is the last one.' He leaned into her.

She swallowed as his handsome face came nearer. He pulled her to him with one arm, softly yet masterfully like a dancer, taking her breath away. The softness of her breasts pressed against his strong hard chest. He searched her eyes briefly before his gaze fixed on her mouth. His grey eyes steely and searching, his pupils slightly dilated. She felt his warmth before his mouth touched hers and his aftershave tantalised her. The softness of his lips on hers still took her by surprise even though she'd been expecting it and sent a shock wave that rippled through her body and pooled deep inside her. She gasped lightly and melted into him, instinctively pulling him into her, her arms wrapped tightly round his body.

He began to stroke her cheek softly with his thumb then as his lips pressed harder against hers his hand reached further back, into her hair and the back of her neck. Her lips parted slightly, and his tongue played with hers, teasing her. She could vaguely hear Abbie saying something, but she wasn't sure what it was. Desire was ripping through her like she had never felt before, dulling all of her other senses. She wondered whether she was actually dreaming. Things like this didn't happen to her.

Time stood still for Lucy; she couldn't remember ever being kissed like that. It stirred up so many emotions inside her. She was embarrassed in front of Jackson; he'd never seen her kiss a man before. She'd had a few kisses since she had broken up with his dad before he was born but nothing serious.

She touched her mouth; her lips were swollen. Then reality kicked in. He had put a piece of paper in her hand and stormed off, trying to shake Baxter off his trouser leg as he went. She could hear him grumbling about something as he made his way to the car. She looked at Abbie to see if she had noticed that she was having a mini meltdown, but she was too busy scrolling through the photos. Oohing and aahing at each of her precious shots.

'You know,' she said, still not lifting her eyes from the camera screen, 'you were absolutely meant to be a bride and I know he is extremely annoying and can be a right misery but you and Dom look great together.' She showed the shot of Dom kissing her and Lucy had to agree, they did make a gorgeous couple – if only she liked him.

Chapter 14

The detail captured on the painting of the signal box was amazing, as though Gracie had somehow stepped into Lucy's head and painted it exactly how she saw it.

Lucy was delighted with it and hung it up on the living room wall in Railway Cottage until it could take pride of place in its new home. Abbie had taken a photograph of it and managed to edit it as the background of the competition entry for the unusual wedding venue. She had chosen the picture that also featured Jackson and Baxter as she thought it added to the charm – after all a huge shaggy dog was an unusual wedding guest. Using the painting as the background had added a magical effect too.

Work on the inside of the café was almost finished. Lucy and Grandad were having a tour of the place. Downstairs was pretty much complete. The entrance, which had a working train door that beeped when you pressed the button and then slid open automatically was on the road side of the building, just opposite Railway Cottage, and opened up into a long rectangular room. The back of the building was completely bricked up and always had been. The front had windows that stretched the full length of the place and overlooked the railway. Although currently covered in white paint to stop people looking in, she could tell they would allow streams of light in and brighten the place up immensely.

Reclaimed railway sleepers made up the floor of the building and at the far end, just before the toilets, was a metal staircase with railway sleeper steps that led up to the next floor. The kitchen sat behind mock train doors off to the right and looked very professional with gleaming stainless-steel worktops and appliances that stood proudly on the original terracotta flooring. From there a serving hatch opened up on the railway side of the building.

The blue velvet railway seats and tables had been fitted along both sides of the building, just as they would be on a railway carriage. They even had the white flaps over the top with First Class printed on them.

Each table had a little lamp on it, which Lucy imagined would create a wonderful ambience. The mock windows had been created on the bricked wall and the screens had been fitted. They would concurrently play DVDs of train journeys from all around the world, which Lucy had bought. Customers could travel virtually to China, Paris, Venice, London and Edinburgh too – it would certainly add to the authenticity of being in a train carriage.

Grandad and Finn had been busy laying the miniature tracks that would serve the drinks to the tables in the booths along the windows. Each table had a number and they could program the train to stop at the correct number with the drinks on it. Lucy and Grandad were both licensees as they had recently passed the course and their names were displayed proudly over the door. They tested the train out and sat at one of the tables and sure enough the little train arrived with the two Diet Coke cans they had put in there; the train even had a little light on the front. They chinked their Coke cans together and laughed.

'People are going to love this, Lucy

Lucy enjoyed seeing her grandad like this. His pale blue eyes sparkled because of this new lease of life he'd found. He looked around proudly, surveying everything they had achieved so far.

'Lucy, I'm so pleased you moved here as I'll be honest, I was ready to go. I was so bored without your nan. I mean your mum and dad would visit me every week before they went away but they see me as an old duffer who wants to do old man things like play dominoes. When you get to my age you don't change inside, you know. Sometimes I feel on the same wavelength as Jackson. A lot of people write us oldies off, which can make us feel useless.'

She looked at him tenderly and thought about Dom and the way he spoke about his gran the other day. She blushed at the unwanted ripple that just flashed into her body at the mere thought of him.

'Yes, I know people like that too, Grandad.' She covered his hand with hers. 'The thing is: I see us as friends. You are one of the most interesting and entertaining people I know, and I value our friendship so much. I mean who would have thought that one day we would become business partners.'

'It's all thanks to you, darling; you've woken this old man up from a long and dreary sleep.'

She linked her arm through his. 'Well, Grandad, it's a two-way thing because my life has certainly not been boring since you've been around. I'm so sorry I never came to visit you for such a long time. I've really missed you but life just kind of got in the way.'

'I understand,' he said kindly. 'It's so much harder when the little ones come along.'

They picked up their drinks and headed up the creaky wooden steps. They were solid yet quaint. Following the noise of banging they joined Finn and his workers up at the top floor. The seats and tables were arranged as below along the window wall and the bricked wall had screens like below but there was more open space, which could be used as a dance floor.

'I was thinking we could play videos of the bride and groom on the screens if requested,' said Lucy.

'That's a great idea,' replied Grandad. 'I can just see it in my head.'

Lucy pulled a notebook and pen out of her bag and made a note to buy a disco ball as a finishing touch. 'I've ordered some black blinds with fairy lights in them, because of an evening they will block the floodlights from the station as they're powerfully bright.'

'That's a good idea. I'm looking forward to seeing them.'

Finn noticed them and waved hello. He and his team started packing away. One of them had the hoover out to pick up any mess they'd made.

'We're just about done here then,' he said. 'Tomorrow we can start on sanding the wooden fascia boards outside and after a couple of coats of paint we'll be done.'

'You've done an amazing job, Finn. Thank you so much; it's even better than how I imagined it.' Tears welled up in her eyes as she said it. Her grandad hugged her tightly.

'Your nana would have been so proud of you, as am I.'

Lucy wiped away the tear and hugged him back. She and Grandad had sunk everything they had into this place. It was imperative that it should be a success, or she'd never forgive herself.

'And I'm proud of you, Grandad – you really are the best.'

Finn was heading downstairs.

'Have you been in touch with the local press yet? They'll be able to help with advertising. They love things like this.'

Lucy froze. Panic swept over her in waves. Her grandad didn't notice but Finn saw her expression and tried to change the subject.

'Or then again word of mouth would be just as good, I suppose,' he countered.

'Yes, I'll think about it – thanks, Finn. Give my love to Gracie.'

'I will do. Bye.'

'Bye. Grandad, let's go and pick Jackson up from school and take him out for tea as something tells me we are going to be very busy from here on in.'

Chapter 15

Lucy never understood people who didn't like lists. Her dad thought they were a complete waste of time that would be better spent actually doing the things on the list. However, Lucy loved them and took great satisfaction in taking her pen and striking through each item – and with two businesses on the go she had plenty of items to be ticked off. Wedding Belles had taken on a couple of small weddings lately, which had kept her relatively busy, but now she needed to decide what she was going to do about the running of the café.

She and Abbie sat upstairs in the seats by the window. The view of rooftops gave way to a patchwork of rolling fields, a church spire glinted in the sunlight

'What a fantastic place to people-watch,' said Abbie as she lifted her gigantic cappuccino up to her lips.

'I know, isn't it amazing?' replied Lucy. 'I could sit up here and watch the world go by forever. I think this is going to be my happy place from now on.' She looked at the folders and papers spread out on the table in front of her and shuffled them into some kind of order.

'So these are all the wedding business contacts I've set up in the local area – and yes you're in there too, look photography, stationery and wedding favours.' She flicked through pages and pages of cards advertising everything from cake makers, to dress shops and beauticians.

Abbie's eyebrows rose at the impressive number of contacts Lucy had already made.

'So do you have any plans for the launch?'

'Well I was thinking we could invite them all to a party to showcase what's on offer.'

Abbie beamed and clapped her hands together. 'Oh I do love a party, and the place is looking fantastic. I can't believe how much you've achieved in a relatively short space of time.'

'I know – it's been amazing hasn't it? Everyone's been working so hard.'

'So, what's left to do now, apart from me taking photographs of the outside?'

Lucy dug out her list. 'I need to interview for staff and organise uniforms. The aprons match perfectly with the granite grey paint we've used on the fascia boards outside and they will have "The Signal Box Café" embroidered on them in silver thread. The tablecloths will be white, oh and look here's a sample of the takeaway bags, which are the same colour as the aprons.'

'Aw that's so cute,' said Abbie as she held the handles on the bag and ran her fingers along the silver writing.

Lucy struck through a couple more items on her list that she'd completed.

'Ah yes, I need to confirm the menus for the evening meals. As the café is on the incoming side of the platform it's perfect for providing takeaway meals for tired commuters coming home from London. We will be providing bacon or sausage rolls and coffee in the morning so customers could either cross the platform or we could provide a trolley service for them. I don't think my nana's hostess trolley would be appropriate now so will need to get a more professional one.'

She added, *Buy trolley*, to her list and continued.

'As for the weddings, I can provide a completely bespoke package for them.' She smiled and looked around the room. 'This venue is even more amazing than I could ever have imagined.'

Abbie clinked her coffee cup to Lucy's. 'I'll drink to that.' Her face disappeared behind the huge cup as she finished her coffee.

A voice came from below. 'We're ready.'

Lucy and Abbie jumped up and raced down the stairs. It was time for the unveiling of the sign.

The fascia boards looked resplendent in rich granite grey, the old-fashioned swinging sign striking with its granite background and metallic silver lettering, which spelt out 'The Signal Box Café'.

Beautiful window boxes painted various pastel shades underlined each window at the front and sides of the building. Each one laden with a colour burst of flowers. The likeness to the picture painted by Gracie was uncanny. Grandad had been quite emotional when she showed him the three pictures of the signal box, especially the one painted by Dolly Davinci, which he appeared in. They now took pride of place overlooking the café. The placemats and coasters looked fabulous too. Upstairs had the actual signal controls that Grandad had used preserved in a glass box on the wall.

'I really want to get married here,' Abbie gushed.

'Me too,' replied Lucy, her eyes widening as she tried to take in this wonderful achievement.

As they left the building and Lucy was locking up, they bumped into a young man.

'Hi there,' he said. 'My name is Greg Waters. I'm looking for the owner.'

Lucy held her hand out to him. 'Lucy Woods, I'm co-owner of this place. How can I help you?' He shook her hand firmly.

'Pleased to meet you. I'm from the local paper, the *Bramblewood Echo*, and we'd like to do a piece on your new café.'

Lucy's face dropped.

'Oh no thank you, we certainly haven't got the budget at the moment to advertise in newspapers.' She tried to walk away.

'No you don't understand, it's a feature piece we want, which means it won't cost you any money at all.'

'That sounds perfect,' said Abbie, handing him a business card. She turned to Lucy and noticed her cheeks were burning. 'It would be great publicity for the café.'

'No,' Lucy said abruptly. 'We're fine thank you, Mr Waters.'

He looked quite taken aback as though he couldn't believe anyone would turn down this golden opportunity He delved in his pocket for a business card and handed it to her.

'Here, just in case you change your mind.'

'I won't,' said Lucy before storming off to Railway Cottage. Abbie took the proffered business card.

'I'll try and talk her round,' she promised him.

Lucy couldn't stay mad for long when she poured herself a cup of tea and saw an article in the local paper.

The Tooth will out at Sycamore Lodge

Residents at Sycamore Lodge were left feeling very uncomfortable and unable to eat their dinner due to a mishap with their dentures. The falsies were usually labelled up in separate named dishes and put through a steriliser before being taken back to each resident on a trolley.

CCTV footage has shown that two residents may have had too much to drink, knocked over the trolley and tried to replace them but have obviously caused a mix-up.

Mrs King the manageress has apologised for the incident and assured families it will not happen again. 'I will do my utmost to find out who the perpetrators are,' she was quoted as saying.

Lucy giggled and hoped that this wouldn't mean she would be summoned back to Sycamore Lodge.

Chapter 16

Dominic Cavendish worked hard, played hard and exercised hard. Every day he would spend his lunch hour in the gym that was situated in his office building near Liverpool Street. Lockers were provided and they also offered a laundry service, so he didn't have to fight through the commute every day with sweaty gym gear in a cumbersome bag.

At the weekends he liked to go for a run. For years he would come home and kick his trainers off outside his four-bedroomed riverside house. Every year he invested in a new pair of the most expensive running shoes, which he would take into work for his gym sessions, and then he relegated the old pair for weekend outdoor use.

This system had always worked well for him; in all the years he had done it his trainers had always remained safe. That was until now. On Saturday at 11am, as regular as clockwork, he sat hungover and bleary-eyed on his front step. He'd tied the lace on the first trainer and yawning he patted the ground with his hand for the second. He opened his eyes to search for it, looked around his front garden and finally under his car. The shoe was nowhere to be seen. Scratching his head, he tried to make sense of the situation but simply couldn't understand it. Was there a one-legged thief hopping about with his three-hundred-pound trainers on? Well at least one hundred and fifty pounds' worth of them anyway. He was most disgruntled at having to revert to his tatty old spare ones; this would now make him late for his run, which would throw his plans for the day out completely.

An hour and a half later and dripping with sweat, he arrived back at his doorway and stood gulping his bottle of water. He opened the door, sat on the step and took off his trainers when he noticed his other pair were now reacquainted. The left one looking just as it had this morning whereas the right one was now a bundle of rags attached to half a sole. He raised an eyebrow and ran his fingers through his hair. Surely, he would have noticed that there this morning? Something shiny caught his eye. He bent to pick up a dog tag with the name B Woods on it, along with a contact number. He pulled out his phone to give the owner a piece of his mind.

Jackson had promised his mummy faithfully that he would stay on the green and not go near the river when walking Baxter that morning. He knew she was trusting him to not get into any trouble. So, when he found Baxter with a training shoe in his mouth, he panicked and spent ten minutes trying to get it back off him. Baxter thought it was great fun and chewed harder and faster in his excitement..

'Bad boy, Baxter, Mummy is going to be mad at you.' He scolded when he finally snatched the shoe from his furry friend. Heretraced his footsteps to look for the other one and on finding a house with just one trainer outside, he threw it as hard as he could; his hand covered his mouth as it bounced off the front door and landed with a thud next to the other one. At least Mummy would never know about that. He ran all the way home.

*

Lucy was sitting at the dining room table, busy arranging the launch party for the following week, when her phone rang.

'Hello, Prue, don't panic I've located the bridesmaids' dresses. They were on their way to Edinburgh for some reason and are being couriered as we . . .' she answered distractedly, clamping the phone to her ear with her shoulder as she rifled through paperwork.

'Hello,' interrupted the man.

'Oh, I'm so sorry, I thought you were someone else. How can I help?'

'I've found a dog tag next to my front door with your number and wondered if I could return it to you.'

Panic shot through Lucy and all her nerve endings contracted. Where were Jackson and Baxter? She was sure she had seen them come back home earlier but then she'd been on the phone most of the day with missing bridesmaid dress woman. She jumped up to look through the window and saw them playing happily in the garden. Relief flooded her.

'Oh, thank you but I don't want to put you out. I'm assuming you're just round the corner from me, so I'll pop round and pick it up.' He gave her the address and signed off. She popped into the garden and called Jackson.

'Did you realise that Baxter had lost his name tag? I'm just going to pop round the corner and collect it. Do you want to come with me?'

Jackson's cheeks went pink. 'Erm no I didn't notice. Not really thank you, Mummy, my legs are a bit tired so can I please stay here?' he answered.

'Okay, I'll only be five minutes. Remember, do not answer the door to anybody.'

'I won't, bye.' He resumed his game with Baxter.

The sun shone brightly, and the birds sang joyfully. Lucy realised a little break would do her good; she literally hadn't stopped for weeks, she still had paint in her hair from decorating the interior of the Signal Box Café. It felt good to stretch her legs after sitting down working for hours. As she walked round the corner to the lovely mock Tudor houses she marvelled at the view before her. Not many people could say they had a river on their doorstep with boats moored up and wildlife in abundance. The smell of spring was in the air; the sun reflected off the gentle ripples, which sparkled like diamonds. She found herself singing as she walked along.

As she got nearer to the house she realised with a small amount of trepidation that it was Dom's. He opened the front door and their eyes met as quickly as two magnets snapping together.

'I wondered if it was you,' he said unsmiling, 'as soon as I put the phone down I thought, "Woods, now where have I heard that name before?" and then I remembered Dougie Woods and then when you were rambling on about bridesmaids' dresses and I thought, "Yes it must be."'

'Well thanks for letting me know about the dog tag – we didn't know it had come off. I can't think how it came to be here. How is your gran by the way?' she said without taking a breath. His mood certainly differed from the last time she saw him.

He was stubborn and obviously didn't want to be entering into conversation as he ignored her question. He reached to the hall table behind him and in one hand he held up the dog tag and the chewed rag in the other.

'I think it was maybe when he was doing this.' He shook the thing that used to be a shoe for emphasis.

Lucy covered her mouth with both hands and her eyes could not have opened any wider. 'I am so sorry. Please

97

let me know how much I owe you. I had no idea; my son was walking him this morning.'

'Well I suggest you keep a closer eye on both of them; in fact include your grandad in that one too. What is it with the males in your family? I can only imagine what your husband is like.'

Lucy's eyebrows, like her hackles were raised. She gave him a glassy stare and unleashed the full force of her anger.

'How dare you! The males in my family are decent and loving and respectful, unlike you, and for your information I don't have a husband and it's no wonder your wife left you. You are enough to put me off men for life. I wish I'd never let you kiss me.' She wiped her mouth on her arm, her face twisted into a look of disgust. 'In fact I'm deleting it. Yes that's right, it has been deleted from my memory. It never happened so you'd better make sure you delete it from yours as well, as you don't deserve to have the memory of a beautiful kiss from me.' She snatched the dog tag from his hand and stomped down the path.

She used the walk home to try and calm down. How he was related to Abbie or Violet she would never know; they were both so lovely and he was impossible.

Dominic watched her go down the path. She irritated him so much. She was all romance and flowers and living in a little dream world. She did have a temper on her though and that bloody dog was a liability. He would be glad if he never saw any of them again. He peeked at her one last time. Her golden curls were bouncing, and he couldn't help noticing she had a sexy wiggle even when she stomped. He tore his eyes away and slammed his door. She might have deleted the memory of the kiss, but he certainly wasn't going to.

'Bloody women, bloody kids and bloody dogs!' he muttered under his breath as he threw what was left of his trainers in the bin.

Chapter 17

It was time for the launch party; Grandad had permission to stay out for the night so insisted on taking the single room even though Lucy offered him the double. Jackson bunked in with her. The excitement in the air was tangible.

She and Abbie had spent a long time yesterday stuffing goody bags with freebies and business cards and leaflets from all of the local businesses that had wanted to take part. A couple of catering companies were providing food. They had local cake makers providing cakes and wine companies supplying champagne and prosecco. It was a real joint venture.

The staff looked resplendent in their uniforms, white shirts, black trousers or skirts and waistcoats in granite grey with the silver logo of the Signal Box Café embroidered on them. They also wore signalman hats. The new chef Lewis was a gentle giant who had come highly recommended; he had two assistants, Maisie and Lee. Waiting staff stood at their stations ready to welcome guests. Local balloon companies had provided impressive displays and a DJ had set up upstairs. Cleaners Val and Lotus had done a brilliant job and the place was gleaming. The wedding businesses had set up small stands upstairs and had been invited an hour earlier than the general public. Grandad and Jackson wore their signalman hats and stood at the door waiting to let everybody in.

They had fixed a ribbon across the front of the doorway, which someone had suggested that the local mayor should cut; however, Lucy knew there was only one person whom she thought deserved that privilege and that was her grandad. A hush swept over the crowd as he began his speech.

'Firstly, I would like to thank you all for coming today. As many of you know I spent many years working happily in this place and am now delighted it has found a new lease of life thanks to my beautiful granddaughter Lucy. This is all down to her insightful vision and it just goes to show that dreams can come true.' He choked back a sob. 'I hope we see each and every one of you visiting us here for many years to come. We love this community and want to be a strong and vibrant part of it. So, it is with great pleasure that I now declare the Signal Box Café, well and truly open,' he concluded and along with Jackson cut the ribbon to the sound of cheers from all the guests.

Just stepping through the door was an experience in itself. At the press of a button the reclaimed train door whooshed open. It was just like being on a real train. The film of the journey from London to Edinburgh played on the screens down the left-hand side of the wall. The windows on the right allowed light to flood in. Some of the guests sat down in the seats and the little trains were kept busy supplying tiny bottles of prosecco. Lots of people were taking photos and videoing the arrival of their drinks. The chef had prepared a selection of canapés for the day: cocktail sticks with bite-sized morsels of steak and potato, blinis with prawns in a Marie Rose sauce, mini goat's cheese and pepper quiches and tiny pies with a variety of flavours.

Lucy gave a small speech. 'Welcome, everybody; I would also like to thank each and every one of you for attending today and for supporting us. As some of you know I will still be continuing with Wedding Belles, my wedding planner business, as well as looking after this place and I hope you will all feel happy to recommend us as a most unique wedding venue.' Over the sound of cheers, she raised a toast: 'To the Signal Box Café.'

Glasses were raised and the guests echoed the toast.

After an hour the stallholders made their way upstairs. The DJ was having a break and a young girl called Lydia sang her original songs whilst playing the guitar. Her voice was rich with a jazz feel, which created a mellow ambience.

Lucy had been chatting to a lady called Camilla who was known locally as Camilla Cupcake; as well as delicious cupcakes she also made the most delightful novelty and wedding cakes and was well thought of in the area. Lucy helped her set out her cupcakes on a stand upstairs and popped down again to prepare to greet the other guests as they came in.

The first people she recognised were Finn and Gracie. Their business cards were in the goody bags and Gracie had offered a portrait as a raffle prize. Gracie's pictures hung on the wall in pride of place along with other railway-inspired paintings from the gallery, which were for sale. Gracie clapped excitedly as the little train delivered her a drink before it chugged back to the kitchen to be refilled for the next table.

Abbie and Lucy stood at their stall, resplendent with the Wedding Belles banner proudly on display, heads together looking at some of the pictures she had taken of the event so far. Lucy looked up and nudged Abbie. 'Do you know that man with the video camera?'

Abbie flicked her head up, casually checked out the guy as he spoke to a customer and immediately did a comical double take, which made Lucy snort. Abbie whispered a wolf whistle in Lucy's ear. 'Who the hell is that?'

'He's Dave the videographer. He sorted all the screens out for me. Those are his wedding videos playing on them now. Aren't they beautiful?'

'He sure is.' Abbie fanned herself with a Signal Box Café leaflet. He had dark hair that formed in curls at the nape of his neck and brown soul-searching eyes.

'He literally couldn't take his eyes off you, Abbie. I think he's got the hots for you.'

'Really?' she shouted far too loudly. He looked over and away again, quickly trying to stifle a smile as he spoke to a couple.

'You know who he looks like don't you?'

'Of course I do, your absolute favourite person in the whole wide world, and I reckon he wants you to be his Demelza.' She laughed. 'I have a funny feeling, Abbie, that you two are a match made in wedding photography heaven.'

Abbie nudged her. 'Oh shit, shit he's coming over.'

'Ow your elbows are so poky. Sorry I've got to go. See you later, Dem . . . I mean Abbie.' Still giggling she nodded and smiled at Dave as he made his way over to her friend.

Lucy popped down to the kitchen and helped replenish the canapés. When she came out, she saw Greg the reporter. She glared at him and he held up his hands in mock surrender.

'Look they're empty – no notepad, camera or secret microphone, I promise. I come in peace.'

Her face relaxed; he had a cheeky grin and wasn't bad-looking. He had short dark hair and brown puppy dog eyes that he was taking full advantage of by trying to make her feel sorry for him. It worked, slightly. She shook his hand and offered him a canapé. He took a steak one and kissed his fingers afterwards in appreciation.

'Delicious,' he said.

'I'm sorry if I was rude. It's just been so stressful trying to organise this place,' she replied.

'And you've done a brilliant job. But please bear with me; how would you feel if you could write the feature yourself? Just a press release and you supply one picture; it seems such a shame that you should miss out on this publicity. It can be completely impersonal if you like. The focus would be on the building and your grandad. I mean what a story: he was the original signalman and now he's co-owner of the best new wedding venue in the county.'

Her eyes snapped up to meet his. 'D'you think?'

'I don't just think, I know. In case you hadn't noticed not much happens around here, so I can assure you this is huge.'

She scratched the back of her neck. He seemed genuine enough. She could hear her grandad chatting animatedly to their guests and knew he deserved some well-earned recognition for the place. It would make his day to be in the newspaper.

'Okay,' she said, 'I'll do it for my grandad.'

'That's great – you won't regret it, I promise. Also, I was wondering whether you would maybe like to come out for a drink with me sometime.' He looked down at his shoes as he spoke and then hopefully into her eyes.

She thought for a minute or two. He was good-looking, not very tall, only about an inch or two taller than her. She liked the way he dressed – casual and relaxed – if she did go out with him she would probably choose to wear her flats.

'So, what do you think?' he asked.

She pulled herself together, shook her head. What was she thinking? She had far too much on her plate to even think about going out with someone.

'I'm sorry, I wish I could, but I don't have a babysitter.'

Rosie from the café on the river had arrived with her mum and dad, the owners of Odds'n'Sods, a shop in Market Square that sold everything.

'Lucy, I'd love to babysit for you,' she said, kissing her in greeting. As if on cue, Jackson spotted her and ran into her arms for a cuddle.

'Rosie, come with me; the train will deliver your drink.' He took her hand and led her to a table.

She turned back to Lucy with a huge smile on her face. 'Honestly I'd love to.'

'Well?' asked Greg, still waiting eagerly.

'I'll think about it, but I'm really not looking for a relationship at the moment,' was the best response she could manage.

'That's okay, me neither – just let me know when you decide.' She excused herself as more guests were arriving. She smiled as her grandad's friend Violet entered, dressed elegantly as usual. It was obviously a special occasion to her. She looked as though she would be quite at home in the queen's garden party.

'Hello, Violet, how lovely to see you,' she said kissing her on both cheeks and greeting her with a warm smile that disappeared when she caught sight of who was behind her.

'Gran insisted on coming here,' he said.

'And she is very welcome,' Lucy replied with emphasis on the word 'she'.

His eyes darted around the room before settling on her. He looked like he would rather be anywhere else but here.

He scratched an imaginary itch on his forehead and began to speak before hesitating again as though he couldn't find the words he was searching for.

'Look, I just wanted to say I'm sorry. We seem to have got off on the wrong foot. My gran has given me a good talking-to about your grandad and she said exactly what you told me: that she is old enough and capable enough of making her own decisions.'

Lucy's mouth fell open; she held her hand up to his forehead as if to test his temperature.

'Was that really Dominic Cavendish apologising for something? Are you sure you're feeling okay? Maybe you should go and have a lie-down.'

Her hand felt cool on his forehead. When she removed it, the softness of her touch remained as if it could soothe all his worries away. His mind took him back to when he had kissed her. She had yielded to him so naturally and it was the most beautiful kiss. So why on earth did he end it and walk away? He was such a miserable sod. Why couldn't he just be nice to her? His conscience was quick to respond, 'because women bring you nothing but trouble; that's why.' He knew it was true.

He wanted to grab her hand and place it back on his skin. He also wanted to entwine his hands in those soft golden curls and bring her pink lips to his. All of her hearts-and-flowers nonsense was clouding his judgement and blocking his common sense, but he didn't care. He just needed to know how to get out of this hole that he had dug for himself as far as she was concerned.

'Look, I was wondering if we could go for a drink or something, maybe tomorrow, so I can show you that I'm not the awful miserable git that you think I am.'

Although flattered that this was the second date she'd been asked out on in the last half an hour, she wasn't ready to forgive him quite so easily. Seeing Greg was standing nearby she linked her arm through his and turned him to face Dom.

'I'm sorry but I already have a date for tomorrow, with a dog- and child-friendly man, thanks for asking.'

Greg smirked at him and kissed her cheek lightly before he moved off and mingled with the other guests.

Dominic glared at Greg then turned to Lucy. 'Okay but let me know if you change your mind.' He turned to walk away as he spotted some friends waving to him. 'Oh, and by the way, Lucy, that thing you asked me to delete, I tried really hard to but I couldn't. I'm sorry.' Her blue eyes met his and lightning sparks flew between them. He broke the gaze and joined his friends.

He sat down to join them for a beer; and was extremely impressed when the little train chugged along to deliver it to the table. He had to hand it to Lucy, this place was amazing, a touch of hearts and flowers for the girls and train sets for the guys; this was the perfect mix. He'd come to realise that she wasn't just beautiful, she was smart and incredibly capable and someone he needed to keep at arm's length. The last thing he needed was to get involved with a woman. Luckily she was out of his league and wasn't interested in him anyway, though he didn't think much of the creep she was with.

Lucy sneaked a look at Dom when he sat down with the other men. He was laughing a lot, his face completely transformed; there were quite a few good-looking guys in this town, she noted. Her stomach was still doing flips from what he said about the kiss. Why did he grate on her so?

The support from local people was amazing and Lucy was thrilled. She had already taken five bookings for weddings to be held at the Signal Box Café for this year and seven for the year after. She hadn't expected business to take off as quickly as this and wondered whether she could cope. Customer feedback acknowledged that people were looking for a unique venue and this place had the added extra because Lucy was a professional wedding planner who could provide a completely bespoke service.

After the party Lucy thanked and congratulated each one of the staff for working so hard.

Back home she was running her bath and rummaging through her goody bag. The wedding people had added lots of extra treats; the love potion bath bomb was fizzing around the water now and smelt of strawberries and cream. She found a little bottle of pink prosecco with a plastic champagne flute and one of Camilla's smaller cakes known as cupcake kisses. This was raspberry and champagne flavour. She placed them on the ledge surrounding the bath.

The launch had been amazing but her feet were aching. She slipped into the strawberry-scented bubbles. This was blissful. She could switch off for once as Grandad was staying over and reading Jackson a story. The combination of Grandad's silly voices and Jackson's giggles melted her heart. She popped open the prosecco, waited for the fizz to drop a little before topping up the glass. She took a sip, allowing the bubbles to swirl around her mouth, tickling her tongue as they popped delicately.

Now it was time for the cupcake. She opened the clear plastic casing but noticed a business card stuck to the bottom of it. She turned it the right way up and sat up abruptly, almost soaking the cupcake and the bathroom floor. Her lip turned into a snarl. That bloody man was impossible. She raged as she tore up Dominic Cavendish's business card, which proudly stated he was a divorce lawyer. She wished she had caught him smuggling them into the goody bags, as she would have given him a piece of her mind.

A flashback to the way his thumb had stroked her cheek when he kissed her invaded her mind. She instinctively touched her lips again but then quickly shooed that thought away as fast as it had appeared. She opened her mouth wide and bit into the delight of Camilla's cupcake kiss and wondered who needed a man when you could have cake like this.

Chapter 18

It was heart-breaking dropping Grandad off at Sycamore Lodge. Although he put on a very brave face Lucy could tell that he'd been delighted staying over at Railway Cottage, his real home. She asked him again over a cooked breakfast if he wanted to come back, but he assured her he was fine. Maud hadn't left his side the whole time he was home and he enjoyed stroking her and taking care of her. Lucy's worries soon disappeared when she saw Violet greeting him enthusiastically with a kiss and a hug. She could swear her grandad blushed a little.

Lucy was regretting agreeing to this date tonight, especially as she'd only done it out of spite. She had no idea what to wear and had thrown various unsuitable outfits all over the bed. She didn't want to wear anything even remotely revealing, as that would give the wrong impression. She settled on some black jeans and a green jumper with cream lace around the bottom that she felt quite pretty and comfortable in. She smoothed serum into her hair so that the curls weren't quite as crazy as usual; she remembered to put on her flat black ballet shoes as she didn't want to be towering above him. She swept some mascara over her eyelashes and used her finger to pat some cherry balm on her lips. A quick squirt of perfume and she was ready to go.

Rosie had turned up half an hour early with a huge bag of goodies from Serendipity, a new storybook about trains and a DVD that she said she'd been dying to watch but felt silly watching on her own as it was meant to be for children.

As soon as she rang the doorbell Jackson had been on a high. He raced to the door to meet her and led her by the hand up to his room.

'Hold your horses, Jackson,' she said. 'I need to get my shoes off first.' She kicked them off, shrugged off her jacket, which she hung on the bannister, and followed him up the stairs two at a time. Baxter stood at the bottom of the stairs barking until they came back down again, desperate for some attention from this exciting visitor. Maud stayed curled up in bed showing no interest whatsoever.

'And now I want to show you the huge train set, Auntie Rosie. It's in the garage and Grandad has been building it for twenty years. It's called a minit-chair railway. No, Baxter, no jumping on Auntie Rosie – that's naughty and Mummy will tell you off. This is the living room, and this is the kitchen, and this is the garden.'

Rosie loved listening to the incessant chat and allowed Jackson to lead her to the garage where she enjoyed playing with the impressive railway she'd heard so much about.

When Lucy popped her head into the garage a few minutes later she laughed as she saw them wearing the signalmen's caps and happily playing.

'Hi, Rosie, thanks so much for this. I've never left him with a sitter before, but he seems so happy with you.'

'Don't you worry about us, lovey; we're going to have a ball aren't we, Jackson?'

'Peeep peeeep.' He nodded as he blew the whistle to start the train again and pushed his glasses further up his nose.

'Can I get you a tea or anything?'

'No, I'm fine thanks.'

'Okay well help yourself to anything, and Jacks, you be a good boy for Auntie Rosie.'

She blew a kiss to him and walked down the high street to the wine bar where she had arranged to meet Greg. Her hands were shaking; it had been a long time since she'd been out with a man. She could only hope that he wouldn't be expecting too much.

The Grape Escape was a trendy establishment; pink bulbs glowed from under the white marble bar area onto high stools. Blue lights shone down on the wide choice of drinks that were displayed along the back wall. White tables and chairs were arranged in the centre of the room with booths lining the walls. Each table had a blue or a pink lamp on it and a disco ball reflected colourful shapes around the room. They didn't serve meals, but they did do tapas and nibbles.

Greg was sitting at the bar waiting for her. He was having a mojito; he jumped up when he saw her and pecked her on the cheek. She tried not to choke on the strong smell of aftershave that engulfed her.

'Hi there, how are you? Would you like a cocktail?' He handed her the list and watched her as she perused it. Her mouth moved as she read the contents of the drinks.

'Ah, I think I'll have an after eight martini please.'

'Coming up,' said the bartender as he prepared the drink, shaking it noisily and pouring it into the glass for her. She thanked him and Greg could see she was eyeing the high stool in front of him.

'Shall we sit at a table?'

'Oh yes please.' They chose a table in the window, the neon sign that read 'The Grape Escape' reflected backwards on their faces.

She sipped her drink nervously. 'Mmm, this is delicious.'

'That's good, oh by the way thank you for sending me that press release – and I've got the photos from Abbie. They should make a great feature. The place looks brilliant and I think people will enjoy the historical aspect to it too with regards to your grandad working there for all those years.'

'Yes, he loved working there. That's why it means so much for us to be able to bring the place back to life again. It was mostly thanks to an inheritance from my nana that we were able to do it. That's one reason why I felt I had to make it a success.'

'Sounds like a wise investment. Anyway, tell me about you. I know you have a little boy but that's pretty much it. How old is he?'

Lucy felt guarded and more than a little uncomfortable; he was entering private territory here.

'He's eight years old and he's the love of my life. So, what about you: do you have any kids?' She was the expert at steering conversations away from herself.

'No not yet. I can't ever imagine being ready to give up so much and put someone else first. I mean I don't think I'm selfish, to be honest I'm probably just immature.'

'And how long have you worked at the newspaper for?'

'Nine years – ever since I left uni. I'm waiting for my big break though, as it can get a little mundane in a small town like this. I mean I'm practically invited to the opening of an envelope round here. Not a lot happens, apart from a bunch of pensioners running riot on mobility scooters of course.' He laughed.

'Oh yes, I nearly died when the manager of Sycamore Lodge showed me the headline and told Grandad off.' Her face flushed and she realised she'd said too much.

'Oh, that was your grandad? I should have recognised him seeing as I wrote the article. That's hilarious.'

'What can I say? My grandad is rebellious, but I love him.'

Lucy was persuaded to have one more drink and decided a glass of wine would be less risky than another cocktail as the first one had already made her feel a little light-headed. She steered the conversation to the Signal Box Café.

'Designing and opening the café was the proudest moment of my life, apart from having Jackson of course.'

'It's a brilliant concept. Our readers will love it and if I were you I'd make sure there is someone answering the phones on Wednesday when this week's edition is printed, as I'm sure you'll have tons of interest.' He cleared his throat. 'So, you must have been pretty young when you had Jackson.'

She could sense the heat rising from her neck and looked into her drink. 'I was old enough.'

'It must be hard though, bringing him up alone and managing a business.'

Her shoulders tensed, her protective instincts asserting themselves. After taking another sip of the wine, she placed the remaining half a glass on the table, stood up and pulled her bag strap up to her shoulder.

'I really must be getting back to check on Jackson.'

Greg realised he'd overstepped the mark and tried to persuade her to stay.

'No, I'm sorry, I've only ever left him with family before now. I need to get back. Plus, I have an early start in the morning as we're serving breakfasts to the commuters,' she said as she scraped her chair back.

'Okay but I insist on walking you home.' He swallowed his wine in one gulp and wiped his mouth with the back of his hand.

'No really I'm fine, it's . . .'

'I insist. I pride myself on being a gentleman. I know it's not far, but I will see you to your door.'

She gave in and they left the wine bar to walk along the high street.

'You know I was talking to my mum and she said that she remembers your grandad being the signalman and working in the signal box.'

'Oh, how fascinating?' She smiled. 'That's lovely. Some of my best childhood memories were of this place. I used to always come here for holidays to see my grandparents. I'm truly pleased for you both and hope the breakfast shift goes well tomorrow.'

They approached Railway Cottage just as the train was due so had to wait as the level crossing barriers had come down. The red flashing lights reflected on their faces. They stopped talking as the sirens made it hard for them to be heard. The signal box stood tall and proud alongside the station. Lucy couldn't resist looking at it every time she passed, and she could see it from her bedroom window every morning. Tonight, the fairy lights twinkled like stars as they lined the contours of the roof and peeked out from between the flowers in the pretty window boxes. The place was magical.

The train arrived, allowing them to cross the road as soon as the barriers lifted. Busy commuters made their way down the long platform. She noticed some people looking with interest at the previously derelict building.

As they stood awkwardly outside the cottage Greg put his arm around her and moved forward for a kiss. She managed to manoeuvre herself away from him and giggled softly as she said sorry. She then recognised one of the commuters looking at her and quickly changed her mind. She threw her arms around him and went in for a snog.

His eyes first registered surprise before closing as he enjoyed this unexpected treat.

Her eyes remained open as they surveyed the commuter, his steps slowing as he realised who she was, before shaking his head, looking away. The hollows of his cheeks tightened as he ground his teeth and crossed the road. Her heart was pounding but not because of this kiss as she had hardly noticed that. She had seen a flash of something in Dom's eyes and that made her feel good. That would teach him. She came back to reality by realising her lips were still attached to someone. She gently pushed him away by his chest, but his head stayed forward for as long as he could. He was very reluctant to break off the kiss.

'Wow, what did I do to deserve that?' he asked, before trying to lunge in for some more. She blocked him with her hand over his mouth; he kissed the palm of her hand, which tickled.

'I had a lovely night, thank you but now I must go.'

'Bye then. Can I call you?'

'Maybe but I'm quite busy for a while; in fact maybe it's best if you don't. As I said before, I'm not looking for a relationship.'

'I understand, you have a lot on. Maybe we could grab a coffee sometime?'

They said goodbye and she watched him walk away. From inside the house she could hear the movie that Rosie had brought round playing loudly. She knew how much both of them had been looking forward to it and didn't want to spoil their night by ending it abruptly so she decided to pop into the café for half an hour and enjoy some blissful peace.

As she unlocked the door and pressed the button to allow the train door to open, she realised she had never been inside it on her own. She didn't need a light on as the station floodlights were bright and the blinds were open. She ran her hands across the velvet of the seats; they were as good as new and had had a deep industrial clean. Popping into the kitchen she put the kettle on and made herself a cappuccino, treating herself to a dusting of cocoa on the top and a couple of chocolate biscuits.

She took a seat in one of the cubicles, breathed a huge sigh and her shoulders dropped a couple of inches. This place would be ideal to catch up on paperwork, or simply to have some time to herself. She couldn't remember the last time she had been so calm. The Signal Box Café seemed to be wrapping her in its open arms and giving her a much-needed hug. The barrier was coming down again for the train, which was heading into London. She watched it pull away and could see people walking down the platform. Some were talking on phones. There was a couple who looked like they were arguing and a lady with a baby in a pram. They were soon followed by a group of teenagers laughing and joking amongst themselves. Lucy had always loved people-watching so she held the huge bowl-shaped cup of cappuccino in both hands and relished the moment.

Thoughts of that special kiss wormed their way into her head, but they were chased away by the kiss she'd had with Greg. That had been nice hadn't it? The blush burned her cheeks and rushed to her ears; she was ashamed to say she couldn't remember it. She was too busy keeping her eye on Dominic bloody Cavendish to worry about what her lips were doing. She tried to think of excuses as to why she did it. Was it to make Dom jealous? No, it couldn't be that because she couldn't stand him, even though he was the best kisser she'd ever had he was unbelievably arrogant.

She put her hands on her burning cheeks to calm them down. What was the point of blushing if there was no one there to see it? She already knew how embarrassed she was and she didn't need her blazing cheeks to tell her.

Chapter 19

The Signal Box Café was well and truly declared open. Since 6am Lucy had been cooking up a storm with takeaway sausage and bacon rolls, fresh pastries, coffees, teas and fruit juices – all being served to excited commuters through the little takeaway hatch on the platform. At the top of the hatch was a granite grey canopy with the Signal Box Café's name embroidered in silver. It not only looked striking it would also be useful for protecting customers from the elements.

One of the waitresses had taken a whole batch of the rolls onto the opposite side of the platform on a trolley for those commuters who hadn't had time to pop over. She had already made five journeys that morning and had returned empty within minutes.

'A couple of the drivers asked if they could put breakfast orders in for the rest of the week,' she told Lucy, handing her an order form.

'Yes, that's a brilliant idea. Well done.'

Inside the café was just as busy with some of their more prepared customers leaving home earlier in order to have a breakfast treat before a long day in London. Customers sat in the booths and had a choice of full breakfasts, porridge or pancakes. At 7.45 Lucy popped into Railway Cottage to get Jackson up for school. She was surprised to find him up and dressed but then he had been so excited about the café opening.

With one hand in his mum's, he pushed his glasses up with the other and skipped excitedly along the way.

'Can I really have pancakes and sausages with maple syrup like they do in America, Mummy?'

'Anything is possible at the Signal Box Café,' she replied with a smile.

She sat him in one of the empty booths.

'Now, what do you want to drink?'

'Orange juice please.'

She soon returned with the sausage, pancakes and maple syrup, and scrambled egg on toast for herself. The screens were playing a journey across China, which some of the customers were mesmerised by. Jackson clapped as he heard a little 'peep peep' and saw the miniature train approaching with his orange juice in it.

'Grandad is so clever,' he said as he collected his drink from the train.

'He certainly is,' agreed Lucy.

'Mummy,' he said between mouthfuls of pancake and sausage, 'I think that you're very clever too.'

She clasped her hands to her chest. 'Thank you, darling, that's a lovely thing to say and I think you're even cleverer than me.'

'Was my daddy clever too?'

Her heart fluttered and she didn't know where to look, then checking her watch she quickly gathered her half-eaten breakfast together.

'Oh dear is that the time? We need to get you off to school.' She ran into the kitchen to let the staff know she needed to pop out.

Jackson was wiping the syrup off his face with his napkin.

Lucy rushed him back over to the cottage so that he could brush his teeth and they proceeded in the opposite direction of the high street for the ten-minute walk/skip/ jump to school.

When they'd lived in Brumstoke they'd had to drive to the school, which had been huge and impersonal. Bramblewood primary school was nestled down a leafy country lane and surrounded by fields. There were only about one hundred and fifty pupils in the whole school. The church was just around the corner and the children would attend assemblies there once a week. Holding hands in twos they would meander along like a little navy stream on a map.

'So how was last night?' Lucy asked.

'It was cool. Auntie Rosie was so funny. We watched *Toy Story* because she's never seen it, so I showed her my Woody and Buzz Lightyear and we played with them when the film was on. She brought scones and cakes and we drew some pictures. She said she wished that she had a little boy like me, so I asked her why she didn't have any children and she said that she wasn't married. So, I said that you weren't married, and you still had a little boy.' He picked up a large stick and trailed it along the dirt on the footpath behind him.

Lucy's cheeks turned pink. 'And what did Auntie Rosie say?'

'She asked me if I saw my daddy.'

'Well you shouldn't be telling people my business, Jackson, and whether or not I'm married is my business and no one else's; it's private do you understand?'

He nodded sadly and threw the stick into some bushes.

Her heart jerked with motherly guilt and she hugged him.

'I'm sorry, Jacks, I'm a bit overtired today – that's all. I had to get up so early this morning.'

At the playground, Lucy smiled at one of the mums who had been in the café that morning with her two children.

'Hi again.' She smiled back at her. 'I just wanted to let you know how impressed I was with the Signal Box Café. You have done an amazing job and the way the drinks arrived at the table was genius. I was wondering whether you do children's parties because my son is nine in a few weeks and we would love to have his party there.'

Lucy hadn't yet booked any children's parties but knew she should embrace another great source of revenue. Her head was buzzing from the early start and with the actual potential that the Signal Box had. If people hired the place they would be able to use upstairs for magicians and other entertainers. She delved into her jacket pocket and pulled out a business card, which she handed to the lady.

'I'm sure that won't be a problem as long as it fits around the weddings.'

'That's absolutely fine – midweek would be great. Also,' she whispered so her son couldn't hear her, 'could you let me know where I could get one of the little trains? They were brilliant.'

'They are, aren't they? My grandad made them for me. He's pretty amazing.'

'Well could you please ask if he would consider selling them?'

'Yes of course. I'll be in touch.' She turned to Jackson who was playing with the lady's son as they were in the same class.

'Bye, Jackson, have a lovely day.' She wasn't allowed to kiss him at school as he got embarrassed, so she patted his head and waved goodbye. She walked extra quickly to get back to the café.

When she returned, she was surprised to see her grandad there, then quickly snapped her hands to her mouth as she remembered she was meant to collect him so he could help out in the mornings.

'Oh, Grandad, I'm so sorry, it was such a rush this morning I completely forgot to come and get you. How did you manage to get here?'

'That's okay, don't worry, love. Violet got her grandson to release us and she's popped in for breakfast.'

Her eyes quickly followed in the direction of where he had gestured. Her stomach flipped in anticipation of seeing her nemesis there. She hadn't quite realised how much she had hoped to see him, until the dull empty feeling punched her tummy when she saw Violet sitting alone in one of the booths. She waved to them, her gold bangles jingling loudly with the movement.

'Hi, Violet, how are you?' she asked, kissing her cheek lightly.

'Very well, dear. I must say this place is marvellous.' She held up her glass of apple juice as if in toast. 'Congratulations to you and Douglas on this wonderful achievement.'

'Thank you so much. Grandad, you sit down, and I'll bring you both breakfasts. You can have the morning off.'

Grandad kissed her on the cheek and sat in the booth opposite Violet.

Chapter 20

Dominic Cavendish could not get a certain someone out of his mind. Everything he did seemed to have some sort of connection to her. Even getting the train into work every day reminded him of her. Well how could it not? The signal box had been virtually invisible before, a derelict building that had pretty much blended into the background. He had never even realised it was there, not once paid any attention to it whatsoever. He'd had a vague recollection of it being used years ago but had never given it a second thought. Now it was imposing, a very impressive-looking building with a whole new sense of purpose and it reminded him of her.

He thought back to last night when he'd come home from London. He didn't usually work weekends but he was working on a stressful case at the moment so had gone in for a couple of hours and had been invited to join colleagues for a few drinks afterwards. It was the first time he'd seen the café at night, twinkling fairy lights pinpointing its silhouette against the dark sky. He lazily observed it as he walked along the platform and that's when he'd seen the couple outside Railway Cottage.

He could tell it was her a mile off. He'd never seen anyone with those amazing golden curls. He remembered the feel of her hair in his fingers as he swooped in for a kiss, soft and silky, as was her skin. Now she was kissing this guy and he hated what it was doing to him. She really rubbed him up the wrong way. He asked himself why he'd been so obnoxious to her. His conscience replied: 'self-preservation, my friend.' His ex wife had started off all sweetness and light, but it hadn't taken long to discover she was a heartless money-grabbing bitch. He remembered the headaches he would have following one of their arguments. Too much hard work. And Lucy was a wedding planner of all things. He shuddered as though someone had walked over his grave and quickened his pace.

When he received the phone call from his gran this morning to ask him to come and pick her and Douglas up he was not very happy. He was already running late and now he would be even later. As he dropped them at the station he couldn't resist the smell of bacon, which was tantalising everyone on the platform, so he ordered a roll for himself. His eyes scanned all the members of staff but he couldn't see her anywhere. Dougie had noticed his eyes searching the room.

'Looking for anyone in particular?' he asked.

'Er no, not at all,' he replied though he couldn't hide his disappointment.

Sitting on the train he was relishing his bacon roll until a large blob of tomato sauce landed on his blue silk tie. *That bloody woman,* he thought as he tried his best to wipe it with a napkin.

Chapter 21

Mortification was the only word that Lucy could think of when she saw the piece about the Signal Box Café in the papers. The article had been fab, as promised word for word from the press release that she had sent in. The problem was the pictures. There was a lovely one of the exterior with Grandad standing outside proudly in his original signalman's uniform. A couple of interior shots with all the wedding businesses that had been present on the day, but the one that had completely embarrassed her was the wedding picture of her with Dominic kissing. How on earth had they got hold of this one?

After ten missed calls Abbie finally answered her phone. She sounded panicky.

'Lucy, I'm so sorry. I promise you I didn't send that one in. It must have still been on the memory stick I used to send the others to him. I'm so sorry and I am dreading seeing Dom as he will kill me. I promised him that these pics would not be shown locally. Please say you'll forgive me. In fact, let me take you out tonight please – honestly my stomach is churning about this.'

Lucy was hyperventilating; there were thousands of copies of this newspaper. How many could she realistically collect and burn? She knew it was a bad idea to have the local press involved. She had specifically said she didn't want to be in the feature and Greg knew that.

The only good thing to come of this was that the phones in the café and her mobile had been ringing non-stop with people interested in booking the place for weddings. Lucy's weekends would soon be filled with viewing appointments.

It took her a good few hours to sort through all of the answerphone messages and ring people back. She tried not to think of the article and instead concentrate on what she was here for. The café wasn't open at lunchtimes as they were mainly concentrating on the commuters for breakfasts and dinners for now, which would mostly be takeaways.

She had been sorting out the food choices with Lewis, the chef, and they had worked together to create an appetising menu. Lucy's nana had originally come from Liverpool and had passed down her secret scouse recipe; this was a delicious stew made from lamb or beef with potatoes, carrots and onions and served with red cabbage in vinegar, beetroot and a thick slice of crusty bread. This was going to be on the list of specials for dinner, which would change every day and included boeuf bourguignon, chicken curry and rice, chilli con carne, lasagne, and fish pie. Jacket potatoes with an assortment of fillings would be available every day.

The menus were printed and they were ready to go. Lucy made the scouse herself and it had proved to be very popular. A lot of people had never heard of it and hadn't realised that's why people from Liverpool were called Scousers.

Lucy loved seeing the meals packed into their environmentally friendly sectioned takeaway boxes and the customers carrying them off in the little dark grey paper bags with the Signal Box printed in silver. Most people used the takeaway service as they were tired after a long day in London and it was a perfect solution for those who didn't want to cook, but some customers decided to have company with theirs and dined in.

The novelty of the trains delivering the drinks never wore off and brought smiles to the faces of weary commuters. Lucy burst through the double doors from the kitchen to clear some plates and almost bumped into the back of a tall man who was shrugging off his raincoat. Although it was mid-spring the weather was still decidedly cold on some days and it had rained non-stop all day.

'Oops sorry, I'll be with you in a minute,' she said as she negotiated around him.

It wasn't until she was on her way back with stacked-up dirty plates that she realised who it was. His steely grey eyes belied a smile that wasn't apparent on his handsome face. He said hi and she was mesmerised by those chiselled cheeks, which made her feel all fluttery inside. She was losing the argument with the wobbling stacked-up crockery and cutlery she was carrying and they both watched as a dirty knife dropped, spinning in the air as if in slow motion before scraping itself down the trousers of his immaculate designer suit and depositing the rest of its detritus on his very shiny shoe.

She wanted to retrieve the knife and hesitated over whether to put the stack of dishes on his table or carry on and come back for it. She couldn't think straight.

'I'm so sorry,' said Lucy. 'Stay there and I'll get you a cloth.' Her face was beetroot when she arrived in the kitchen. *Why did it have to be him?* she thought as she rinsed out a clean cloth with which to clean up the mess.

She burst back into the café again.

'No, don't do that,' Dom shouted as Baxter licked the tasty morsels from his trousers and shoes whilst he stood and looked defeated.

128

'No, Jackson, you can't bring Baxter in here – he's not allowed.'

'But he wanted to see you, Mummy,' he said pushing his glasses back up his nose.

'Okay well, can you take him back home please and wash your hands because your dinner is ready.' Jackson cheered and took his dog the few steps back home.

Lucy forgot herself for a moment and began sponging down Dominic's trousers as though he were Jackson.

'Right, we'll have this out in a jiffy,' she said scrubbing a little harder on a more stubborn stain.

He watched her, amused by her maternal instinct towards him. Her eyes met his and she remembered who he was and realised what she was doing.

'It's okay, I think I might need to get them dry-cleaned.'

'Oh yes of course, I'm so sorry. I got carried away. Please send me the bill,' she said straightening up and refolded the cloth nervously. 'Now what can I get you? On the house of course!'

'Oh thank you, I must say that scouse smells good.'

'Ah so you know what it is then? There are so many people who've never heard of it.'

'I wouldn't be a true LFC fan if I didn't know what scouse was. I'm a season ticket holder and every time I go to the match, I have a big bowl of it.'

'Oh, my grandad and Jackson are huge LFC fans too.' She realised she was having a normal conversation with him. This was a first. 'I'll get you a portion. Would you like a drink with that?'

'Coffee thanks.'

'Consider it on its way.'

She gave him an extra dollop of scouse for good measure and poured some into a bowl for Jackson who would be here again in a minute. As she walked back into the café she was horrified to see Jackson sitting in one of the window booths opposite Dom.

'Oh no, Jackson, you can sit at your own table. You're not to disturb the customers.'

'Aw, Mum.' Jackson made to leave the table; he held his head in his hands as though exasperated.

Dom interrupted. 'But technically I'm not a customer if this is on the house.'

'You do have a point I suppose, but I'm sure you must want to relax after a hard day's work.'

'No really it's fine; I invited him to join me. Us LFC'ers have to stick together don't we?'

'Please, Mum,' pleaded Jackson, looking at her over the top of his glasses, which had managed to slide down his nose again.

'Okay as long as you don't mind.' She directed the question to Dom and placed the two steaming bowls on the table before pushing her son's glasses back up his nose. She must get them tightened properly. The little train arrived with their drinks on it, a lidded coffee for Dom and an apple juice for Jackson.

A real train had arrived at the platform, so Lucy was busy helping to serve the onslaught of takeaway orders through the hatch. The Signal Box Scouse was a huge hit and had nearly all gone. They would have to make more next time. There were still plenty of jacket potatoes left and only one more rush hour train to come in before they could pack away for the evening, so she decided to come off duty and leave the others to it.

She came back into the café with a small bowl of the scouse for herself and found Dom and Jackson playing Subbuteo noisily at the table.

'I'm Liverpool this time so you'll have to be Everton,' Jackson told Dom.

'Oh no but they're rubbish,' joked Dom as he flicked the blue player and kicked the ball into the goal. 'Yes, he scores.'

Lucy was taken by surprise as her eyes filled up. It wasn't just seeing Jackson sitting and playing with a man other than her dad or Grandad, although that was a strange scene for her, especially the way Jackson's pale blue eyes had lit up and his face was so animated. It was also the smell and taste of the scouse. It reminded her of her nana so much and made her realise how much she still missed her. This was real comfort food – no wonder it was a hit with the commuters. It was like a warm hug in a bowl. She commiserated with her grandad and his loss but was pleased that he seemed to be having a lovely time with Violet. She was such good company for him.

Just as Lucy had mopped the last of her scouse up with the crusty bread and popped it into her mouth, the entrance door opened with its customary beeping sound and her stomach dropped to the floor as she saw a huge pile of newspapers in Greg's arms.

'So, what do you think of the article then?' he asked excitedly. 'I thought I'd bring you a few copies around so you can pass them out to your customers. Ooh something smells good in here.' He inhaled deeply as though to absorb more of the delicious smell.

Dom glanced at him and, realising he was the guy he saw kissing Lucy, accidentally exerted a bit too much pressure on his flicking finger, causing the little Subbuteo man to fly through the air and land surreptitiously in Greg's eye.

'Oh God,' cried Greg dropping the stack of newspapers on to the floor, his hands flying to his eye to ease the pain. Lucy gasped in shock. Her hands flew to cover her mouth, which was gaping.

'You've bloody blinded me!'

'I'm so sorry,' said Dom, 'little heavy-handed there.' He was struggling to keep his face straight, as was Jackson who was half giggling behind his hand and half staring at this man wondering whether he now had a Subbuteo man instead of an eyeball.

Lucy rushed into the kitchen to get some ice. Luckily it had missed his eye, but he had a swelling on his cheekbone, which was red and shiny.

When he realised there was no blood and gore Jackson lost interest and rummaged around on the floor under the table to retrieve his little man.

'No more now, Jackson – please can you put the game away.'

'Aw, Mum, do I have to?'

'Yes you do. It's time for your homework, so come on, pack it in.'

Jackson rolled his eyes and reluctantly packed his game away.

'Sorry,' said Dom. 'That was my fault but thanks for letting me play.' He put his coat back on.

'That's okay,' replied Jackson. 'I'm just glad that you're not always a miserable git like Mum said.'

Greg snorted; Lucy turned bright red and shouted, 'Jackson.'

Dom shrugged it off. 'Your mum is right, Jackson – I am mostly a miserable git.'

Lucy peered out from between her fingers, which she was now trying to hide behind, just in time to see his grey eyes twinkle as he winked at her on the way out. Goose bumps ran up her arms and she felt tingles in her tummy.

On his way out he gestured to the newspapers.

'Do you mind if I have one of these?' he asked Greg who was still pressing the ice pack to his face and wincing. Greg moved his hand to allow him to take one but Lucy quickly clamped her hand down on the pile.

She gasped. 'No sorry, these are all accounted for.'

'What all of them?' he asked.

''Fraid so, the customers love them.'

'Oh okay. Bye then.'

'Bye.' Lucy breathed a sigh of relief as he left. She wasn't quite ready for that confrontation just yet.

Lucy popped back into the kitchen to make Greg a coffee to go with the half portion of leftover scouse; it was the least she could do. Playing on her pity he had also managed to wangle another date with her in a few days.

Jackson was playing with the Subbuteo figure and he looked at Greg as he was scanning the newspaper for his own articles and features. The swelling hadn't gone down much and was still very red. There was also a small scratch. Jackson scrutinised the figure for blood or skin.

'Do you want to play Subbuteo?' he asked Greg.

'No thanks, kid,' he replied without glancing up from his paper.

'I'm sorry my dad hurt you.'

Greg's interest was piqued; he looked at him, puzzled, and pointed behind him to the door. 'Oh was that your dad?'

'Nooo silly, not Dom, I mean him.' He held up the Subbuteo man.

'How can he be your dad?'

Jackson tapped the side of his nose. 'I mean the real one.'

'What you mean – your dad plays football for Liverpool?'

Jackson nodded conspiratorially, checking the door to make sure his mum didn't come out.

'Why else do you think you're eating scouse?' He held his finger to his lips. 'Sh don't tell my mum I told you or I'll be in big trouble.'

Greg could hardly contain his excitement; this was big news.

The evening shift was nearly over at the Signal Box Café and although Lucy had enjoyed every minute she was looking forward to a night out with her friend. The last few months had been constant hard work and probably the most satisfying time of her life but it was the weddings that she needed to concentrate on. The staff training was almost complete and apart from a few little hiccups it was going well. The whole team were working well together. She didn't open for lunch because she didn't want to encroach on other eating establishments in the area as they had all been very supportive of her new venture.

As they were about to shut the takeaway window a final customer came running up, Lucy recognised that handsome smile immediately.

'Hi, Finn, how are you? Come round the other way.' She walked to the front door and greeted him with a kiss on his cheek. His face was beaming.

'How's Gracie?'

'She's amazing; I've just dropped her home from the hospital with our new baby.'

Lucy's face lit up with anticipation. 'So, what did you have?'

'We've got a son and he's absolutely perfect,' said Finn, emotion cracking his voice.

Lucy enveloped him in a hug, squeezing him tightly. Tears filled both of their eyes.

'That's such great news, Finn. I'm so happy for you both. What's his name?'

Jackson looked up from his homework. 'Boys are the best,' he added.

'Thanks, Jackson.' Finn smiled. 'His name is Matthew. He was eight pound seven ounces, has a mop of black hair like me and mother and baby are doing fine. Poor Gracie is starving so I hoped I could catch a couple of your daily specials.'

'You most certainly can, how does boeuf bourguignon sound?'

Finn groaned with pleasure.

Lucy put two huge portions of the casserole into the takeaway boxes with plenty of buttered charlotte potatoes. She placed them carefully on top of each other into one of the larger takeaway bags.

She handed the bag gratefully to Finn, who sniffed the air appreciatively.

'This smells delicious. How much do I owe you?' He reached into his jeans pocket for his wallet. Lucy put her hand to his arm to stop him.

'My treat, give Gracie my love and baby Matthew a huge kiss from me and I'll pop in to see them soon if that's okay?'

'Are you sure? Thank you. Yes, you'll be welcome anytime.'

Chapter 22

'Jackson, wake up.' Lucy's voice shrilled through the house. Her stupid phone had run out of charge and the alarm hadn't gone off. She plugged it in, then thundered down the stairs and quickly went to throw some lunch in his lunchbox, before realising she had forgotten to empty it out the night before so crisp crumbs and brown apple cores were making bacterial homes there for multitudes of germs. She tossed it all in the bin, sprayed it clean and filled it up with a tangerine, packet of crisps and a hastily prepared sandwich cut in half and stuffed in a sandwich bag. She usually lovingly cut his sandwiches out with cookie cutters in the shape of trains and rockets and dinosaurs but there was no time for that this morning. She took two drink cartons and a small cake from the fridge. He would have to have breakfast in the car on the way, which would consist of one of the cartons and a cereal bar from the cupboard.

Jackson came running down the stairs like a new-born kitten, bleary-eyed with his hair sticking up. Lucy dampened a paper towel with water to smooth the more stubborn pieces of hair into submission and quickly combed it over to the side, causing him to say 'Ouch,' with each stroke. She still had her pyjamas on but that would have to do. She slipped on her shoes and they both ran to the car with Baxter bounding along behind them.

'Jackson, did you unlock the back gate? Because Baxter was in the garden.'

'No, Mummy,' he sniffed. She didn't have time to put him back in the house and he loved a car ride so she let them both in the back and drove them to school. Thank goodness they were on the right side of the rail barriers as they had just come down and would have made them even later if they'd had to wait.

On approaching the playground, they could see some children walking in with their parents. They were just about going to make it when she noticed that the other children were not wearing their uniforms. This did not go unnoticed by Jackson who, still with the last piece of cereal bar in his mouth, wailed.

'It's World Book Day.' Before he dissolved into bucketloads of tears, which Baxter promptly licked off his face.

Jackson hadn't cried like this for ages, not since he had lost his guinea pig last year. The sound of it tugged at her heart and Lucy wanted to cuddle him and wrap him in cotton wool. How could she have forgotten World Book Day? Had she even known it was World Book Day? She was racked with mother's guilt. This was a major fail. As a single parent she was always extra hard on herself because she knew that Jackson had no one else to rely on. Her mind whirred into action as she tried to plan what to do next.

Instead of parking in the little car park she did a U-turn and headed straight back home. Jackson wailed even louder as he didn't want to be late. She had to speak very loudly in order to be heard over his distress.

'Jackson, calm down, here's what we are going to do: you are going to think about your costume for World Book Day and I am going to get home and phone the school and just tell them a tinsy white lie. I'm going to say you had a doctor's appointment and then we will have time to get you changed and go back.

He wailed again. 'I'm going to be in trouble. You said it's wrong to tell lies. You can't lie to the teachers. What if the doctor tells them it's not true?'

She reassured him, 'No, Jacks, you're not lying so you won't get into trouble and sometimes mummies have to tell little tinsy white ones. So, you will be fine, I promise.' What a hypocrite she was.

They rushed back into the house and the phone was ringing but she didn't have time to answer it as her head was thumping with trying to think of an outfit for her son. The shrill noise wasn't helping. No sooner had it stopped than it started again. She joined Jackson in scrabbling around his fancy dress clothes but he wasn't happy with anything. Then she remembered his little black suit, which he wore to a wedding last year and for the photo shoot they did.

She remembered Grandad's book collection on the bookshelf downstairs.

'How about James Bond?' she suggested excitedly.

'Oh yeah,' said Jackson thrilled. 'But wait, isn't that a film?' he said with echoes of sobs in his throat.

'No, it's definitely a book. There are loads of them, and Grandad has them downstairs.'

'Okay then,' he said smiling once more and wiping his tear-soaked eyes on the sleeve of his jumper.

'Great.' Relief flooded through her. 'Quickly, put this on.' She threw the suit and a white shirt to him and he scrambled out of his clothes. She swiftly ran to her room and called the school on her mobile as she rummaged around in the wardrobe where she remembered seeing a black dicky bow of her grandad's. After a few attempts she managed to tie it round Jackson's neck but only by standing behind him and looking in the long mirror.

'Look at you, handsome.' She straightened up the bow and wolf whistled. He smiled shyly but she could see he was thrilled with the outcome. She slicked his hair with gel and on the way out she grabbed one of the James Bond books from the shelf and handed it to him.

He held it tightly and proudly all the way into school.

'You really are the best mummy,' he said, allowing her to cuddle him as there was nobody around to see them.

She wanted to give herself a gold star for being a great mum this morning and managing to avoid a huge crisis. Her shoulders, which had been so relaxed yesterday, now felt attached to her ears again she was so tense.

When she got home the first thing she wanted to do was have a relaxing soak in the bath with a cup of coffee. She turned on the taps and plopped one of the strawberry and cream bath bombs into the water. She'd been so impressed with the freebie that she'd ordered some for herself. She remembered the back gate and ran down quickly to check if it had been left unlocked. It had. Maybe Jackson had kicked his football over the wall into the entry again and had forgotten to lock it. She pushed the rusty lock across anyway. The last thing they needed was for Baxter to escape from the garden. She ran up the stairs again. Her bath was beckoning her.

As she got to the landing, she could hear her phone pinging in the bedroom and it started ringing. She remembered the house phone ringing earlier and her heart began to pound. What if it was an emergency? She answered it just in time to hear Mrs King inform her that she needed to see her immediately for a matter of great urgency. Without thinking she jumped into the car and it was only as she burst into Mrs King's office frantically that she realised she was still wearing her pyjamas. Her mum had ordered them especially for her with the words, 'Sh, Wedding Planner Sleeping,' on them. She wouldn't have realised then if it hadn't been for Dominic Cavendish's steely grey eyes scanning her body slowly before settling on the caption emblazoned across her chest and shaking his head.

She self-consciously folded her arms and tried to smooth out her outrageously wild curls. She had a look of being just dragged out of bed, which pretty much summed up what had happened. She sidled up to the available chair next to her grandad and noticed that Dominic, beside him, was dressed as impeccably as ever in one of his designer suits. Violet was shyly peering round at her from the other side of him.

'Sorry I had a school emergency, hence the erm . . .' She gestured with her hands to her attire.

'Is everything all right, love?' Grandad's eyes crinkled with concern.

'Yes, don't worry all sorted now,' she replied.

'When you're quite ready, I'll begin,' said an unamused Mrs King.

Dom had his hand over his mouth and she could sense that he found this funny. His eyes looked more like a pale blue and there was definitely a twinkle in them.

However, as soon as Mrs King started talking, he quickly reverted back into miserable git mode. All four of them snapped to attention, backs straight and shoulders back. It was like being summoned in front of the headmistress.

'Miss Woods and Mr Cavendish, I would like to thank you both for joining me so promptly this morning.' She looked Lucy up and down disapprovingly, her mouth pursed tightly as though she had just sucked on a lemon.

'Now as you both know we take great pride at Sycamore Lodge in making our residents comfortable and happy, but the only way we can achieve that is by applying certain rules that we think it is only fair for everybody to be expected to follow.

'I have mentioned before that we operate an extremely strict three strikes and you're out policy and I'm afraid that we are now in a regretful position of politely asking your grandparents to leave the premises.'

Dom and Lucy looked at each other in shock before both looking back at Mrs King.

'Oh come on, Dolores, it was only a few puffs of a cigar,' Grandad said in his defence.

'And mine was only a menthol,' added Violet looking at Dom and then over to Lucy, 'which aren't even real cigarettes.'

'Well that hardly seems like an offence worth being evicted for surely?' Dom asked looking at Mrs King who had gone very red at this point, her head shaking nervously.

'I'm afraid it's not the fact that they were smoking so much as where they were smoking them.' She managed to spit out almost in one go, as though each word tasted like vomit.

'We are consenting adults,' said Violet jumping up and grabbing her lover's hand. 'And what's more is that Douglas has asked me to marry him and I've said yes.'

Mrs King continued as Dom and Lucy also got to their feet, 'This is true. Your grandfather—' she pointed a bony finger at Lucy and then at Dom '—was found in your grandmother's bed this morning and as if that wasn't bad enough they were both smoking. Thankfully the smoke alarms alerted us to this embarrassing incident but I'm afraid there is no going back on this. Sycamore Lodge does not need this kind of scandal.'

Lucy's jaw had dropped open and she was staring at Mrs King in astonishment. Dom looked furious and Grandad and Violet were cuddling and having an actual necking session.

Mrs King's face looked as though she had swallowed a wasp. 'So I'm afraid I'm going to have to ask you both to pack up your things and leave Sycamore Lodge with immediate effect.'

'You need to wake up to the realities of human beings, Dolores,' said Grandad. 'You have lots of lonely people here who would be much happier if they could settle down with each other but because there are only single rooms you won't even let Martha and Jeffrey sleep together and they're married. I think it's a bloody disgrace.'

Dolores King was not going to be swayed and she raised her hand to put an end to the matter.

'Come on then, Grandad, I never liked you being in here anyway. Let's go home,' said Lucy.

'But, Douglas,' said Violet taking his hand.

'I've promised Violet that we could be together, Lucy.' He looked downhearted.

'That's fine, Grandad, it's your house and you can do whatever you like. No more being treated like a prisoner or a child.' Grandad looked at her and smiled. This had only ever been for a trial period anyway.

Neither of them had much to pack so before long they were ready to go. Mrs King had given them each a letter, so they had it in writing exactly what was going on and why they had been evicted. The other residents formed an orderly line so they could all say goodbye to their great friends Dougie and Violet, who had certainly livened this place up.

'Please say you'll come and visit us,' said Jeffrey as he shook hands with Dougie.

'We will, maybe we'll come and break you out of here sometime.' He chuckled. Grandad handed Jeffrey a half bottle of whisky from his bag. Jeffrey winked at him and ran off to squirrel it away to his room before Mrs King had a chance to confiscate it.

'It won't be the same without you, Dougie,' said a smart elderly gentleman holding out his hand. Dougie shook it and patted him on the back. 'I'll miss you too Old Bill but it won't be the last we see of each other.'

Grandad rummaged through his belongings and handed a bag to Lucy.

'It's a surprise for your friends,' he said.

Lucy looked inside to discover it was a smaller version of the trains they had in the café. It was painted a shiny black and in delicate silver lettering it had 'The Signal Box' painted on one side and 'Matthew' painted on the other. It was exquisite and took Lucy's breath away.

'Grandad, it's so beautiful. They are going to love this. You should start selling them. I've already been asked if they were available anywhere.'

'Jackson helped,' he said. Lucy's heart swelled with pride for the two special men in her life.

Grandad smiled a proud smile.

Chapter 23

Grandad was excited to put the key in the lock at Railway Cottage; he couldn't wait to be home again. Violet had followed them in Dom's car, and he was now standing at the bottom of the path holding her suitcases.

'Are you sure about this, Gran?' he asked.

Violet stood tight-lipped and nodded determinedly, 'I'm absolutely certain, Dominic. Douglas and I have become very close lately and who knows how much time either of us have left. We want to spend our twilight years together.'

As they stepped into the house, they could hear an unfamiliar noise and the beautiful smell of strawberries and cream hung in the air. The noise was quickly identified as running water; it was seeping down the stairs and dripping onto the hall carpet.

'Noooo,' Lucy screeched, thinking back to this morning. 'I've left the bathwater running.' She thundered up the stairs three at a time and pushed the door open. The bathroom was completely flooded, and the bath was still brimming over. She quickly turned the taps off and managed to pull the plug out.

'Be careful where you stand, Lucy,' she heard Grandad shout from downstairs. She ran down to join him, her feet squelching on every step. He flicked the light switch a couple of times. 'It looks like the electrics have blown.'

'Oh no, it's all my fault.' She followed her grandad to the kitchen, her eyes closed in disbelief, her hands clasped at each side of her face. How could she have caused so much damage? The kitchen was flooded, and large pieces of the ceiling were now smashed and scattered over the worktops and floor.

Grandad was speechless and was trying to take in the total devastation around him. Violet was stroking his arm in an effort to bring him comfort. Dom stood in the dining room, the cases at his feet, rubbing his face as if trying to think of something helpful to say.

Lucy's heart had never sunk so low. She could almost feel it near her pelvis. She felt as though she were going to throw up. It was now her turn to wail.

'Grandad, I'm so sorry, I was running late and it was World Book Day and I needed your dicky bow and I had to rush Jackson to school and the lunchbox was dirty and he was crying and then I wanted to have a bath and then Mrs King rang and I ran out of the house in my pyjamas and I'm so, so, sorry.' She bawled.

Grandad took her in his arms and held her tightly, soothing her.

'Don't worry, love; there is nothing here that can't be fixed, and there's no way one overflowing bath can do all this. It's most likely been a burst pipe or something and the electrics here are more ancient than I am.'

'I've destroyed your house, Grandad. It all started with the alarm not going off. I'm such a rubbish mum and an even worse granddaughter.' Her sobs were coming from deep in her chest now. Her nose was running and mingling with the tears that she thought would never stop. She couldn't breathe or swallow properly due to the lump in her throat the size of a tangerine. Grandad kissed the top of her head.

'Do you honestly think that you're the first person to have done this?'

She nodded.

'Well I can tell you that you're not. The first time your nana did it your dad was just a baby. The first she knew was when water was dripping on her head in the kitchen when she was making his lunch. The second time was when your dad was a toddler and he jammed all his toys in the bathroom sink and left the tap running and my turn was when your nan went to visit her parents with your dad when he was about ten and I was left home alone. So please don't worry – this is just your initiation into Railway Cottage. It can all be fixed.'

She tried to return his smile but simply couldn't. Devastation washed over her.

Dom and Violet were being practical. He was picking up the large pieces of plaster and wood that had fallen and Violet had gathered towels and blankets from the airing cupboard and was trying to soak up the worst of the water.

The gas was still working so Grandad put the kettle on to make a pot of tea. 'Now you pack a bag for you and Jackson for a few days and we can check you into a hotel – there's a nice little B&B in Market Square.'

'What about you, Grandad?' she asked between hiccupping sobs.

'I'll be fine here,' he said, having settled her in the living room with a cuppa.

'Me too,' added Violet.

'Oh no,' said Dominic. 'There is no way you are staying here, Gran. You'll get pneumonia with all this damp air; you can stay with me for now.'

'What a splendid idea,' she replied. 'Dominic's house has room for all of us, isn't that right?'

'Well, I just meant . . .' His eyes were practically bulging out of his head.

'I'm so proud of my wonderful grandson for opening his home to me and our lovely friends,' said Violet as she kissed him on the cheek. Dominic looked around the room at the devastated faces and knew he had no choice.

'Okay then, Gran, maybe for a few days.' His eyes rounded on Baxter as Lucy held him by the collar to stop him trying to lick up the scented water. 'But what about the hairy hound?'

'Oh he's no trouble. Look at him, he's lovely,' said Violet stroking him as he rolled over to give her access to his belly.

Dominic begged to differ but kept his mouth shut. 'Come on then,' he said loading up the car with his gran's cases.

'I really don't think this is such a good idea,' Lucy whispered to Violet. 'Dom doesn't like children or dogs, or me for that matter. It's okay – Jackson and I will go to the B&B.'

'I won't hear of it,' Violet responded strongly. 'This was mine and Douglas's fault for getting into trouble at Sycamore Lodge; you should never have been called over there, especially as you've had such a stressful start to the day. So come on, pack some things for you and that delightful little boy of yours. Besides he does like children. Between you and me that was one of the bones of contention that caused he and Clarissa to break up. He wanted them and she didn't, plus she was ever such a contrary Mary and an absolute bitch to boot.' She put her fingers to her lips in a shushing motion.

Lucy put her fingers to her lips in solidarity but was thinking that was an interesting snippet; she smiled weakly and did as she was told. She could hear Grandad on the phone to the insurance company explaining what had happened; he seemed in good spirits despite everything.

Parking up on Dom's drive was very alien to her even though he was waving her on to it. She wasn't happy to be there but decided to make the best of the situation for both her grandad's and Jackson's sakes. She knew it would be a huge adventure for Jackson and she planned to stay out of Dom's way as much as possible.

Dom's gran had given him a good talking-to in the car, instructing him to be nice.

The first thing Dom did was take Baxter's bed and put it in the utility room.

'Sorry, dog, but my carpets are all new and I don't want them covered in your hair or dirt.' Baxter circled his bed before finding a comfortable position and settling in to his new environment. He looked expectantly at Dom with big brown eyes, begging for a little attention, his tail wagging frantically. Dom turned his back on him to show everyone to their rooms. He took his gran's cases up to the largest of the spare rooms, which had a lovely en-suite shower room and a double bed with fitted wardrobes. Dougie followed with his suitcases and the atmosphere in the bedroom was a little awkward with the two men in there. Dom couldn't believe his gran was now shacked up with another man in *his house*. He gave an involuntary shiver at the thought of it. Dougie shook his hand.

'Thanks for this, son, it's much appreciated.'

'Well it's not for long is it,' he replied, trying not to let his discomfort show.

★

Dom opened the doors to the other spare rooms. He ushered Lucy in.

'Here you can have this one.' He pointed to the slightly bigger of the two, which had a smart leather sofa, a desk with drawers on either side and a comfortable leather swivel chair on wheels. There were a couple of floor to ceiling bookshelves, which were stuffed full of books. Lucy imagined they would be in alphabetical order but didn't want to look too closely. There was also a built-in mirrored wardrobe. The walls, as in the rest of the house, were painted magnolia and the curtains in this room were black and grey. He opened out the sofa into a bed, which had matching bedding to the curtains.

'You should be reasonably comfortable in this,' he said as he smoothed the quilt cover over the bed.

Lucy could neither look at it nor him. She stood stiffly by the door like a soldier on sentry duty, her face glowing. It felt embarrassingly over-familiar being in a room with him and a bed. She could feel herself burning up.

'I feel awful putting you out like this,' she said starting to feel tearful again.

'Can't be helped I suppose. Those two are a nightmare.' He nodded his head in the direction of their grandparents' room. 'I will admit that it's six of one and half a dozen of the other, but my gran wouldn't have dreamt of doing this before your grandad came along.'

'Ah but was she happy then?' she countered. 'Was she living a fulfilling life? Because she certainly seems to be now thanks to my grandad.'

Dom couldn't argue with that point.

He showed her the other room, which was the smallest of the house and had a single bed in it.

'Jackson should be okay in here, shouldn't he?'

'Yes he'd love it thank you but he can come in with me – it's really no trouble.'

'No don't worry, he might as well.' He went to leave the room but turned back to say, 'Look I know you don't want to be here but whilst you are then please just help yourself to anything. You and Jackson can have the bathroom to yourselves as we have en-suites.'

He looked into her sad blue eyes and instinctively went to stroke her hair but stopped himself at the last minute. Now that would have been mildly inappropriate, he thought. She gasped and her eyes opened wide as she saw his hand came towards her. She looked away when he swerved it away again.

'Let's hope those two gramps don't make any noises through the night,' he joked. 'I swear I couldn't cope with that.' He shuddered. 'I feel like I'm their bloody dad.'

Lucy laughed.

'Come down when you're ready. I assume you'll want to get dressed sometime today.' He glanced at the caption on her chest again and shook his head. 'I'll go and make some coffee.' As he went down the stairs, he could hear the gramps giggling and put his fingers in his ears and starting singing, 'Lalala,' very loudly.

Dom's power shower almost knocked Lucy back at first. It was wonderful, and she realised how weak and slow Grandad's one had been. Her curly hair was so thick and usually it took ages to rinse all the shampoo out but not with this hi-tech gadget. Her skin felt slightly sore afterwards but exceptionally clean. She stepped out onto the landing at the same time as Dom stepped into the hall; they were at the top and bottom of the stairs. She was wrapped in one of his immaculate white towels and another was wrapped in a turban around her head.

Dom tried to look away but couldn't take his eyes off her. Her arms and legs were still damp from the shower and her skin glowed. Her face was youthful and dewy. Her big blue eyes stared at him like a deer caught in headlights. He knew he'd have to look away or she'd think he was a right perv. He looked at his watch and said, 'What coffee would you like? Cappuccino, latte?'

'A cappuccino would be lovely thanks,' she replied, still frozen to the spot until he walked away.

Lucy dressed quickly and entered the pristine kitchen; the smell from the coffee machine was enticing. He was leaning against the worktop when she came in; his DAB radio was playing rock music, which surprised her. He handed her the mug with the steaming milky coffee; he'd even sprinkled some cocoa powder on the top. She felt quite shy being in his house and found herself shifting her weight nervously from one foot to the other.

'Thanks.' She took the drink from him, preferring to stare into the cocoa-covered froth than into his eyes. She couldn't think of what to say to him.

'I really am so sorry about this. I feel devastated.' Her eyes filled up and she sniffed. He stood in front of her, his close proximity taking her breath away for a second.

'Look your grandad's right, there's no way you could have caused all that damage.' He stroked her arm gently leaving traces of fire up and down her skin. She trembled and her eyes slowly looked up to meet his sympathetic gaze.

Violet entered the room and they jumped apart; she searched through his cupboards and fridge. 'We are going to need to do a shop. There's not a thing to eat in this house. Dom, I don't know how you survive.'

He opened a drawer and pulled out a handful of takeaway leaflets. 'This is all I need, Gran, and some decent pub grub on my doorstep.'

She tut-tutted him. He winked at Lucy with a cheeky grin. He was like a completely different person when he smiled.

'And you so healthy with all the running you do.'

'Let me treat everyone to dinner tonight please. I can pick some up from the Signal Box Café later. It's the least I can do.' Lucy looked pleadingly at Violet who could see she genuinely needed to contribute.

'Okay then, that would be a lovely treat, wouldn't it, Dom?' She elbowed her grandson who didn't seem to be paying attention.

He was trying not to look at Lucy because when he did, he found he couldn't look away. Her golden hair was like sunshine and her eyes, as blue as the sky on a cloudless day, seemed to draw him in hypnotically. Her thick black lashes framed them perfectly.

'Er yes that does sound good, thank you,' he replied still not making eye contact with her but taking every opportunity to steal glances at her when she looked away.

'Well your grandad and I will get down to the shops then and pick up some basics.'

Lucy gulped her coffee down, almost burning her throat; she couldn't be left alone with him. That would be so awkward.

'Right well I must dash too as I have to sort a few things out before I pick Jackson up from school.'

She ran upstairs to pick up her bag, popped to the utility room to collect Baxter and as she was on the way out she sensed Dom behind her.

'Lucy, before you go, I need to do a bit of work in the room that you're in. Do you mind? It's just that the printer is in there and all my files are in the desk.'

He'd called her by her name; she'd never heard him say it before – well only as a child when he used to tease her, but not as a man. Goose bumps rose up on her arms and she felt like a feather was stroking slowly down her spine. She liked the sound of his voice saying her name. It held a certain intimacy. She answered quickly before he noticed she was turning to mush.

'Of course, that's fine. Thanks again. I'll make sure we're out of your hair soon.'

He reached for the door as if he was going to wave her off but she held on to the knocker and shut it quickly behind her. She shivered when she got outside even though it wasn't cold.

She popped back to Railway Cottage to pick up a few things and her stomach sank again at the thought and the sight of what she'd done. The smell of damp was now seeping into the air, which had overtaken and contaminated the lovely homely smell that usually greeted her. How could she have been so stupid? Grandad had decided that Maud should stay at Railway Cottage as she was too fretful anywhere else and if she had gone to Dom's they would have had to keep her in. So they agreed they would take it in turns to pop round and feed her and spend some time with her so she didn't get too lonely.

Maud was perfectly happy to have her house back all to herself even though certain parts were now unusable by humans. After feeding her, Lucy walked along the river and marvelled again at what a beautiful area this was. The sun was glistening on the ripples, which danced along the river and warmed the skin on her face. Her hair would be dry in no time. Baxter plodded along happily, every now and then stopping to sniff at, and wee on, random leaves and trees and happily greet other dogs that came past.

She soon arrived at Davinci's and saw that it was shut; she walked to the front door of the adjoining house and knocked gently in case the baby was asleep. She saw Finn come to the window and smile in greeting when he saw her. A few seconds later he opened the front door and kissed her cheek.

'Come in, Lucy, how lovely to see you.'

'Could I put Baxter in the garden please. He's a little muddy and I don't want to bring him through the house.'

Finn led the way down the tiled hall to the large kitchen, which had patio doors leading out to the garden; he filled a bowl with water and put it on the ground where Baxter lapped it up thirstily before sniffing and weeing on the flowers in the borders.

Lucy opened the door into the large living room. Sunlight flooded in through the big bay windows, and Gracie was sitting on one of two dove grey settees, the baby at her breast. She raised her head and smiled at Lucy. She looked a little washed out but incredibly happy.

'Oh I'm sorry, you're feeding. I'll leave you in peace.'

'No, please stay, Lucy. With this hungry little one I always seem to be feeding. It's so lovely to see you. Sit down and tell me something, anything that isn't baby-related.' She moved some baby items onto the coffee table and patted the cushion next to her. Lucy sat down and laughed.

'I remember those days; luckily I had my mum and dad to help me or I would have gone crazy. I did persevere with the breastfeeding though and it was worthwhile.'

Finn popped his head round the door. His face wore a permanent smile of new baby joy, but his eyes looked quite tired.

'Tea or coffee?' he asked Lucy.

'Coffee would be lovely thanks.'

'So what's been happening with you then, Lucy? How's the Signal Box Café? That food you sent us was delicious by the way.'

'Oh I'm glad you liked it. It's going amazingly well and the wedding planning business is going from strength to strength too.'

Finn brought in the drinks and placed the tray on the coffee table in front of the settee she and Gracie were sitting on. He offered the plate of biscuits round and they each took one.

'We loved the venue so much,' said Gracie, 'and we were wondering whether it would be possible to have Matthew christened there one day. Well obviously not christened there but to have the celebration there afterwards.'

'I would be absolutely honoured,' Lucy replied with a beaming smile of pride. 'Just let me know the date as soon as you have it and I'll book it in.'

Matthew had finished feeding and was lolling back in a completely satiated state; his lip was still performing a sucking motion. He was nothing short of perfect. Gracie sat him up with his chin tucked between her thumb and forefinger, his little face all scrunched up. She patted his back and rubbed it gently until a huge burp rattled loudly around the room. One deep blue eye opened in surprise for just a few seconds before closing again, and he drifted back into the land of slumber.

'There's a good boy,' said his mummy proudly.

'How can something so little make such a huge noise.' Finn laughed.

'Would you like to hold him?' asked Gracie.

'I would love to; that is if I can remember how. He's so tiny I almost can't recall Jackson ever being this small.' She held out her arms and Gracie lowered her baby into them, ensuring his neck was supported in the crook of Lucy's arm.

Gracie took the opportunity to pick up her herbal tea and try and drink it whilst it was still hot. She also picked up another biscuit to nibble on.

Lucy stared in awe at this tiny being. It had been so long since she'd gone through this. Seeing Finn look at his little family with such love and adoration made her pang for something she could never have had. But she couldn't change that and nor would she want to now. She and Jackson were a team; they didn't need anybody else.

'He is the cuddliest baby in the world.' She laughed as he snuggled his little blue Babygro-covered body into her. She held him higher so she could smell him. 'They really should bottle that smell.' She kissed his soft downy hair.

'Well as long as no one ever bottles the nappy needs changing smell.' Finn laughed again.

'Oh I nearly forgot.' Lucy remembered the bag she had brought with her; she picked it up with her spare arm and handed it to Gracie. Inside the gift bag, wrapped in pale blue tissue paper, were two presents and a card.

'Ooh one each.' She handed the heavier one to Finn to open and she opened the softer one. 'They are beautiful, thank you so much.' She held up a little three-piece outfit with matching bibs in the shape of neckerchiefs. 'I'll bring him to see you when he's wearing them.'

'Oh, I would love that,' she said.

'Oh wow, now look at this,' said Finn as he unwrapped the shiny black train with his son's name painted on it in silver. 'This is amazing.'

'Oh yes,' agreed Gracie, 'I know who'll be getting lots of pleasure out of this.'

Finn put a biscuit in the back of it, placed it on the floor and aimed it towards Gracie before turning on the engine. Gracie laughed as the train chugged over to her, the headlight shining on the polished wooden floor.

'Now this will come in very handy for passing the remote control to your daddy won't it?' she said to Matthew who was completely zonked.

'This is something we will treasure forever. Thank you so much, Lucy.'

'Well it is a Dougie Woods original you know,' she said with a gleam in her eye.

She could hear Baxter barking in the garden so decided it was time to go.

'I'm sorry for bringing Baxter but it's a bit of a long story. To cut it short, I've flooded my grandad's house and we have to stay with someone for a while and he doesn't like dogs – well he barely likes people – so I had to get him out.' She could feel her eyes filling up and felt silly.

'You should have said, Lucy. I could help.'

'No, Finn, that wouldn't be fair. You're off having time with the baby and I would never ask you to miss out on that. They don't stay tiny for long.'

'Well I don't have to do the work – I have a whole team of men who can sort it out for you. It's only a phone call, no trouble at all.'

'We'd appreciate that, thank you.' She gently handed the baby to his dad, his deep blue eyes truly mesmerised by this tiny bundle.

Gracie gave her a hug. 'Thanks again for the lovely presents and thank your grandad too.'

Lucy collected Baxter from the garden and left via the back gate. She walked past the window. She felt a pang of loss as she saw Finn with his arm around Gracie, both gazing adoringly at their baby son's face. What a beautiful family, she thought, it would be an absolute pleasure to have baby Matthew's christening at the Signal Box Café. The walk back down the river and onwards to Jackson's school was just as enjoyable as it had been earlier. The sun was still shining, which had melted the ice, and the colourful wild flowers were beginning to appear along the towpath.

When she told Jackson that they would be staying at Dom's for a little while he jumped up and down with joy.

'Can we collect my Subbuteo on the way there please, Mummy? Has he got an Xbox?'

'We can but remember he is a very busy person and won't have time to play with you, so you mustn't get upset if he says no and you mustn't keep asking him all the time. Okay?'

'Okay but if he has got an Xbox can I play on it pleeeeease?'

Squeezing his hand lovingly she smiled and wondered if Dom knew exactly what he had let himself in for.

Chapter 24

Dominic Cavendish had been trying to catch up by working from home after a completely disruptive start to the day, but he was finding it a little hard to concentrate. His home office was usually a bland room with no distractions in it. However, the sofa bed was out and Lucy's bag casually lay on it. Her wedding planner pyjamas were folded neatly on top. She had hung some of her clothes in the wardrobe and had put the towels on the radiator to dry.

He'd lived on his own for two and a half years now, so it was very strange to have another person in the house, never mind four people and a hairy hound. He didn't know why but he just couldn't concentrate with her things in the room. He felt like an intruder, but he needed access to various files and the printer, so it wasn't easy to use another room.

He noticed a picture of her and Jackson from when he was a couple of years younger on the bedside table. Their faces were so similar. Their eyes sparkled with laughter. It was such a happy picture, full of joy. He picked it up and looked closely into her eyes; they were a piercing blue with a darker blue circle around the edge of the iris. She had beautiful eyes, so open and expressive. Her nose was crinkling up in the picture and she looked remarkably cute.

He remembered her as a little girl, she would play with Abbie and they would fawn around after him and his friends but they were far too cool to hang around with girls so he would be quite mean to her. He hoped she had forgotten because he would be embarrassed if she could remember. He had been such a sod when he was younger, always getting into lots of mischief. He had secretly thought she was cute all those years ago but would never admit it for fear of being teased by his friends.

There was something in the air that unsettled him. He took a deep breath. That's what it was; he could smell her perfume, fresh, clean and flowery. It was driving him mad. He inhaled again and closed his eyes. His mind wandered back to the time he first smelt that scent. It was when they had shared that kiss. Abbie had pointed out that he should have just pretended but how could he when those delicate pink lips were begging to be kissed. He simply did as he was instructed to do. He re-created the scene in his mind, lolling back in his comfortable chair with his legs stretched out before him. Suddenly the door burst open and in came his gran with a cup of coffee and a biscuit.

'There you go, love. We don't want you wasting away now do we.'

He sat up abruptly as her surprise entrance dragged him out of his very pleasant daydream.

'Thanks, Gran.' He took the coffee and smiled at her.

She took the picture frame out of his hand and smiled to herself. 'She's a sweet girl, isn't she? And that little boy is adorable; I could eat him up.' She placed the picture back in his hands and he returned it to the bedside table. A flush of guilt and embarrassment swept across his face.

'Oh yes I accidentally knocked it over I was just putting it back. They're okay, I suppose. Did I hear Dougie leaving earlier?' He was eager to change the subject.

'Yes, dear.' She began tidying up his desk. 'He's gone back to Railway Cottage to let some builders in. Lucy's friend Finn got them round super quick. Apparently it could have happened any time and it was just a coincidence that the bath was running. It seems a crack in the pipe caused a slow leak, which had rotted the chipboard on the bathroom floor; unfortunately the pipe eventually burst and caused the chaotic scene. It all needs replacing but it's not as bad as it looked, thank God.'

'Lucy will be relieved. She looked so devastated.'

'She did, didn't she, poor girl but it really wasn't her fault. Hopefully it won't be long before we are all out of your hair.' She pinched his cheek playfully. 'Such a handsome boy, just like your grandad with those bright grey eyes and chiselled cheeks.'

'Do you think . . .?' She hesitated, 'Oh it doesn't matter, don't worry.' She went to leave the room.

Dom wasn't used to seeing her looking so worried; she looked older and slightly frailer. He put his coffee down on the desk.

'What is it, Gran?'

'Oh, nothing I'm being silly.' She pulled a scrunched-up tissue from out of her sleeve and sniffed, holding it to her eyes to absorb the tears that had slowly started to flow. 'I just wondered: do you think he'd mind?'

Dom looked puzzled. 'Do I think who would mind what?'

Her voice was choked as she couldn't hold the tears back. 'Do you think Grandad would mind that I'm with Douglas now?' she sobbed.

Dom had never seen his gran cry so he rushed over to her and pulled her into his arms. She had always been a strong and quite formidable woman in the past but now he realised how incredibly vulnerable and tiny she was. She cried into his chest, real deep heavy sobs and he stroked her back gently.

'Gran, it's been eight years since we lost Grandad and I think he is looking down at you now and wishing you all the happiness in the world. You two loved each other so much and no one can ever take that away from you, but you are allowed a second chance at a different love. I'll admit I was very unsure of Dougie at first, but I can see how much he cares about you and I can see how happy he makes you. So—' he gave her a little squeeze '—do you remember Grandad's favourite quote?'

She blew her nose on the tissue and smiled as she nodded her head.

'If you see something good,' he began.

'Then just go for it,' she finished.

'Exactly, Gran, so you go for it; and in the meantime, you're welcome to stay here for as long as you like.'

'Thanks, love. There is something else too. We've been talking and have decided we would like to get married as soon as possible and I was wondering whether you would give me away?'

'I've heard of people selling their granny but you want me to give mine away. What is the world coming to?' He laughed, happy that she sounded a bit more upbeat.

She laughed too but more with a sense of relief at having got that off her chest.

'Of course I will. In fact, it will be my pleasure. I mean I don't agree with weddings, but I can hardly have my gran living over the brush can I?' He laughed again and kissed her forehead. She slapped him playfully on the back of the head.

'Oi cheeky!'

'I was also wondering whether we could give notice to the tenants in my cottage as we were thinking we could move in there together as there's no way we can all fit in Railway Cottage and I know Douglas feels strange about me moving in there because of the memories of his wife, and Lucy and Jackson have settled in so well there.'

Dom's first thought was what a headache this would be but then he admonished himself. When looking in his gran's worried eyes he realised he needed to show some compassion.

'I'm sure that will be fine, Gran. I'll speak to the estate agent and get it sorted. They're on a month-by-month rolling contract anyway so it shouldn't be too difficult. Just leave it to me.'

Since his mum and dad had moved to Scotland six months ago he had felt responsible for his gran. They had offered to take her to live with them but she chose instead to move into Sycamore Lodge because she didn't want to be a burden to anyone. She had been slowing down a lot, which she had put down to old age, but now he could see she had just been bored, as she had certainly perked up a lot since she'd met Dougie.

Chapter 25

The fragrance in the flower shop attracted Lucy like it would a bee; the seductive scent drew her in until she felt as though she had stepped into a glorious bouquet. The aromatic scent of roses hit first, followed by the fresh soapy scent of freesias and sweet-smelling gardenias. Guided by her nose she explored each of the displays in the shop and felt exhilarated by the time she got to the counter. Had she been a bee those flowers would have been beautifully pollinated. What looked like a huge colourful bouquet with legs came walking towards her. A little voice called out from amongst the floral display.

'I won't be a minute – sorry, love.' The bouquet was gently deposited in a large tub of water and the owner of the legs and the voice greeted Lucy. 'Hi, how can I help you?'

'Oh hi, I'm Lucy from the Signal Box Café. I've come to collect the wedding flowers and wondered if you got my invite to a little wedding fair I'm holding on Saturday?'

'Oh of course, Lucy, yes I did, thank you. I'm Flossie. It's lovely to meet you and I'd love to come.' She wiped her hands on her apron before extending one to Lucy. 'Weddings are my favourite occasions and talking of whichyour flowers are all ready.' She gestured to the displays on a long table.

'Oh they look amazing.'

'I'll just finish writing this card out .'

Lucy couldn't help but notice the writing on the pad that Flossie was copying from: *To my darling Violet, I love you. From your Douglas xx*

Lucy's heart skipped for joy. Although she wished her nana could still be here, she knew that she would want Grandad to find happiness again.

Whilst they spoke Lucy watched in amazement as Flossie prepared a beautiful bouquet out of some loose flowers that were left over from her other orders. She efficiently swathed them in pink tissue paper and cellophane and handed them to Lucy. The finishing touch was a business card, which she inserted on a long green stick so it was just visible amongst the flowers.

'This is for the Signal Box Café,' she said.

'Wow that was amazing, thank you; I do love artistic and creative people, which is one of the reasons I love my job so much.'

'It's easy when you know how,' she answered modestly.

They exchanged bundles of leaflets and Lucy invited Flossie to pop into the café anytime for a look around. 'Here, these are for your goody bags.' Flossie gave her an assortment of miniature silk rose pin brooches of varying shades, each with a tiny ribbon with the name 'Flossie's Flowers' printed on it.

'They're so pretty. Thank you.'

'Come on, I'll help you load the arrangements into your car.'

Back at the café Lucy placed her beautiful flowers on the kitchen windowsill in a vase and arranged the other flower arrangements tastefully around the room.

Today was Ray's big day. Abbie and the other staff were busy setting everything up. Large pink helium balloons in the shape of flamingos were dotted around the room and within an hour the place was buzzing with excited guests sipping champagne and wearing pink carnation buttonholes and the registrar had arrived. Lucy's heart had flipped when Dom turned up with some of his friends that she recognised from the pub. He nodded a hello to her and Abbie when he caught their eye. Bunting was arranged along the far wall, which spelt out, 'Will you marry me, Beau?'

Lucy received the text from Ray to say they were on their way over and she and Abbie shushed everybody. The room was silent apart from a couple of giggles here and there. They heard the whoosh of the door opening and the two handsome men stepped through it to the sound of 'Surprise!' being shouted by seventy people. Beau's hands flew to his face. Abbie and Lucy pressed pink roses, laced with sprigs of baby's breath with a tiny pink flamingo, into each of their buttonholes. Beau looked at Ray and then to the bunting. His eyes widened as he read the words and filled with tears as Ray got down one knee.

'Beau, I know I told you we were coming to someone else's wedding but as you have probably realised by now, all these gorgeous-looking people are here for you and me.' The crowd laughed. 'The thing is when we met all those years ago, we weren't allowed to get married so we did the next best thing. Today is the tenth anniversary of our civil ceremony and so I know I've always said we haven't got the time to get married, but when someone lands an amazing wedding venue on your doorstep you just have to make time. So, Beau, the love of my life and the other half of my rainbow, I would just like to say happy anniversary and will you marry me?' He opened a ring box, which contained two matching wedding rings studded with a large diamond in each one.

Beau pulled him to his feet and hugged him tight. 'Yes, of course I will, you soppy old bugger.' The guests cheered and Lucy and Abbie led them to a rainbow balloon arch under which stood the registrar waiting to officiate as they exchanged their vows.

After the ceremony both grooms made speeches and Beau mentioned how his life had been grey and cloudy before his Ray of sunshine came along and, together, they had chased away the rain and brought the colours of the rainbow to each other's lives. 'Soppy I know,' he said, 'but true!'

Ray was able to share the news that he had booked a honeymoon to Flamingo Beach in Aruba, which set Beau off crying again. They cut the flamingo cake and Abbie took photos of the occasion.

A live band played upstairs in the evening whilst guests danced. Beau spoke to Lucy and told her why they called the pub the Flamingo's Leg. It was because they were fed up of names like the King's Head, which is what it was called when they first took it over, or the King's Arms. They knew those names were traditional but wanted something different. 'Well it's certainly that.' She laughed. 'But what I want to know is, which leg are you talking about – the one he's standing on or the other one?'

Beau laughed too. 'That depends on what mood I'm in.'

'Excuse me,' said Lucy after hearing a glass smash from behind the bar. The barman had a nasty cut and had gone quite pale. Lucy treated it with the first aid box but thought he might need stitches. 'I'll run him over to A and E,' said Abbie. 'Will you be okay here?'

'I'll be fine thanks.' Lucy stepped behind the bar with ease and quickly worked her way through the queue that had formed. Colours from the disco lights swirled around the room in time to the music. The atmosphere was filled with excitement and positive energy and her heart burst with pride. This place had so much personality but could also adapt to the various wedding themes she hoped to have here. A song she loved came on and as she had no customers, she decided to join in the dancing from behind the bar. She glowed with happiness. As she spun around again, she realised she had a customer.

'Don't stop on my account.' Dom's grey eyes were looking right into hers.

She carried on dancing. 'I couldn't stop if I tried.' She laughed. 'When I worked at the hotel, we all used to dance whenever this song came on, no matter where we were.'

'I've noticed you dance a lot around the house.'

'Oh yes, Jackson and I love our crazy hour. We blast the music and dance non-stop. I'm sorry if that bothers you.'

'No, it doesn't bother me at all. I think Jackson's a lucky lad to have a fun mum like you. I'm just down that no one asks me to join in.' He pulled a sad face then laughed. 'I have the gramps waltzing around together, you and Jackson going crazy to ABBA, and who've I got to dance with?'

'There's always Baxter,' she suggested.

Dom mocked offence.

'No I'm serious, have you never seen him dance? He'd be the perfect height for you as well. Next time you see him, just say "dancies" and he'll jump up to you.' Her eyes sparkled with mirth and he grinned. It felt good talking to him on her turf. She could be more herself.

'Do you want another of those?' She nodded to his almost empty beer bottle.

He took the last swig and nodded. 'Yes please and whatever you're having.'

'Thank you, I'll have a glass of prosecco. Have you had a good time?'

'It's been great. I've got to hand it to you, this place is fantastic. You and your grandad should be proud of yourselves and yes I'm sorry I doubted yours and Abbie's talents.'

'Wow, Dom, are you okay? I mean a compliment from you is as rare and as valuable as a handshake from Paul Hollywood.' She opened the bottle and placed it in front of him. 'The Signal Box Café has become so important to us both now. Grandad has been quite lost since losing my nana. This place has revitalised him, along with your gran of course.' She laughed.

'What was she like? Your nana, I mean.'

'Oh, my nana was the loveliest person. She would take me round the market every Monday and we would buy hot sausage rolls and eat them from the paper as we walked round the stalls. Then we would throw coins into the fountain and make wishes.'

'What did you wish for?' Dom was listening intently.

'Oh, I can't remember now,' she lied. 'Anyway, then we would take Grandad's lunch to him in the signal box and he would let me help him with the barriers. They were such happy days for me. That's why I had to make this work.'

'Well, it looks like it's definitely working, and I think your nana would be very proud of you. Look I know I'm a miserable git sometimes. I mean that wedding photograph had the guys ripping the piss out of me and I'll never forgive either of you for that, but I wish you and Abbie every success, and if today is anything to go by then you've got no worries.' He raised his bottle to her. 'Just don't tell Abbie I said that as we don't want her head to get too big.'

Lucy was touched by his kind words but before she could digest them she became rushed off her feet as many of the guests rushed to the bar to beat last orders. She ploughed her way through them as fast as she could, but the queue was never-ending. Then she heard his voice.

'What can I get you?' Dom asked the next customer in line as he stood next to her behind the bar.

She smiled at him and nodded her thanks. His eyes met hers, he winked at her and stayed until the last customer was served. He even helped her clear up and they walked home together.

'I still feel guilty you know,' she said, as they walked past Railway Cottage.

'You know it wasn't your fault, don't you?'

'Yes, but even so, I still feel bad especially as you've kindly put us up.'

'I know, it's been terrible. I mean look at this.' He patted his belly. 'I think Gran's a feeder. She keeps filling me up with pies and other stodge. Oh sorry,' he said as his hand knocked into hers when he put it back down by his side.

'That's okay,' said Lucy, trying to ignore the tingles that his unexpected touch had left behind. 'She's a fabulous cook,' she agreed. 'I miss cooking, at home I mean.'

'Well the meals you bring home from the Signal Box are delicious but you're always welcome to cook at mine; in fact why don't we cook a meal for the gramps? You, me and Jackson.'

'That's a great idea.' Lucy bit her knuckle at the thought of spending time with him. 'Wait, where are you going?' she asked as he headed in the wrong direction. He took her arm and linked it though his.

'Just a little detour,' he said. A couple of minutes later they reached Market Square. The fountain looked magical with colour-changing lights shining up through it. The splashing was soothing on the soul. Dom rummaged in his pocket and pulled out a couple of pound coins. He gave one to Lucy. 'Try and remember this wish.'

'I'll try.'

'Okay after three: one, two, three, go.' They simultaneously flipped their coins into the fountain. Lucy's eyes were closed; Dom's open and looking at her. 'And no wishing for me to delete that memory, because that's not going to come true,' he teased.

'Oi you.' She giggled, slapping him playfully on the arm.

'Come on, I'll race you back,' he said. 'Ready, steady.' He ran off and then shouted, 'Go.' She squealed and chased after him.

Chapter 26

The Signal Box Café door whooshed open and Rosie entered full of smiles.

'Hi, Rosie.' Lucy looked at her watch. 'Oh goodness is that the time? I need to walk Baxter before I can go out.'

Jackson ran to Rosie and threw himself into her arms.

'Auntie Rosie, you're here. Mummy said I can go to bed later tonight because it's Saturday tomorrow so that means we can play for longer.'

'Well that is good news isn't it – c'mon then let's get you home.' They held hands to walk over to Dom's house. Lucy shouted a thank you and goodbye to the staff and followed them.

'Lucy, don't worry about Baxter as Jackson and I can walk him for you,' offered Rosie.

Jackson jumped up and down shouting, 'Yes, yes, yes, please, Mummy.'

'Are you sure?' she asked Rosie as she turned the key in the lock. 'That would be extremely helpful, thank you, and thanks for looking after him. Grandad and Violet have gone to the theatre.'

Rosie put her hand gently on Lucy's arm. 'I'm positive – it'll be fun. You don't have to do it all on your own you know, love.'

Lucy hadn't realised how tense her shoulders had been until they relaxed. It was nice to have some help and a night out to look forward to. She didn't trust people easily; once bitten, twice shy was her motto. But Rosie seemed like a lovely genuine person and Jackson had taken to her immediately. Maybe she could start learning to relax now and then. She had been so used to it being just the two of them and if it was up to her that's how she would keep it forever. But Jackson was older now and he needed other people in his life. This was his gentle way of letting her know.

As she got out of the shower, she could hear the kerfuffle of Rosie and Jackson putting Baxter's lead on and then the front door slamming. She enjoyed half an hour of peace as she got ready, just concentrating on herself, and she relished it. *So, this is what me time is,* she thought as she carefully applied her make-up, trying on and discarding outfits without having to worry about an eight-year-old boy pointing at her boobs and laughing. It was bliss.

Abbie knocked for her at the same time as Rosie and Jackson returned so there was a flurry of hellos and good-byes and the two friends walked round the corner to the station to get the train.

Lucy looked wistfully at Railway Cottage as they passed. She hoped they could soon move back in. Abbie looked up at the Signal Box Café in awe.

'It looks so beautiful. I love the fairy lights. You've done such an amazing job here, Lucy and I'm so proud of you.'

'Thanks, I'm quite proud of me too. Apart from Jackson it's my biggest achievement by far.'

Sitting opposite each other on the train, they exchanged knowing glances as they saw other passengers pointing to the striking building and nodding their approval as they discussed it with each other. It was certainly getting noticed and making a good impression.

In the wine bar Abbie told Lucy that Dom had called

her from work the other day, fuming about the picture being in the paper. He'd apparently accused them of making him a laughing stock. She had relayed their whole phone conversation to her.

'What sort of divorce lawyer prances about in a bloody wedding poster?' Abbie said in a deep voice mimicking her brother. 'I told him to stop making such a fuss as after all it'll just be tomorrow's chip paper.' She turned to Lucy. 'Oh sorry, no offence.'

Lucy's hands were covering her face. 'None taken – so what did he say to that?'

'Oh, you know he carried on ranting.' She adopted the comedy deep voice she used for him again. 'It had better be, you know, Abbie. Your friend has brought me nothing but trouble since she moved round here, and Gran's been kicked out of the lodge thanks to her bloody grandad. And you haven't helped trying to make me into a Prince Charming in her fairy-tale world.'

'Huh, Prince Charming! Really?' Lucy's face was burning. Her stomach twisted into knots and she took a huge swig of wine.

'Oh, don't worry,' replied Abbie. 'I put him in his place. I was like: "I don't think *charming* is a word that people would normally associate with you, Dominic, so you have nothing to worry about there." And then you won't believe what I said next!'

Lucy's eyes narrowed. 'Oh no, I dread to think. What did you say?'

'Well I had to put him in his place so I just said to him, "The thing is, Dom, I only meant for you to pretend to kiss the bride. It was you who swept her off her feet."'

'Oh no, you didn't say that?' she shrieked, the wine almost spilling.

174

'I did, and he was like spluttering. I think he nearly choked on his beer to be honest and then he asked me if you'd said something.' She refilled both of their glasses; Lucy was grateful as she had emptied the last one in two gulps. Abbie continued, 'So I said, "Why would Lucy say anything? She was being professional, just doing what had to be done. She has a lot at stake with the Signal Box Café – but, Dom, you can't fool me. I'm your sister and I know that that was no fake kiss." And he was like: "You're being totally ridiculous." And I was like: "Bye, lover boy."' Abbie laughed. 'He was practically growling at me.'

'Sounds like you put him in his place. I feel a bit bad though if he's upset about it, being in the paper I mean.' Lucy played with a cardboard beer coaster and tried to spin it on the table so she wouldn't have to look Abbie in the eye.

She laughed. 'Lucy, you don't have to worry about Dom. Over the years I've learnt to give my big brother as good as I got, and I enjoyed having something to tease him about for a change. I mean as if he'd ever stand a chance with you.' She laughed, tossed a handful of nuts in her mouth and crunched loudly.

Lucy managed a half smile and repeated, 'As if.'

Abbie stopped mid crunch and with her forefinger under Lucy's chin she tilted her face to meet hers. 'Hold on, you don't fancy him, do you? Do you?'

'No, I don't; in fact I can't stand him most of the time but oh I don't know, he is quite good-looking I suppose, and he really helped me out at Ray's wedding.' Her cheeks were blazing.

'You know what it is, it must be wine goggles because I've just remembered you said he looked like a model when you first saw him, and you were drunk then.' Abbie turned her hands into circles and put them round her eyes.

'Yes, you're right – that's exactly it. Next time I see him I'll be sure to take them off and he'll be as ugly as Ugly Macugly face.' They cracked up laughing.

Abbie squeezed her hand. 'Oh, Lucy, what have I done? Why did I get him to kiss you? Dom has already caused me to lose two of my friends in the past by dating them. Women think they can change his mind about relationships, but he's embittered; his ex-wife broke him. He's like a curse on my friendships, as they then feel too uncomfortable being with me because of the connection to him. I can't lose you though – you're my best friend.'

'And you're mine too and very precious to me. You have no worries about all of that; besides he hates me and most of my family.'

'No, he doesn't hate you at all. I mean would he have let you move in if he hated you. But I will agree he is a pain in the arse to be avoided at all costs.'

'I don't think he had much choice as your gran put her foot down. However, I'll drink to him being an arsehole and the being avoided bit.' Lucy clinked her glass against Abbie's.

Chapter 27

Daylight came too soon for Lucy the next morning. Her head was throbbing and her throat was painfully dry. This was why she never went out drinking. She ran her tongue along her teeth, which felt like sandpaper. She got up, brushed them and headed downstairs. Jackson chatted to Baxter as he poured his food in his bowl. He was such a good boy and no trouble really. By the time she entered the kitchen Jackson had poured himself a bowl of cereal and was curled up on the couch watching telly and laughing at the cartoons.

She put the kettle on and gazed around the room blearily: spilt milk and cereal on the countertop, water sloshed over the floor around the dog's bowl. Her bare foot crunched on something. She dreaded to think what it was. She lifted her foot and tentatively looked underneath it. It was okay – just some more cereal. Before she could get the dustpan and brush out Baxter had made light work of it. He eagerly sniffed around the tiled floor looking for more unexpected treats.

She poured herself a strong coffee and quickly cleaned up. She didn't want Dom to have anything to complain about. Thankfully, he hadn't surfaced yet whereas she had a busy day ahead and needed to wake up fast. While the coffee was cooling, she ran upstairs to get showered and dressed.

Lucy managed to make herself look decent in double quick time. She thanked Grandad for looking after Jackson for the day and told her son to be a good boy, but neither of them took much notice as they were so engrossed in a train set they'd brought round from home.

She opened up the café where Abbie was standing waiting for her. She was carrying large wedding portraits she'd had printed and framed, which would be displayed upstairs. As she unveiled them Lucy squirmed on seeing the one of her and Dom kissing.

'I know what you're thinking but I'd only ever done one other wedding at the time, so I needed this one blown up for advertising. It's so beautiful though, Lucy, just look at it.' She waved her hands across it glamorously like a magician's assistant and kissed her friend on her flaming hot cheek.

Lucy had to agree as a professional wedding photograph it was hard to beat; if she could just try and forget that it was her in the picture it might be okay. When Abbie went downstairs to get some more bits, Lucy looked closer at the picture; their faces fit each other so well. She ran her finger along his thumb, which had stroked her cheek so gently and with her other hand she touched her actual cheek. Shivers ran through her body as she tried to re-create that feeling. She knew it would never happen again as he was pissed off about the picture in the newspaper.

The sound of the café door whooshing open snapped Lucy back to the present. She could hear Abbie talking to Camilla and Flossie. They came upstairs. Camilla had a banner stand and a box of cupcakes, which she arranged decoratively on a cake stand. Flossie arranged her exotic and traditional blooms on her table.

'This place smells amazing,' said Lucy as the scent of vanilla mingled with roses and freesias filled the air. Abbie had arranged their Wedding Belles banner stand and her large portraits with some smaller images of the Signal Box Café, which showed it off to its best. Lucy brought up some ice buckets with prosecco in them and she placed them next to a tray of glasses she had fetched from the small upstairs bar area. She cast a quick glance around the room and with a satisfied smile she was ready.

Couples were booked in every hour for a forty-five-minute consultation and a fifteen-minute break in between.

The first couple were desperate to book as soon as they pressed the button and realised it was a real working train door. They had twin sons aged six years old who were train mad and they thought the venue would be perfect.

Two couples were slightly older and were onto second marriages, one of them a train driver, which made the choice of venue very poignant. Two young women had been searching everywhere for an unusual venue and agreed it was a magnificent quirky venue for them. Three other couples were young, just starting out on their lives together and wanted somewhere tasteful and unusual that wouldn't break the bank. The Signal Box Café fitted the bill perfectly.

The final couple were a little bit different. An eighty-nine-year-old man with a walking stick was accompanied by an extremely top heavy forty-two-year-old who was wearing more animal print than the whole of London Zoo put together. She had bright red jammy lipstick on, blue eyeshadow and a bleached blond beehive. Her arm was linked through his. Her pointy red talons clicked together as she walked, which made Lucy feel quite queasy.

'Oh, Albert, this place is fabulous, I love it.' She had a glass of prosecco in one hand and a vape and a cupcake in the other, all of which were in competition to be inserted into her mouth.

'Well I meant what I said, anything for you, my Little Miss Fun Bags. Let's do it,' he said.

The girls had remained professional but couldn't help laughing after they'd gone. Albert it seems was a very rich man and whilst his teeth may not have been his own, the mansion and fleet of vintage cars most certainly were. They had loved the place and booked on the spot.

'I can't wait to do their invitations for them.' Abbie chuckled. 'Dear So and So, Albert and Little Miss Fun Bags request the pleasure of your company at their wedding in the Signal Box Café.'

Camilla laughed too. 'What a hoot they were.'

'I had a phone call the other day from a woman asking if she could marry the Signal Box Café,' said Lucy. 'I said, "I'm sorry do you mean you'd like to get married *in* the Signal Box Café?" And she said, "No I actually want to marry it as I've been in love with it for years."'

Abbie giggled. 'What did you say?'

'I told her no, she bloody couldn't because he's mine,' said Lucy smiling. 'This job has certainly been enlightening. There's actually a condition where people want to marry inanimate objects. That's definitely one of the strangest requests I've ever had. But the good news is that our bookings are going through the roof.'

The girls sat down in one of the window booths and relaxed with a prosecco and one of Camilla's strawberry dream cupcakes each. It had been a busy but productive day. Camilla, Flossie and Abbie had given out their business cards too and everyone had been impressed with their services. Their diaries were already being boosted from the people who had attended the launch; it was proving to be a good symbiotic relationship.

Chapter 28

As a wedding planner Lucy sometimes received offers of complimentary treatments and samples from businesses hoping for recommendations. After spending three hours of pure torture in a salon called Beauty and Denise, she decided they wouldn't be going in her folder. She came out of there looking like a drag queen stuck in a wind tunnel.

She was running late now and would have to go straight to the Indian restaurant after picking Jackson up. Looking at her reflection in the rear-view mirror as Jackson told her about his day, she wondered why she couldn't have been one of those organised mums who always had a packet of tissues and a packet of wet wipes in their bag.

'Josh's mum just booked his party at the Signal Box Café,' she told Jackson, looking at him in the rear-view mirror. She saw his face cloud. 'Do you like him?'

'Not really, he's a bit mean sometimes.'

Lucy's jaw tensed. 'Why what does he do?'

'I don't want to say.' He was looking out of the car window watching houses and trees go by.

'I need to know, Jackson, if he's being mean to you; then we can maybe sort it out.'

'Well he said that I haven't got a daddy and he thinks that's funny.'

Lucy's stomach churned. Her poor boy, he looked so tearful; her heart was being ripped out of her chest. She drove into the car park of the restaurant and went to the back door to help him out. She pulled him into a tight hug and then held him at arm's length, her hands on his shoulders, her thumbs stroking his face.

'Jackson, I know we don't talk about this but that is my fault and I realise that you are growing up now so one day I promise that I will tell you everything, but I'm not ready to do that just yet. However, one thing I will tell you is that you do have a daddy, so Josh is talking rubbish. Give me some time to get my head around it, sweetheart, and I promise you we will have that chat.'

Jackson smiled his wonderful crooked smile and melted her heart again, so much so that she forgot about her debacle with Beauty and Denise.

They entered the restaurant. Lucy sent Jackson over to the table, and she half hid behind the door to the ladies. 'Ask Abbie to come to the toilet please, Jackson?' she whispered. She could see her sitting next to Dave all loved up. Jackson was too caught up in the excitement of being fussed over that she could tell he'd forgotten.

'Psst.' She tried to catch Abbie's attention, but she wasn't looking. She tried louder. 'Psst.' Abbie looked round but not in her direction. She tried once more and finally caught Abbie's eye. She frantically waved her over, and watched as she disentangled herself from Dave.

'What are you doing?' Dom appeared behind her. She jumped and banged her head on the door. She half wished it had knocked her unconscious, so she didn't have to deal with this situation. She contemplated a fake faint. 'I didn't know it was fancy dress. Who've you come as? Ru Paul?'

'Haha very funny.' She laughed. He smirked and walked over to the table. She could hear Jackson shouting his name excitedly, wanting to sit by him.

'Lucy, what's happened?' Her friend pulled her into the ladies.

'Beauty and Denise, that's what.'

'I don't understand, did you ask for a tiger face paint?' Abbie looked at her in the mirror.

'How dare you, this is contouring from the Stardust bridal package, I'll have you know.' Their eyes met in their mirrored reflections and they howled with laughter for at least five minutes. Each time one stopped, the other started.

Lucy was holding on to her side. 'Oh no I've got a stitch now from laughing so much. You should have seen the state of it, Abbie, it was hellish. I'm telling you; the pink zebra has gone into extinction thanks to the number of pelts they've covered that place in. Everything, even the towels – and she was clacking away chewing the gum. She broke a brush doing my hair and look at it, it's like Patsy from *Ab Fab* and Donald Trump had a baby. Oh, thank God for that,' she said as Abbie produced a pack of facial wipes from her bag.

'I never go anywhere without them.' She was still giggling. 'Now let's get scrubbing.'

They had managed to untangle most of the beehive and scraped it back into a stiff ponytail. The heavy black eye make-up would be impossible to get off here, as it would make a terrible mess.

'There you go,' said Abbie, as she patted her skin dry with a paper towel. 'Still looks slightly prostitutey but a marked improvement.'

'Thanks, friend.' Lucy smiled, relieved that at least her skin could breathe again.

Everyone at the table fell silent as they took in the new-look Lucy. Dom had been about to eat a poppadum, but it hovered in mid-air as his mouth gaped. Lucy sat opposite Dom and next to Grandad who kissed her on the cheek.

'Well I don't know about you, but I need a drink after the day I've had. Can I have a gin and tonic please?' she asked the waiter who was looking at her hungrily like she was a one-off bargain at the supermarket.

'What did you use to brush your hair, a toilet brush?' asked Dom rudely but with his tongue in his cheek and a twinkle in his eye.

'Don't be rude, Dom,' said Violet. 'This hairstyle is how the young ones are wearing it now isn't it, Lucy. I saw it on one of those vlog things when I was in the hairdresser's.'

Lucy had to laugh. 'Ah, Violet, that's very kind of you to say, but no, this is the result of me visiting the worst beauticians I've ever seen in my life. They wanted me to recommend them to do bridal make-up.'

'Maybe for bride of Frankenstein,' mumbled Dom unable to keep his face straight. Abbie nudged him in the ribs.

'Oi that's my beautiful friend you're talking about there.'

'Abbie, don't worry, he's right. He saw me before. I can laugh at it now but I didn't even have a tissue to wipe it off and then I had to rush to the school and then because half the playground wanted to speak to me I was running late.'

Lucy talked to Grandad and noticed that Jackson and Dom were chatting away about football.

'Remember when you flicked the man in the eye,' Jackson said giggling.

Grandad looked at him with interest. 'What's that?' he asked.

'Grandad, it was so funny. I was playing Subbuteo with Dom and then he flicked the man and it landed in Mummy's boyfriend's eye.' Dom and Jackson laughed again at the memory of it.

'It wasn't exactly funny, and someone was hurt,' said Lucy. 'Anyway he's not my boyfriend,' she added, flushing a little.

'He said he was, when you went to get the ice he said, "Isn't she a good girlfriend?" Didn't he, Dom?'

Dom nodded as his mouth was full of curry and rice.

'Well he isn't, he's just a friend and he should never have said that.'

Dom raised an eyebrow at that comment and made eye contact with Lucy. A flash of electricity rocketed through her body and she had to look away, aware of his eyes searching for hers. She regretted the kiss with Greg; it was childish of her.

Grandad raised a toast to celebrate the coming together of their two families and Lucy experienced that warm sense of belonging as she observed the way they interacted with each other. Grandad was chatting to Abbie; Violet and Lucy were discussing Jackson; and Dom and Jackson were laughing and playing card tricks with Dave. Sharing naan breads and passing the dishes around to each other was very intimate; Jackson had never been to an Indian restaurant before and loved trying all the new exotic flavours.

She was so happy for her grandad. Sometimes he had quiet moments when she knew he was thinking about her nana and fighting the inner turmoil he had about remarrying. But she had made him promise that he would find happiness again after she'd gone. It had been a long ten years without her; and it would be nice for him to have some company for whatever years he had left.

They had set the date for the wedding in one month's time at the Signal Box Café. It was such a romantic setting and could potentially be the Gretna Green of the South East albeit with a different theme. The two families chattered eagerly about the ceremony. Dom would be giving Violet away, Grandad's friend Jeffrey from Sycamore Lodge would be his best man and Jackson would be pageboy.

Lucy and Abbie were delighted to be bridesmaids and Dave was photographer and videographer. It was only going to be a small wedding, but Lucy knew it would be beautiful.

Dom didn't say much about the subject. He was too busy playing I spy with Jackson and they were giggling like naughty schoolboys because Jackson had used the word 'wig' for the letter 'w' and Dominic guessed it when looking at the other customers and accidentally said it too loud, causing the man wearing a toupee to look at them distastefully.

Dave had to go as he had work to do, so Abbie asked Lucy if they could stay out and have a few drinks and a catch-up. Lucy was on her second gin and tonic already and they'd had a celebratory bottle of bubbly that Grandad had bought; she was feeling mellow and thought it was a great idea.

'Yes,' said Grandad, 'I'll take your car back and we'll look after this one.' He put his arm around Jackson.

'Dom, can I play Xbox with you pleeeeease?' he begged.

'Jacks, I told you that Dom is too busy, so you mustn't ask him about the Xbox,' said Lucy.

Dom held his hand out to Jackson for a handshake. 'You can play as long as you don't mind losing,' he said laughing.

Jackson giggled and went to shake his hand in return, but Dom raised his hand quickly, put his thumb on his nose and wiggled his fingers at him, sticking his tongue out at the same time.

'You've got to be quicker than that,' said Dom. They laughed and left the restaurant chatting together with not even a backwards glance at Lucy.

Lucy and Abbie finished their drinks and wandered along to the Grape Escape. Lucy figured, as it was dark in there, she might not look too scary or cheap. On the way out they saw Greg waiting for a takeaway.

'Hi,' he said, kissing both of them on the cheek. 'Lucy, you promised me another date, don't forget.' He touched an invisible scar on his cheek just by his eye, in order to tap into her guilt-ometer again.

'Well you have got babysitters on tap now,' Abbie said, thinking out loud.

'Yes, thanks, Abbie. I don't think I promised anything, Greg. Everything's a bit up in the air at the moment.'

'Please give me one more chance, Lucy. I really like you. Shall we say the day after tomorrow?'

Abbie gave her a nudge. 'Come on, Lucy, I need a drink – just say yes.'

Greg looked at her pleadingly.

'Oh, all right then, yes, but just as friends,' she added.

'You won't regret it.'

As they stepped outside and headed for the wine bar Lucy turned to Abbie. 'Why did you do that? I don't actually want to go out with him.'

'Because, my lovely, you are turning into a nun. You need to start dating, Lucy. Let someone spoil you and treat you nice. It doesn't matter if he's not the one you've been waiting for your whole life. He's not bad-looking, he's got a good job, he's single and you've already snogged him. Men like that don't grow on trees you know. He might not be Mr Perfect but he's Mr Not Bad and that'll do for now. Just practise dating with him. I know it's been a long time for you.'

Lucy thought maybe she was right and wondered what harm it could do to go out as friends.

They were soon sitting in the dimmed lighting of the wine bar sipping cocktails and giggling. Abbie took a selfie of them to prove to Lucy that she didn't look like a slapper. The pink and blue neon lights worked wonders on hiding the scary mask she was wearing.

'So, what I want to know is who is the best kisser: Greg or my brother?' Abbie teased as she slurped the brightly coloured remains of her cocktail through her straw before waving the empty glass in the barman's direction.

Lucy was struck by a jolt deep within her at the mention of Abbie's brother and the word kiss in the same sentence. She almost choked on her drink but recovered quickly.

'Don't be silly, Abbie, we hardly kissed.' She brushed imaginary fluff off her leg.

'Hardly kissed? What do you mean you hardly kissed? You were at it for ages. Maybe time goes at a different pace in your world, Lucy, but I thought I was going to have to shout "cut".'

'Are you serious?' She giggled. 'It went really quickly for me. I'm sure his lips hardly even touched mine.' She laughed nervously. Now the flashbacks were coming back: Dom stroking her cheek, causing flutterings to tickle her from within. Then she tried to think of the other kiss with Greg but all she could remember was what her eyes were seeing at the time and not what her lips were feeling. She could see Dom walking along the platform, the way his eyes flashed with anger or maybe jealousy – she didn't quite know what – before he continued to walk away.

She needed to get a grip. This was Dominic Cavendish, hotshot divorce lawyer who thought she was a silly girl with her head stuck in a heart-shaped cloud of flowers and happy ever afters.

'Don't forget, Abbie, one of those kisses was fake and one was real.'

Abbie nodded in drunken agreement. 'That's true.'

Lucy thought better of clarifying which one was which.

Chapter 29

Dom held Jackson's hand carefully with the knife as he showed him how to chop the peppers whilst Lucy sliced up the ingredients for her speciality: Mexican chicken. Mariachi band music was blasting out of the speakers and Dom had stuck lime wedges in bottles of beer for him and Lucy and in a bottle of coke for Jackson. He was in charge of making the chilli con carne, which was half of his cooking repertoire, the other half being bolognaise.

'Wait something is missing.' He stopped stirring his chilli and marched out of the room.

'What is it?' shouted Jackson as he followed him up the stairs like a little puppy.

Five minutes later Lucy heard giggling outside the kitchen door and in they came sporting sombreros, brightly coloured ponchos and thick black moustaches.

'Here's one for you, Mum,' said Jackson. She bent down so he could put the poncho over her head and stick the moustache on. He was giggling so much that she was worried he was going to wet himself. She stood up and Dom plonked the sombrero on her head. She couldn't see his mouth as the moustache was so thick but she could see from his eyes that he was smiling and as he gazed into hers she felt sensations inside her the likes of which she'd never experienced before. She could feel the heat rising and she hadn't even tried the chilli yet.

Jackson had run into the living room and given Dougie and Violet their outfits and they joined the youngsters in dancing around to the fast-paced music. The food cooked and the smell of the delicious spices infused the room, which rang with the sound of fun. Lucy shrieked with laughter as Dom tried his best to dance with Baxter, holding on to his paws whilst he growled at his moustache. After the meal they played board games and the laughter continued as they had to act out funny words and sayings. They were just like a real family, thought Lucy.

Later when she was going through Jackson's school bag she found a letter from his teacher, which said that Jackson had volunteered his dad to come in and talk about his job and that the children were all excited that he was an astronaut; the teachers were pretty excited too.

Lucy's heart plunged into her stomach. She gathered her thoughts and hastily wrote a note to say that it wouldn't be possible due to him working away so often and that she and his father weren't together.

Poor Jackson – her heart wept for him. He had recently been asking questions about his dad, but she simply couldn't talk to him about it. She'd never told anyone who he was. She and Jackson were a team and they didn't need anybody else but she couldn't deny that it was lovely to be part of this bigger family now.

Chapter 30

Jackson was in his element as Grandad and Violet were spoiling him rotten. They had insisted on picking him up from school and taking him for his tea to Flowerpots. As well as being the local garden centre there was also a little section of animals they could visit, including a variety of birds in cages and sheep, pigs, rabbits and goats. His favourites were the marmoset monkeys as they put their tiny hands through the cage to take nuts from his hand, which made him giggle in delight. There was also a little steam train that people could ride on, which was very popular. They spent a lovely few hours there and when they returned, Grandad insisted that Lucy go out with her young man, as he called him.

'We're here now for you, Lucy. You don't have to do it all alone anymore.'

Lucy sensed that relaxed feeling again, the one where her shoulders dropped, and her teeth didn't quite clench together so much.

Alone at last, she decided to have a lovely soothing 'love potion' bath. This time she would stand guard over it though; she would never ever make that mistake again. Thankfully Grandad's repairs were getting done and they would be able to move back soon. She was looking forward to that but had to admit it had been quite pleasant staying here, apart from the initial awkwardness.

Later on, Greg had pulled up outside the house and was beeping his horn to let Lucy know he'd arrived. She cringed at the sound. Her shoulders gradually made their way up to her ears again. Surely a gentleman would have knocked for her. She came down the path just as Dom was walking up it. He looked into the car and then huffed when he saw who it was.

'You off out with your "friend",' he said sarcastically, using his fingers to emphasise the quotation marks. His grey eyes were narrowed and mean, looking nothing like the ones that had made her melt the night before.

'Yes, but Grandad's looking after Jackson and Baxter. Is that okay with you?' she snapped immediately on the defensive. Why did he have to be so horrible sometimes? She felt that she would just start to get to like him a bit more and then he would be arsey and she would completely go off him.

She wasn't even looking forward to this stupid night out anyway. She couldn't be bothered with any of it.

She opened the car door and climbed into the passenger seat. Greg looked her up and down appreciatively and leaned over to kiss her; she expected him to aim for her cheek and was a little taken aback when he went straight for the lips. She instinctively looked towards the house to see whether Dom had seen and was disappointed to see the back of him walking away from the living room window, probably in disgust. The thought of him seeing her and Greg the last time now made her feel pretty foolish.

He started the car and drove out to a small restaurant in the countryside called 'The Charming Man'. It was hundreds of years old and formerly the gatehouse for a mansion called Belvedere Manor, which nestled a couple of miles away down a long and winding driveway. With its thatched roof and original beams, the restaurant was filled with character.

It was the sort of place that would have been perfect for a romantic meal with someone you loved, but Lucy did not feel that way about Greg at all. During the lulls in their conversation her mind drifted to thoughts of someone she would much rather be with. She explained to him that she felt they could only ever be friends. She even insisted on paying half towards the meal but that didn't stop her having to wrestle with an octopus when they got back into the car and smack his hand off her knee on the journey home. He refused to get the message and referred more than once to their next date and the fact that they had rooms in The Charming Man so maybe they could arrange to stay for the night.

Relieved to pull up outside Dom's house, she jumped out of the car before Greg lunged at her again. She turned up the path to see Jackson coming out of the house with Dom holding Baxter's lead.

'We're taking Baxter out for a late-night walk, Mummy.'

'Oh, are you now?'

'Dougie said it was okay as Jackson has a day off tomorrow and he was so excited about walking him at night. Is that all right with you?' Dom asked, unsmiling.

'Yes, it is, isn't it, Mummy?'

'Yes, okay then, but be good!' She smiled as the two buddies walked off into the night with Baxter.

Grandad was still up when she got in. He looked tired but happy.

'How's my girl?' he said, giving her a welcome-back hug.

'I'm good thanks, Grandad. How are you?'

'All the better for seeing you but why the furrowed brow and faraway expression?.' His eyes filled with concern,. 'Come on, let's have a cuppa.'

Lucy followed him into the kitchen where he put the kettle on to make a drink.

'How was your date?' He reached up to the cupboard to get the cups out.

'It wasn't really a date. We're just friends,' she answered, clicking a couple of sweeteners into her coffee and reaching into the drawer for a teaspoon. 'And to be honest I'm not sure I even want to be friends with him.'

Grandad looked at her closely; she was looking down stirring her drink but she seemed sad.

'You are allowed to date you know, love. No one is expecting you to stay single forever.'

'I know, Grandad, but it would be hard to bring a man into mine and Jackson's relationship now. This guy is definitely not for me anyway. And I'm quite happy with things as they are; I haven't got time in my life for a man.' She snapped out of her reverie and jollied up her tone. 'Anyway enough about me; did you have a good time at the garden centre? What did you get up to?'

She smiled as he told her about taking Jackson to feed the animals and what he'd had for dinner. He laughed as he added, 'And then he came home and had another dinner because Violet had made some chicken pie and he devoured it.'

'Sounds delicious – and he could eat for England that boy.' She looked at her watch. 'It's getting late. I wonder when they'll be back. Dom must be getting fed up with us. Jackson hasn't wanted to leave his side since we moved in here.'

'I think they've only gone to Market Square to the fountain. You should have seen Dom with Jackson, love; he was brilliant with him. They've been playing Xbox for ages and the shrieks and giggles from them made Violet and I laugh so much.'

Lucy flushed remembering Dom taking her to the fountain, then felt a bit left out, which she knew was a stupid way to feel.She wondered whether she'd have had a better night if she'd stayed here with them. But then Jackson was now learning to be who he was without having his mummy there all the time and he was making other relationships, which could only be a good thing. His support network was growing. She chatted with Grandad for a bit then waited up for Jackson and Dom to get back so she could read him his bedtime story.

'I want Dom to read me a story,' he said as he was still holding his hand when they came in.

'No, Jackson, you can't take up any more of Dom's time – he's a busy man.'

Dom mouthed to her that it was fine by him if it was all right with her, so she reluctantly nodded and as soon as Jackson had kicked off his shoes he bounded up the stairs two at a time with Dom behind him.

Lucy popped into the kitchen to wash up the couple of cups in the sink. Jackson was so at home here he didn't seem to need her anymore; she sighed heavily and despite having eaten a huge meal she felt hollow and empty as she trudged up the stairs to bed.

Chapter 31

Dominic Cavendish couldn't wait to get home. He'd bought a new Xbox game that was more age-appropriate for Jackson. He hadn't expected a kid to be such good fun but they shared a love of the same football team and it seems the same wicked sense of humour. Jackson managed to make Dom belly-laugh at least once a day either by telling silly jokes or just by the way he questioned everything in his own little eight-year-old way. He allowed Dom to see the world through his eyes, which was quite refreshing for him.

They'd been staying with him for a little while now and he had really got used to them being around. The house was beginning to feel more like a home – lots of noise and laughter and delicious cooking smells. Dom was even enjoying the untidiness of being in a lived-in home instead of a show home. He was relaxed around all of his guests except for Lucy and he couldn't quite figure out why not with her. He found her stunningly attractive, but he didn't think that was it.

Deep down he knew what it was, but he didn't want to admit it. He had developed strong feelings for her but instead of letting her know he picked on her. It was just like when they were kids; he didn't quite know how to behave when she was around. He was safer with Jackson, that cute little funny kid. They had become mates now and even that nutty dog was growing on him. Violet had discovered Dom the other day rolling around wrestling with Baxter on his precious living room carpet.

As Dom had walked up to his house, he hadn't realised who the car parked outside belonged to. His defences rose when he saw Lucy coming down the path and heading straight for it. That's when he snapped at her. What did she see in this guy?

He looked forward to getting in and playing the game so he called for Jackson but there was no answer. There was something odd about the house. There was nobody here.

It felt so empty, even though that's what it had always been like before. He hadn't realised how hollow his life was. He went from room to empty room and made himself a coffee. Then he heard a snuffling noise behind the utility room door and his heart did a little leap for joy. Baxter was still here. He grabbed his lead and a couple of his toys and took him to the green outside his house where he played fetch with him for a good half an hour.

On opening the fridge he found a chicken and vegetable pie that his gran had made for him along with instructions on heating it and what to serve with it, she'd even prepared vegetables, mash and her amazing home-made gravy. It was his favourite meal; she'd regularly made it for him when he was younger.

He looked at the dining table, which had been more of an ornament until the family had moved in, as more often than not, he would eat his dinner on a tray in front of the telly. He set a place for himself and put the food in the oven. There was still some left so he thought maybe Jackson would like to try it when he got back as he was always hungry. He plugged his phone into the speaker and turned his music on. The house was unbearably empty and quiet; he'd never noticed that before.

He could hear Jackson coming up the path before he saw him; he was skipping along holding Dougie and Gran's hands and chatting non-stop.

As soon as he entered the house he kicked off his shoes, shrugged his coat to the floor and burst into the living room to see Dom. Dom was sitting in the armchair pretending to be asleep, even though he was almost as excited as Jackson was.

'Dom,' he whispered, 'are you awake?' He crept as close as possible and gently lifted one of Dom's eyelids, then shrieked as Dom jumped up and tickled him, growling and doing a dinosaur impression. Jackson was giggling hysterically and told him about the animals he'd seen on his trip to the garden centre.

He pushed his glasses up his nose and sniffed the air. 'Something smells lovely in here, Dom. What did you have for your dinner?'

Dom rubbed his tummy to emphasise how full he was. 'Oh, it was delicious. I had my gran's very special chicken pie and it was yummy.'

'I'm sooo hungry. Violet, are you my gran too?'

Violet's hand rushed to her heart. Delighted, she hugged and kissed him on the spot. 'Well yes I will be, officially when we get married, but you can call me Gran now if you want to.'

'Gran, one day will you make me some chicken pie please?'

She answered him with a squeeze.

Dom heard the conversation and smiled at his gran.

'Does this mean I have to call Dougie Grandad?' he joked, making Jackson laugh.

Dougie walked in with a tray of coffees and set it down on the coffee table.

Dom went to the kitchen and got Jackson to follow him. His face lit up when Dom plated up the leftover dinner for him and heated it in the microwave.

'Now as soon as you've finished this—' he pointed to the dinner '—we can play this.' He held up the Xbox game as though it were a magic chalice.

Jackson's eyes opened wide. All the kids in school played this one and he could never join in the conversations because he didn't have a clue what it was about.

He gulped the meal down as fast as he could and Dom realised he shouldn't have mentioned the game until he'd finished eating. He had a lot to learn about kids.

'Right we can't play for too long as you need to get to bed soon.'

'No, it's okay; it's an inset day tomorrow so we don't have to go in.'

'Great, come on then, let's go.' They went to the conservatory and spent the next couple of hours shouting and laughing as they played the game.

Dougie and Vi were cuddled up on the sofa and smiled at each other.

It was when they were on their late-night dog walk that Jackson had confided his problem to Dom.

Chapter 32

The letter had totally taken Lucy by surprise; Grandad had picked the post up from Railway Cottage and brought it back to Dom's house.

'Dear Miss Woods, You have been nominated by Miss Abbie Cavendish as having the most unusual wedding venue and we are delighted to be able to tell you that the Signal Box Café has been shortlisted and is now in the final three of our competition,' she read out loud to Grandad and Dom, as they drank their morning coffee. 'The other two finalists are a converted cow shed in Shropshire and a cave in Cumbria.'

Grandad cheered. 'Well done.'

'That's fantastic,' said Dom. 'Good luck.'

She placed the letter on the table in disbelief. 'I'd forgotten all about the competition – I've been so busy with everything else.'

Grandad picked it up and continued reading it. 'So, they want to come and pay a visit next week. That's so exciting, Lucy. We'll have to make sure it's all spic and span.'

'Are you not going into work today?' he asked Dom.

'No.' He finished the last of his coffee and rinsed out the cup. 'I'm working from home today. Got a few meetings locally and then I'll be locked in my office. Oh, that's if it's okay with you, Lu?'

She looked at him, her heart in her mouth; he'd just called her Lu, which seemed so affectionate. He was looking at her waiting for her answer. She temporarily couldn't speak.

'Lucy's going out with your gran and sister looking for wedding dresses.'

'Yes, I am. Sorry, Dom, I'm still a bit dazed about making it to the finals but I will be out all day.'

Jackson came thundering down the stairs and Lucy handed him his lunchbox. He waved goodbye to his grandad and Dom. Dom winked at him and Jackson tried to wink back but either kept both eyes open or closed. He would keep practising.

He and Lucy walked up the lane to the school. The sky was blue but for a few tufts of candyfloss clouds. Wild flowers lined the pathway and trees formed a leafy green archway overhead. Either side of the pathway were farmer's fields. Horses grazed lazily in them. Sometimes the horses would come right up to the fence and they would feed them apples or Polo Mints. Jackson loved to stroke their long noses and would giggle when they snorted at him.

The noise of children chatting, laughing and screeching got louder as they neared the school. They were allowed to play in the playground until the whistle blew when they had to stand like statues and be called in class by class. Lucy stood by the gate and waved to Jackson as he headed for the playground.

'Bye, Mum.' He waved.

He seemed a little happier about school now; although he still didn't like talking about the other kids, so she didn't push him. She saw Josh run up after him and speak to him so hopefully they were talking now.

As she turned to go, she saw Jane head over to her. The party was tomorrow, and Lucy was dreading it.

'Hi,' said Jane. 'All set for tomorrow?'

'Yes, all good, I'll see you there.' Lucy turned to go.

'Josh said that it's Jackson's turn for bring your dad to school day today. He's very excited about it.'

Lucy's heart lurched; her body was reeling, the ground disappearing from her feet, but she tried not to show it.

'Oh no there must be a mistake. I did write to the teacher and let her know.'

'Oh, that's a shame; Josh was so looking forward to that. I mean it's not every day you get to meet an astronaut is it. Well I suppose it is for you and Jackson.' She laughed. 'Anyway, must dash. I'll see you later. Bye.'

Lucy was about to explain that she wasn't with Jackson's dad, but she was too stunned to speak, and Jane had already gone. She could feel her pulse throbbing in her neck, and it was making her dizzy. She made a mental note to phone the teacher when she got back.

When she arrived at Dom's she opened the door to hear Abbie and Violet talking excitedly.

'Here she is,' said Abbie giving her a warm hug. 'We're ready.'

Violet hugged Dougie goodbye.

'Have a lovely day, ladies.'

'You too,' said Violet. 'And don't forget to pick Jackson up at four.'

'I won't.'

Lucy did not feel in the mood for this now, which was such a shame as they'd all been looking forward to it for so long. She unlocked the car to let Violet and Abbie in.

'I won't be a minute,' she said as she went back up to her room and rang the school. Her anxiety levels were rising when there was no answer but eventually an answering machine clicked on declaring that there was nobody to take the call right now. She left a message for Miss Rooney telling her that she was sorry, but Jackson's dad was unable to attend the school today and that she would call again later to explain in more detail.. At least that should hopefully get Jackson off the hook. She then tried her best to push the situation out of her mind.

She joined her two companions for the day in her little red Mini and off they set. As they drove along the far end of the high street, they noticed Dom outside the theatre waving goodbye to another man and he was carrying the biggest garment carrier they had ever seen. It looked quite heavy too; Dom lugged it into the back of his car. He hadn't noticed them go past.

Boutique Brides was a very elegant yet understated little shop. Originally a rose-covered cottage the downstairs of which had been transformed into every bride's dream. Lucy was hoping to add the boutique to her wedding folder if they liked it there.

Each room had racks and racks of beautiful dresses: traditional brides in one, bridesmaids in another, and another room was dedicated to mother of the bride outfits and to more mature brides. Large cheval mirrors with ornate silver frames and comfortable dark grey velvet chaises longue sat elegantly in each room. Sunlight flooded in through ivory voile curtains.

A lady called Greta welcomed them in and sat them down in the mature brides' room.

'Would you like a glass of champagne?'

'Ooh yes please,' they chorused.

Greta was very professional but at the same time approachable and friendly. She began an informal chat in order to find out a little more about Violet and what vision she had for her wedding. When she mentioned that it was to be held in the Signal Box Café, Greta rushed over to an array of wedding magazines that were arranged neatly on a baroque, glass-topped coffee table. She flicked through it until she found the page she was looking for and there across a double-page spread were the three competition finalists, including the picture with Lucy and Dom in it. Greta pointed to the picture and looked at Lucy. 'I have to say you made a wonderful bride and such a handsome husband too.'

'Oh no we aren't married. This was a publicity shot,' Lucy explained quickly.

'Well maybe you should be.' Greta laughed. 'You look wonderful together.'

'He's actually my grandson and Abbie's brother, so who knows maybe one day it will happen,' teased Violet.

'Not if I can help it,' added Abbie. 'He's stolen enough of my friends already.'

'Apart from the fact he hates weddings and he's a divorce lawyer and he and I don't exactly hit it off that well together, I'd say there's not much chance of that.' Lucy could feel her cheeks betraying her by flushing and really wished they wouldn't.

'Well I will make a point of voting for you in the competition as I think it's an amazing venue.'

'Thank you,' said Lucy. 'You must pop in if you get a chance.'

Greta promised she would.

For the next couple of hours, they were treated like royalty, trying on a whole range of dresses before Violet walked out in a pale gold delicate lace-over-silk dress with a bolero made from the same lace. The dress fitted her lovely slim figure then gradually flared out slightly; it was mid length, which was extremely flattering for her shapely ankles. Around the waist was a diamante feature, fashioned to look like a belt. Violet looked and felt beautiful.

Both Lucy and Abbie gasped when they saw her and just knew that this was the one. Tears rushed to Lucy's eyes as she imagined how delighted her grandad would be when he saw her. Greta was able to provide a clutch bag and shoes, which matched the outfit perfectly. Violet would be wearing her ash blonde hair up in a chignon and Greta had a beautiful diamante barrette, which was in keeping with the accessory on the dress.

Lucy and Abbie's dresses were a similar style to Violet's but without the lacy outer layer. Cream silk with thin straps, they were knee length and flared out from the waist. They also had matching shoes. Large mirrors were arranged around the room so they could see themselves from different angles. Lucy and Abbie were trying to out-twirl each other in their beautifully feminine designs.

After Greta had taken their measurements, they arranged a final fitting date. Greta was delighted when Lucy invited her to be included in her Wedding Belles planner album. She gave her a handful of leaflets and insisted she took one of the wedding magazines as a souvenir seeing as she was featured in it.

Next stop was a few doors down into Rocking Horse tea rooms, which was another old converted cottage with a vintage rocking horse in the window. They ordered after-noon tea, which was brought out on a couple of delicate china cake stands. The tables were laid with mismatched vintage crockery that only added to the charm of the place.

'So, Gran, how did you feel in that dress? You looked so beautiful,' said Abbie.

'My grandad is going to be speechless when he sees you. You looked stunning,' agreed Lucy trying to decide between a roast beef or cucumber sandwich. She put both on her plate and began with the cucumber one.

'It's funny really,' replied Violet with a wistful look in her eyes, 'I thought I'd feel silly trying on wedding dresses. I mean I'm no spring chicken, and I had absolutely no idea what sort of outfit would suit me but I have to say that I did feel pretty special in that one.'

'You honestly looked amazing,' said Abbie popping her smoked salmon sandwich in her mouth and eyeing up the scones on the next level up on the cake stand.

'Thank you, girls, for everything. Your opinions mean a lot to me because I trust you not to make me look silly on the day,' she said cutting her egg sandwich in half and eating it delicately.'

'Oh my God,' said Abbie as she chewed. Lucy and Violet looked at her slightly startled. She put her hand over her mouth as she spoke. 'These scones are org . . . I mean amazing. They have chocolate chips in them.'

'Ooh,' said the others as they took one each and spread them thickly with cream and jam. Lucy stifled a giggle as she cottoned on to what Abbie almost said in front of her gran. 'When's Grandad getting his suit sorted?' Lucy brushed scone crumbs from her jeans.

'Dom is taking Douglas, Jeffrey and Jackson to the suit hire place on Saturday apparently,' replied Violet.

'Oh, how cute will Jackson look in his little suit,' said Abbie.

'They will all look so handsome,' agreed Violet. She gestured for the waitress to bring them the bill. 'Could we also have a box to take these cakes home in please. They were delicious, but we couldn't manage them all.' The waitress smiled and did so. Violet had insisted it was her treat and the two girls thanked her.

Having been so distracted Lucy had completely forgotten that she had wanted to speak to the school to explain why

Jackson's dad wouldn't be there, but she supposed it was too late now.

She excused herself and tried anyway. As Miss Rooney spoke, Abbie and Violet were shocked to see Lucy's face drain of all colour.

'What do you mean he's been and gone?'

Abbie touched her arm lightly and mouthed, 'Are you okay?'

Lucy's voice had risen to a shriek. 'But where's Jackson?' Her stomach clenched. She was going to throw up.

'He's playing in the playground,' replied Miss Rooney.

'Are you absolutely sure?' Lucy's heart was pounding now and she had pushed her chair noisily away from the table.

'Yes, I can see him from my classroom; he seems a lot happier now that the other children believe him. He's enjoying his popularity.'

Lucy couldn't take in what she was saying as she was waiting for the opportunity to speak. 'Look, Miss Rooney, Jackson and I don't see his dad; please don't let him in again. I did send you a letter a little while ago explaining this and left a message this morning saying he wouldn't be there.'

'Oh, I see, yes of course. I'm so sorry but I never received a letter from you.' Miss Rooney sounded shocked, 'and when his Dad turned up I assumed the circumstances had changed.'

Lucy couldn't believe she was having this conversation; it seemed so alien. How could he have possibly found them? Maybe it was through the newspaper's coverage of the Signal Box Café. Her name hadn't been mentioned but Grandad's had and that bloody picture of her with Dom was massive. Maybe he'd seen that and thought she was with Dom now and was feeling proprietorial over Jackson? If so he had absolutely no rights to him whatsoever.

More ugly thoughts wormed their way into her head. What if he'd snatched Jackson? Had Jackson already been in touch with him? If so how? Maybe he'd sneaked onto Dom's computer and found him. But then none of this made sense. Jackson knew nothing about his dad – no name or anything.

Abbie and Violet were very worried and had followed Lucy out of the teashop.

'Is everything okay, dear?' Violet hugged her and Lucy broke down.

'The school said that Jackson's dad turned up for the "bring your father to school day" but the thing is Jackson has never met his dad and doesn't know anything about him. I'm scared he's found us and has maybe been contacting Jackson. This is why I didn't want any publicity in the paper, Abbie.' Her heart broke and she sobbed, releasing years of pent-up emotion. Between them Abbie and Violet tried to settle her again. Stroking her back and soothing her with kind words.

'I should probably ring the police.'

'No wait,' said Abbie, 'The teacher said that Jackson is okay so why don't we go back to Dom's and chat with Jackson when he gets home. Let your grandad pick him up as planned and we'll get you home and cleaned up for when you see him. In fact, we could check with your grandad – maybe it was him and the teacher was confused.' She held her friend's face in her hands and tried to wipe the tears away with her thumbs like little windscreen wipers.

Lucy nodded; that sounded like a plausible idea. Abbie took her keys and drove them back to Dom's house. They could hear him on a teleconference in the office so

Abbie took Lucy straight to the bathroom and left her to freshen up.

She tried some deep-breathing exercises to relax herself before Jackson came home; she was trembling from top to toe and didn't have a clue what to say to him. Abbie had given her a hug and left as she didn't want to be in the way. Violet began preparing dinner after making Lucy a strong coffee and was singing in the kitchen, trying her best to keep everything normal.

As she heard Grandad's key in the lock and Jackson's voice, her hands started shaking again. She ran to the door and grabbed him into a hug.

'Good news,' said Grandad, 'we can now move back to Railway Cottage as they've finished all the work and it looks as good as new and in fact even better than it did before.'

'Aw,' said Jackson, trying to escape his mum's hug and pushing his glasses back up his nose. 'I like living here. Dom is so cool.'

'Well it's been very kind of Dom to put us up but I'm sure he'll be glad to get us out of his hair,' Lucy answered.

'I was thinking we could pack your stuff tonight and move you back in tomorrow. How does that sound?' suggested Grandad.

'Yes great, but what about you; aren't you coming too?'

'Well that's the thing – Violet has suggested we stay here a bit longer as it will be a bit of a squeeze with all of us there and if I'm honest I do feel a bit strange having another woman there after your nan. That house holds such special memories for us. I don't want to lose them.'

'That's perfectly understandable, Grandad, but Jackson and I should probably start looking for somewhere for ourselves anyway. It's about time we stood on our own two, or should I say four, feet.'

'No, I wouldn't hear of it. That house will go to you anyway when I'm gone, and it makes me so happy having the two of you living there now. We can move into Violet's cottage in a few weeks when the tenants move out so all will be fine.'

'Thanks, Grandad, but no more morbid talk – you're not going anywhere.'

She went to the dining room where Jackson was sitting at the table with a glass of milk and some of Violet's home-made cookies. He was swinging his legs as he spoke to her.

Lucy waited for a lull in their conversation and sat next to Jackson as he munched.

'How was your day today, Jacks?' she asked softly yet wanting to scream at him.

'It was good, I got to play with Josh, Sam, Ben and all the others and Josh invited me to his party tomorrow.'

'Well that's nice but a bit short notice isn't it? Why so late with the invites?'

He sniffed and wiped his milk moustache on the back of his hand completely unperturbed.

'Everyone else has had theirs for ages but I wasn't invited and now I am.' He seemed quite pleased about that.

'Jackson, I spoke to Miss Rooney today.'

He stopped chewing and looked at her nervously. 'What about?' he whispered.

'I think you know what about, don't you?'

He looked down, his cheeks burning scarlet; he choked slightly on the biscuit and gulped at his milk to wash it down.

'Is it true that someone came to see you today at school?'

Guilt overwhelmed him and he sobbed. 'But, Mummy, all the kids were picking on me. It was like when I was at my other school. They were all saying that I didn't have a daddy and they did. But now they won't do that anymore,

Mummy. You remember you said I did have a daddy, so I wanted to show them.'

His words were like a kick to the stomach for Lucy. He'd never told her why he was being picked on at the other school.

'How did you find him, Jackson, or did he find you?' She held his arms too tight. 'What did he say to you? You are not to speak to him again, do you understand? Do you want him to take you away from me?' Her voice gradually rose until she was bordering on hysterical.

Jackson was frightened; his sobs shook his tiny body.

Violet and Grandad ran into the room at the same time.

'What's going on?' said Grandad trying to hug them as they were both crying hysterically now. Lucy was holding on to her grandad's shirt and crying into his chest.

'Jackson's dad came to the school today for a "bring your father to school day".' She gratefully accepted the tissues that Violet handed her. 'But I don't know how on earth he managed to find us or how long he has been in contact with him for. He could have snatched him today and I would have been none the wiser.'

'No, Mummy, that wouldn't happen.'

'You don't know that, Jackson, and I will not let you contact him again – do you hear me? Or I will have to go to the police,' she shouted.

Dom stood calmly at the door; he had come down to see what all the commotion was.

'You won't need to do that,' he said authoritatively as he realised what was happening.

'What do you mean? You don't know that!' Lucy snapped, blowing her nose loudly.

He had his hands in his pockets as he leaned against the doorframe looking as sexy as hell.

'I do know because it wasn't his dad at the school today.'

Chapter 33

All eyes focused on Dom; he ran his fingers through his hair leaving some strands sticking up.

'But how do you know?' Lucy sniffed.

'Because it was me!'

'What do you mean?' A sob caught in her throat.

'Look Jackson was upset the other night because everyone had been picking on him. They didn't believe he had a dad or that his dad was an astronaut. He told me he was bullied in the other school for the same reason. He asked me to help and I did. I didn't see any harm in it.'

Lucy flashed back to seeing him earlier with the huge garment carrier.

'Are you telling me that you dressed as an astronaut and pretended to be his dad?' She was shaking her head in disbelief, her voice croaky from all the crying.

Jackson cried again. 'I don't want Dom to get into trouble because of me, Mummy.' He ran to Dom and threw his arms around his legs, sobbing. Dom ruffled his hair.

'Don't worry, lad, no one's in trouble.' Grandad turned to Lucy, patted her on the hand and continued, 'And the most important thing is that everybody's safe, so no harm done.' Lucy didn't know whether to laugh or cry especially seeing Jackson now holding tightly to Dom's hand, his blotchy face still wet with tears.

Dom wished he'd dressed up as a magician instead; at least then he could have made himself disappear. He finally answered, 'Yes, I did. I've got a mate who works in the theatre. I asked on the off chance if they had anything to fit the bill and they did. I thought I was being helpful.'

'How dare you!' she shouted. 'And what about the next time he lies to someone? Are you going to dress up as a Liverpool player or a Hollywood film star or a pilot? Lying is wrong, so why would you do that? Jackson, go and pack your things. We're leaving.'

Violet held the young boy's hand and led him upstairs, comforting him as he protested with every step and sobbed. 'But I love Dom, I want Dom to be my dad.'

Dom shook his head, rubbed at his eyes. He hadn't asked for any of this; he just wanted a quiet life. He opened the fridge and took out a beer, flipped off the top and downed half the bottle in one go. 'Look I'm sorry if I've made things worse but maybe the kids will leave him alone now.'

'I can't even look at you,' she screamed as she stormed past him.

'Maybe if you had been more honest with him, he wouldn't have to make up all those lies,' he shouted to her back.

She stopped mid step; he watched her turn to him, but her face showed so much pain she couldn't even answer him. His heart sank. He didn't want to hurt her, but he'd said it with true conviction.

Grandad followed her upstairs to see if he could help. He patted Dom on the back as he passed him as he could see how wretched he felt.

Lucy threw their bags in her car, buckled Jackson in and drove back round the corner to Railway Cottage. She vowed never to speak to that man ever again.

Chapter 34

Back at Railway Cottage Lucy and Jackson had cuddled and cried a lot. Lucy had explained to him that lying was not a good thing and that he simply mustn't do it again. She had told him she was going to explain to Miss Rooney what had happened but he had begged her not to. His tear-swollen eyes implored her not to do it, and so she relented as long as he promised he would never do it again. She popped over to the Signal Box Café and came back with chicken curry and rice for their dinner, which they ate in the little dining room together.

Jackson soon voiced exactly what Lucy was thinking.

'It's so much quieter at this table. I miss Gran and Grandad and Dom.'

'Me too, Jacks, but this is our home and we belong here. Anyway, how about we make some butterfly cakes?' They needed to bond again and they loved baking together.

'Yes,' said Jackson. 'Can I lick the bowl?'

'Not if I get to it first.' She tickled his tummy, making him giggle.

Soon the kitchen was a mess of flour, sugar, eggs and cocoa powder. Icing sugar clouded the air and the smell of baking comforted them and reminded them they were at home and together. They cut off the tops of the cakes, piped chocolate buttercream inside them and then after cutting the tops in half they reassembled them in the cakes to look like butterfly wings. A light dusting of icing sugar finished them off. Lucy arranged them on a plate and got Jackson to hold it so she could take a picture of him with his creations. He pushed his glasses up his nose and smiled that crooked grin. His big teeth were starting to come down a lot more now. He had chocolate cake mix around his mouth and icing sugar on his nose. He looked so cute.

She sent the picture to her grandad and he replied, 'Well done, Jackson, they look yummy. I hope you save one for me.'

'Mummy, can we take some round for them?' His eyes were wide and hopeful.

'Sorry, love, not tonight – maybe tomorrow. Now come on, let's get you bathed and ready for bed. I think you are wearing more cake mix than went in the oven.'

She ran his bubbly bath and he went to his room to choose some dinosaurs to play with. Grandad had organised a surprise for them by using the opportunity to redecorate the bathroom, which was now all white tiles and new white bathtub, sink and toilet. The avocado had gone and he had also installed a new power shower, which would be heaven for Lucy's hair. She left the bathroom door open and pottered about on the landing and in their bedrooms, folding and putting away their clothes, all the while listening to Jackson having fun splashing and roaring as the dinosaurs fought each other.

Jackson got ready for bed and Lucy brought a glass of milk and a butterfly cake up for his supper. It was a bit early for his bedtime, but she wanted to relax and to get him back in the routine of living here, which might seem boring for him in comparison to living at Dom's. Just thinking about Dom made her angry again. How on earth could he have been so stupid? She had been frightened to death that Jackson could have been abducted by his dad. His hurtful words had cut through her like a knife; she hoped she would never see him again.

As if on cue, as soon as she opened the bottle of wine the doorbell rang. Her heart pounded in her chest. What if he'd come to apologise or to try and talk to her? As soon as she opened it Abbie rushed in and gave her a hug. Lucy exhaled deeply.

'Are you okay?' Concern etched across her friend's face.

'I'm fine, you won't believe wha . . .'

'I know,' Abbie interrupted. 'Dom called me and told me everything, and he's very worried about you and asked me to check if you were okay.'

'He's got a nerve, after what he did. He's lucky I didn't get the police on him.' She went through to the kitchen and poured Abbie a glass of the wine, her hand still shaking a little.

'I know it was a stupid thing to do, Lucy, but he explained everything to me and he really believed he was trying to help. He showed me a pic that Jackson insisted he took; here look at it.' She found it on her phone and showed it to Lucy who could hardly bear to look at the screen. Eventually her eyes couldn't resist and they were drawn to the massive smile on Jackson's face as he held the astronaut's hand proudly. She promptly released the dam that was holding back all her emotions and she cried like never before. Jackson had never looked so happy.

The sight of him holding on to his fake daddy's hand unleashed the guilt monster within her that she had managed to keep a rein on for the last eight years. She was always trying to convince herself that it was in Jackson's best interests not to see his dad, although for the first few years they hadn't had a choice. But then it became too late as far as she was concerned. She had been deceived and let down but had eventually struggled through the pain and had fought to be strong, independent and happy, and she wasn't going to let anyone come between her and Jackson. He was and always would be her number-one priority.

Abbie hugged her until the sobs subsided; she gulped more of her wine.

'Where is Jackson now?' she asked.

'He's upstairs watching telly in bed as a special treat. I was so scared, Abbie, I thought that he had come for him.'

'I know you were, but he hasn't and you and Jackson are fine and safe so don't let any more awful thoughts enter your mind.' Abbie didn't know anything about Jackson's father as Lucy had never discussed the details with anyone and she was grateful to her friend for respecting her privacy.

She looked again at the photo on Abbie's phone.

'Can you send this to me please?'

'Of course.' Abbie sent it to her straight away and Lucy looked at it on her own phone. She sniffed and wiped her eyes.

'I'll print it off for Jackson. I'm sure he'll love it.'

'It is a lovely picture and if Dom had known how much trouble he would have caused he would never have done it. He told me a few of the things that Jackson had said about the other kids bullying him and calling him names and one bigger child had a fight with Jackson and called him a liar. He'd kicked him in the leg apparently.'

Lucy immediately thought back to one night last week when she had noticed a bruise on his leg.

'I did see a bruise but he told me he ran into a bench, so I didn't think anything of it.'

'He didn't want to tell you because he knew you would be upset.,' she said gently. 'He's confided a lot in Dom.

Please don't hate him – he's devastated over there as he thinks the world of Jackson. We all do.'

'I know.' She rested her head on Abbie's shoulder. 'But he said horrible things to me like I should have talked to Jackson about his dad and I mean that is absolutely none of his business.' The fire in her belly began building up inside her again.

Abbie sat up and looked into Lucy's face.

'Now I know I could risk our friendship by saying this but I wonder if your anger is being misdirected a little here and that you're really angry with yourself for not having had the conversation with him before now. You wouldn't have to give names or circumstances but maybe there is a snippet of information that you could let him have.'

Lucy felt a spike in her throat, which she tried to calm down because she knew that Abbie was talking out of genuine love for her and Jackson and Dom. She looked down at a piece of cotton she was fiddling with that she had found on the arm of the sofa.

Abbie continued, 'I know it's hard for you and if Jackson wasn't interested then that would be the perfect solution, but he is very interested and sometimes a simple answer is enough. If Jackson asks what does my dad do? And you tell him, then maybe that would take away the mystery for him and he'll probably carry on playing with his toys afterwards. He has such a wonderful vivid imagination; I mean to come up with an astronaut for his dad's job just shows you that our little Jackson knows how to reach for the stars and beyond.'

'He is amazing and you're right. I think I just find the whole thing daunting. I mean who wants to tell their child that their daddy was a shitty human being? It's so hard but you're right, maybe if I break it down into little tiny steps then we can get through all this.'

'You can get through anything; you're a super mum. I hope one day you get to see the funny side of this. Poor Dom had to keep the astronaut helmet on the whole time so he wouldn't get recognised and lucky for him the theatre had wired a mike in there for when they used it in a show so he said he sounded a little like Darth Vader when he spoke to the kids. Even the teachers were in awe of him.' She snorted.

Lucy looked at the picture again and laughed until she cried, her heart aching with pain and joy. Nobody had ever done anything that stupid or crazy but most of all that thoughtful for her son before, but Dom obviously thought she was a rubbish mum.

She brought the rest of the bottle in and a couple of butterfly cakes each. She felt thankful for her amazing friend who was brave enough to be honest with her.

'To friends,' she toasted.

'Best friends,' Abbie toasted back.

They were both very giggly by the time Abbie came to leave and they hugged at the door announcing how much they loved each other. Suddenly they were blinded by the headlights of a car that pulled up outside. They shielded their eyes and realised it was Greg. He switched off the engine and joined them on the step.

'Hi, I was just driving past and noticed the lights were on and realised you must have moved back in so thought I'd pop by and say hello.'

Abbie allowed him to briefly graze her cheek with his lips and she waved goodbye. Lucy managed to side step his advances when she realised he was aiming for a full-on kiss with her. She held her hand up to block him and undeterred he pulled it to his lips and kissed the back of it. She wiped it on her jeans.

'Sorry I haven't been in touch for a while and I know it's getting late, but can I come in for a quick coffee?'

'I'm sorry no, it's not a good time. Jackson's in bed and he has school tomorrow, so I don't want him woken.'

'I promise I'll be quiet, just one quick cuppa,' he pleaded, his big brown eyes desperate to make her feel sorry for him again. 'I just need to talk to you about something, it's important.'

'No coffee, five minutes,' she said, holding five fingers up to him for emphasis.

'Thank you, you won't regret it.'

'So what is it you want to talk about?' she asked after checking her watch.

'Lucy I really, really like you and if you'd just give me a chance, I'm sure you'd be able to see it too.'

'No, I'm sorry Greg, I'm really not interested and I don't want to fall out with you so if that's all it was I think you'd better leave.' She watched his eyes turn glassy as they filled with tears.

'Are you crying,' she asked

'Not really I've just had a really bad day and needed to see a friendly face that's all,' he replied. 'Don't worry I'll go now.' He opened his arms wide, 'Friends?'

'Okay, friends,' she said and reluctantly allowed him to hug her. He held on to her tightly nuzzling his face into her, she patted him on the back in the least romantic way she could so he wouldn't get any ideas, then she realised he was kissing her neck.

'Okay that's enough,' she pushed him away but his lips were still attached to her skin. 'Get off.' She managed to release him and rubbed at her neck which was now damp.

'Come on you can't tell me you don't feel anything.'

'You're right actually, I do feel something. I feel sick.'

He rolled his eyes at her and marched off to his car.

Relieved she closed the door, put the locks on and shivered as though someone had walked over her grave.

Chapter 35

The Signal Box Café was doing a roaring trade. The commuters loved it and many of the locals were customers too, both for eating in and takeaways. Lucy loved seeing people walking along with their little paper bags featuring the name of the café on them, knowing they had a delicious wholesome meal to look forward to when they got home.

After school today would be the dreaded kids' party so she had popped in to check everything was okay. The downstairs would still be open to the public but upstairs would be reserved for the party. It was pretty self-sufficient up there. They had a small bar area, which was above the kitchen, and toilets down the other end near the staircase.

Lucy had briefed the staff on what to do. The mother had organised an entertainer. Camilla had popped round as she had made the cupcakes and the birthday cake, which was in the shape of a Porsche, Josh's favourite car apparently, Lucy surveyed the results of her hard work proudly and it was only after she noticed Camilla looking strangely at her neck that she popped to the loo and noticed a mark like a squashed strawberry. That bloody Greg! She was mortified and texted him. *'I can't believe you gave me a love bite. What are we, twelve?'*

She ran back over to Railway Cottage to try and hide the mark with concealer and a light floral scarf, which she hoped wouldn't look too ridiculous in this warm weather. She heard the ping of a text and checked it to read the words: '*Sorry, wrong person.*' It was from Dom. She wondered if there was an even stronger word than mortification as she would need to invent one if not to describe just how ridiculous she was feeling right now. She could think of no words in reply and so decided to ignore him. She then took a screenshot of the message and sent it to Abbie with the words: '*Look what I sent to your brother. I'm beyond mortified.*' Only to be sent another reply from Dom saying, '*Still wrong person!!*' What was it with her stupid phone? Did it have a magnetic attraction to his or something?

She was still furious at Greg and this time double- and triple-checked it was him she was sending the message to and repeated her text. She didn't get a response.

Grandad was picking Jackson up from school today as Lucy had appointments with another couple of bridal boutiques who would like to be included in her wedding planner album. He would also be dropping him off at the party for her and she would be back in time to pick him up. Jackson had been mega excited about the party and raced over there after he and Grandad had enjoyed one of his home-made butterfly cakes.

Lucy had had a productive afternoon; she was impressed with one of the boutiques but not so much with the other, as the quality of the dresses was not very good. Therefore, the latter wouldn't be going in her folder. She had a busy weekend ahead, which she was thoroughly looking forward to. Four new viewings of the venue and six appointments with couples who had already booked their weddings at the Signal Box Café. She was thrilled to have such a busy diary.

At twenty-five past six, she headed over to the party to pick Jackson up. She could hear the noise of children squabbling and screeching as she entered the door and was horrified to see children running around the downstairs area screaming and throwing cakes at each other, over the heads of paying customers who were trying to eat a relaxing meal.

'Stop that this minute,' she shouted at the top of her voice causing the children to stop in their tracks. 'Get back upstairs now,' she commanded. They did as they were told; she apologised to the customers and ran up behind them, her heart pounding. The sight of the upstairs area brought stinging tears to her eyes. What had happened to her beautiful café? Cakes and trifle were stuck to and dripping off the television screens and the windows. A couple of the staff were trying their hardest to keep the children under control but fighting a losing battle. They were instead focusing on cleaning up the food that had been trampled all over the floor. The leg from one of the buffet tables had been broken and all the food and drink that had been placed on that was now spilt over the floor. The beautiful velvet train seats near the window were splattered with cream and custard. She noticed all the parents had begun to come in after her to pick their children up. Their faces were as horrified as hers was.

She shouted again for the kids to stop screaming and as they saw their parents and quietened down, she heard Jane shouting and arguing in the bar area.

'I know you're having an affair, now just tell me who the slut is. She must be desperate if she wants you. Now give it here.'

Lucy made her way over there to find out what was going on and heard her phone ringing. Jane burst out of the bar, her face purple with rage. A phone to her ear, a man's hand followed as he tried to wrestle it off her.

Lucy looked at the screen on her phone and saw Greg's name come up. She reluctantly answered.

'Hello.' She looked over at Jane again, an expression of pure hatred on her face as she glared at Lucy. It took Lucy a few seconds to register that the person on the other end of the phone was Jane and the man who was trying to grapple it out of her hand was none other than Greg.

'You bitch,' shouted Jane as she hurled herself at Lucy and managed to tug her scarf off. She pointed to the mark on her neck and addressed the other parents who were hurriedly trying to gather their children together.

'My husband gets a text saying that he gave someone a love bite and look – there's the evidence. You're a slut and a whore.' She pointed her finger in Lucy's face. Lucy's fight or flight had kicked in. She didn't know whether to run away and hide or bop this obnoxious woman and her cheating husband in the face. She could do neither, as a frightened Jackson ran over to her and threw his arms around her waist stopping her from moving. She hugged his small frame and assured him it was okay and just a misunderstanding.

Greg was trying to tell his wife that it wasn't what it looked like, but she was squawking unintelligibly in his face like a parrot. Lucy kissed Jackson on the head and told him to go downstairs to the kitchen with Lewis the chef; he did as he was told. She then tried to usher Jane and Greg into the bar area for a bit of privacy; however, Jane was adamant that it should be discussed in front of their audience.

'I'm sorry, Jane, first let me tell you that nothing happened.'

'Why have you got a love bite then if nothing happened, you lying cow?'

'Look I swear, Greg asked me out a few times and we had a few drinks, but he told me he was single and had no children. I promise you.'

'I don't believe you. He wouldn't do that – not deny our children.'

'Of course, I wouldn't,' Greg lied. 'She has been trying to entice me, Jane, but I wasn't interested. Whoever did that to her neck I can assure you it wasn't me. You know what they say, a woman scorned and all that. Because she couldn't have me, she doesn't want you to have me.' He put his arm around his wife who was desperate to believe him then he turned to Lucy. 'I've been doing a bit of digging, Lucy, and it seems you prefer married men. Isn't that right?'

Lucy legs almost gave way beneath her. She felt faint and nauseous at the same time. What was going on in her life?

'If you say so, Greg, but you are a liar as well as a cheat – now get out of my café and think yourself lucky that I'm not sending you a bill for damages.'

The other parents had gradually made themselves scarce and it was just Josh and his brother left running around in the mess now.

Greg was about to argue again when he heard a man's voice shout, 'Do as the lady says and get out. NOW!' he bellowed.

Lucy was stunned to see Dom standing at the top of the stairs; he was looking as sharp as ever in his designer suit. His face was full of anger as his eyes scanned the room; his jaw was clenched tightly, which only made his chiselled features more distinctive. He towered above Greg.

'Now, you two, get your disrespectful, snotty-nosed kids and go.'

Greg remembered the pain of the Subbuteo man hitting him in the eye and didn't fancy his chances with this guy.

They gathered up two bin bags full of presents and their kids, and Dom escorted them off the premises.

'You're all barred,' he shouted after them, to a round of applause from the customers and staff.

When he went back upstairs, he saw a forlorn-looking Lucy with a bin bag, trying to scrape some of the mess from the tables into it before she could even start on the floor. She had asked the staff to go down and bring up scrubbing brushes, cloths and every cleaning implement they owned as well as lots more bin bags.

'Thanks for that,' she said weakly. 'I swear he told me he was single with no kids, and the stupid thing is that I didn't want to go out with him anyway. Thank God nothing happened with him.' She could feel her neck break out in red blotches of embarrassment having remembered who she was talking to. 'He clamped on to my neck last night like a leech.' She shuddered.

Dom's phone rang. 'Hi, Clarissa, can I ring you back? Something's come up.' He listened intently then said goodbye. 'Are you okay?'

'No not at all,' she wept, 'it's a total disaster; I've a full house tomorrow, new viewings and everything, and just look at the state of the place.'

'Don't worry,' he said assuredly, 'I've called for reinforcements and I think that's them turning up. I just need to pop somewhere; I'll be back soon.' She heard footsteps coming up the stairs and soon saw Grandad, Violet, Abbie, Dave and Jackson looking suitably shocked and horrified as they surveyed the mess. Dom had warned Grandad he would need to bring his toolbox and he immediately got to work on the broken table leg. The rowdy kids had also managed to get hold of the trains that delivered the drinks and they were damaged. Grandad assured her that he would have them as good as new in no time. Violet rushed to Lucy and hugged her.

'Don't you worry, darling, we'll soon have this place looking spic and span.' She began by removing the trifle ingredients from the velvet chairs. 'How on earth could they make such a mess?'

Jackson explained, 'The magician was rubbish and so Josh and some of the other kids were throwing things at him and then they all had a food fight, but the mum and dad didn't do anything because they were arguing like crazy. Josh said that they always argue. I tried to stop them, Mummy, but they wouldn't listen.' His lip trembled.

'Don't worry it's not your fault,' Lucy assured him. 'Hey why don't you cheer us up by putting some happy music on?'

Jackson smiled as he connected his mum's phone to the built-in loudspeaker so they could listen to music while they worked. Dom turned up shortly after with a steam cleaner, which worked wonders on the upholstery.

Lucy could have cried when they had finished because the place looked even better than new. She treated everybody to a new dish they had added to the menu, a delicious beef stroganoff, and she opened a bottle of prosecco too.

'Thanks to you all, our amazing family – I'm so grateful to each and every one of you.'

Chapter 36

Jackson was spending the weekend with his grandad at Dom's house and was beyond excited; he was hoping to play lots with Dom too.

They had been to the suit hire shop and all been measured up for their morning suits. Jackson was excited about wearing the same suit as Grandad and Dom.

'Grandad, can we go to Serendipity? I haven't been for ages and I really miss Auntie Rosie.'

'Only if you treat me to one of those gigantic scones, as they are the best in the world.'

'Yay,' he said and ran to get his shoes on.

As they walked along the river to Serendipity, Jackson was feeding the birds with some bread that Gran had given him and an elderly couple walked by, accompanied by a younger couple.

'Hi, Dougie, how are you?' said the elderly man.

'Jeffrey, I'm not so bad. How are you?' He shook his hand and kissed Martha on her delicate cheek.

'Are you all ready for the wedding,' he asked.

'Indeed, we are – it won't be long now. How are you getting on? Have they given you a double room yet?'

'No chance, not with Dolores King at the helm – they make more money out of us being in two rooms than they would if we were in one.'

The younger woman spoke up. 'I think it's disgraceful.

My mum and dad have been married for fifty-five years and they can't even cuddle up to each other at night. I've started a petition to see if they can be moved in together. The rooms are plenty big enough. It's just a case of getting a double bed in there.'

'Well if there's anything I can do, then please let me know won't you,' said Dougie. He was glad he'd escaped.

'I will do, Dougie, cheerio.'

Serendipity looked as pretty as ever. Colourful flowers in full bloom adorned the top of the boat. The smells of scones and hot sausage rolls wafted in the air, getting stronger as they got closer. A long boat moved off from the other side of the river. It was painted burgundy, black and cream and was very smart-looking. Geese scurried to get out of its path and ripples flowed either side of it as it cut through the water and gained momentum. The sound of the engine chugging was soothing. Jackson and his grandad watched as the boat drifted past them. It was called *Precious Moments*. Jackson jumped with excitement as he recognised Finn standing up and steering the boat whilst Gracie sat next to him with the baby in her arms. They waved to him and he excitedly waved back.

'I love living here, Grandad,' he said.

'Me too, and I love you living here,' said Grandad.

They stepped on board *Serendipity*. It was such a serene environment, very relaxing. John Lennon's unmistakable tone emanated from the speakers, Dougie hummed along, he recognised the song from the Plastic Ono Band days. Jackson raced over to Rosie and threw himself into her arms.

'Jackson, what a lovely surprise – I've missed you so much.' She cuddled him tightly. 'Now what have you been getting up to lately?'

'Some kids had a party in the Signal Box Café and they wrecked it and we all had to clean it up and it was a real mess and I know what my dad's name is, cos Mummy told me that if I was good and didn't tell fibs any more then she would tell me stuff. So, I asked her what his name is.'

'Well that sounds like a good compromise doesn't it; so are you going to tell me his name?'

'It's Jack and that's why Mummy called me Jackson because I am Jack's son.'

'Well that's fascinating, Jackson. I love that story.' She looked at Dougie and he shrugged and smiled.

'Here, Jackson, I've saved you and your grandad the best table. Look, you can see both sides of the river from here. Now you go and sit down and I'll bring your food over.' She carried over golden flaky sausage rolls and the huge scones, which were wrapped in a warm cloth and placed in a basket to keep them warm. Clotted cream and home-made jams accompanied them. Their mouths watered just looking at them. She brought Grandad tea and juice for Jackson, then went into the back and brought out some colouring books and pens for him.

'Here I got you a little present. And I also made you something special,' she said. She removed a napkin off the plate she was carrying to reveal some special dinosaur cookies, one of which had Smarties down the back to look like spines and dotted all over the body on the other one.

'Do you know what they're called?'

'Yes, a stegosaurus and a T-Rex,' he answered knowingly.

'Actually, in the real world that's what they would be called but here on *Serendipity*, this one is called a Smartie Rex and this one is called a Jacksonosaurus.' She picked one of them and roared at Jackson who picked up the other and play fought with them.

'Thank you so much, Auntie Rosie, I love you.' He hugged her again.

Jackson didn't notice the tears of joy that his sentiment had brought to Rosie's eyes, as he was too busy eating one of his cookies, but Grandad did and he winked at her. Whilst Jackson was colouring in a complicated picture of two wrestling dinosaurs, Grandad was racking his brain trying to think of a way to help Jeffrey and Martha and then all of a sudden it came to him.

Chapter 37

Dominic Cavendish felt foolish; he firmly believed he had made the best decision for the little boy. Jackson had been inconsolable when they took Baxter for the late evening walk and he had poured his heart out to him. Dominic could see that he had got himself in a pickle and was being bullied, when he said he'd told them his dad was an astronaut; he laughed and asked Jackson how he thought he would be able to pull it off.

'I wished upon a star,' he had replied.

'Well is your dad an astronaut?' He looked down at the boy who was holding his hand. His little pale face shone under the glow of a streetlamp as he looked back up to him.

'I don't know, but he could be, couldn't he?'

'I don't see any reason why not, but as you haven't managed to get in touch with him, what else can we do? We could call the school and say he's sick.'

'But the teachers will recognise my voice and I'll get into trouble.'

'Well they won't recognise mine,' he said in a jokey deep tone.

Jackson laughed for a second or two, and then his face went deadly serious.

'The other kids will keep picking on me. I only have one choice,' he said sadly.

Dom waited patiently for the answer.

'I'm going to have to run away.'

They were in Market Square; the fountain was lit up and looked so pretty. The trickling water was relaxing. They heard laughter and saw a couple arm-in-arm heading into the B&B, opposite them. Dom gestured for Jackson to sit on the bench and he sat beside him. A tired Baxter lay at their feet.

'Running away is not the answer to anything, Jackson. When you screw . . . I mean mess up, you have to be a man and face up to it. I think you know you shouldn't have lied so you have hopefully learned your lesson but will you promise me you won't do it again if I help you out this once?'

Jackson had been trailing his fingers in the fountain expecting a lecture until he heard Dom's last sentence, at which he perked up. The light reflected on Jackson's piercing blue eyes as he gazed adoringly over the top of his glasses up at Dom.

'Will you really help me? Are you sure? Do you promise?'

'Only if you promise me that this is the last time you lie.'

'I promise I will never lie again,' he said as he hugged Dom, keeping his fingers crossed on one hand just in case. 'You won't tell Mummy though will you? Because she will go crazy.'

'I won't if you won't. There's just one other thing too. Can you remind me to tighten your glasses for you?' They shook hands and Dom pulled a face as he realised Jackson's hand was wet from the fountain. 'Eurgh thanks, mate.' He rummaged in his pocket for a few coins and handed them to the boy. 'Here, you can make a wish if you want.'

Jackson smiled a wonky-toothed grin and threw the coins into the fountain.

'Mummy used to wish in this fountain – her nana used to bring her.'

'Is that so?' he replied. 'I wonder what she used to wish for.'

'She used to wish that she could get married.'

Dom rolled his eyes. Typical, he thought. They started to walk back home again hand in hand.

'So remember you're not to worry about a thing. I'll sort it out one way or another,' he said.

'Thanks, Dom.'

After much deliberating, Dom remembered seeing an advert for a show about astronauts that the local theatre group had put on. He texted his friend Gabe to see if they still had the costume. This was one of the most stupid things he'd ever done but that little kid's face had tugged on his heart.

He was shocked at Lucy's reaction when she had found out. He hadn't expected that. Abbie explained to him how frightened Lucy had been, but he was a very pragmatic person and couldn't understand why the woman didn't just tell her son what he wanted to know. He hadn't meant to hurt her and he hated that his house was now so big and empty without her.

She'd been on his mind all day Friday and when he called to the Signal Box Café after work to pick up a takeaway, he'd noticed Jackson through the hatch in the kitchen looking concerned. When he asked him if he was okay, he'd told him a man and woman were shouting at his mummy. Dominic, heart pounding, had run as quick as a flash into the building to see what was going on. On seeing who the man involved was, he remembered the texts he'd got in the morning and realised that this must have something to do with Lovebitegate.

He hoped that by turfing them out, it would go some way to helping Lucy forgive him for what he'd said and done.

Chapter 38

The time for the wedding had arrived and both households were buzzing with excitement. Dom and Grandad had moved into Railway Cottage with Jackson for the night and Lucy and Abbie were staying at Dom's house with Violet. The competition judges would also be there as the rules insisted that they needed to see an actual wedding taking place at each venue. Lucy had organised the whole thing and Violet was incredibly grateful.

Violet sat in the living room on a dining room chair, being luxuriously pampered from top to toe. Hairdressers and beauticians had been flitting around the three of them like pretty butterflies all morning. The doorbell rang and Lucy answered it then walked back into the room with a huge bouquet for Violet. The older lady tried to peer at it with one eye as the other one was being shaded a delicate mauve colour, which beautifully enhanced the green of her eyes.

'Oh, they're so beautiful. He is a treasure, isn't he?' she said, a little tearful. The beautician dabbed at her eye with a cotton wool pad to avoid the tears ruining her make-up. The doorbell rang again. This time it was Flossie with the wedding flowers. She brought in one large and two small bridal bouquets created with cream roses dusted with gold and interspersed with violets, and three fresh flower headdresses made from the same blooms. The fragrance enriched the sense of occasion that was already apparent in the house and added to the excitement.

Lucy had had her hair and make-up done first and was now dressed in jeans and a plain white blouse as she needed to pop over to the Signal Box Café and make sure everything was set up. She opened a bottle of champagne before she left and they toasted the bride who was looking beautifully elegant in her silk robe.

There were lots of people buzzing around the café. The ceremony would be held upstairs, the wedding breakfast downstairs and then back upstairs for the evening reception and buffet. On stepping inside the building Lucy's heart lifted like a helium balloon. The place had been transformed and looked enchanting; the tables were laid with starched white cloths, silver cutlery and crystal glassware. Small goldfish bowls sat in the middle of each one with cream roses and violets entwined in water. Garlands of roses and violets were wound round the bannister of the staircase. Long teardrop crystals hung in the windows and reflected the sun's rays into all the colours of the rainbow around the room.

The three-tier cake stood on a separate table at the far end of the room with a flower arch over it. The cake was one of Camilla's masterpieces. Quilted icing studded with silver balls had been lightly dusted with a pale gold shimmer. Icing violets spilled from the top tier to the bottom just over one corner. The tribute to her grandad was the bride and groom sitting in a steam train engine at the top. Camilla had been clever enough to make it after discussions with Violet and it was perfect.

Upstairs literally took Lucy's breath away. Her plan had been followed to the letter. Neither Grandad nor Violet knew what to expect, as this was her special gift to them, 'the perfect wedding'.

At the far end where the little bar was, stood the most beautiful flower arch imaginable. Cream roses and violets were entwined with greenery and gypsophila. All of the loose chairs were laid out facing the arch, each one enshrined in a cream cover with a sheer purple voile bow tied at the back. Flower garlands were strewn atop the television screens adding to the enchanted feel of the place.

The fixed tables along the window were covered in white cloths with the goldfish bowls for décor. The place looked fresh and inviting; she got out her phone and took some pictures. She couldn't wait for Dave to arrive so he could take some professional ones for them.

She reluctantly left the beautiful room and checked on Lewis in the kitchen. She had originally thought she would be hiring external caterers for the weddings but Lewis had proved to be an extremely proficient chef so she gave him the job. The rest of their team were also keen to be involved. He was raring to go, and everything seemed to be in order. Lucy patted herself on the back. She wasn't exactly the most organised person at home but when it came to planning a wedding, she left no stone unturned and organised it with military precision.

As she came out of the building, she saw her parents had pulled up outside Railway Cottage looking very tanned and healthy.

'Mum, Dad,' she shouted and ran the few steps to join them.

'Lucy, how lovely to see you, and what a fantastic job you've made of the signal box. I know you sent me pictures but they hardly do it justice. It looks amazing,' said her mum hugging her tightly. 'Now what's Daddy's new stepmum like? Is she wicked?' she joked.

Lucy laughed and walked into Railway Cottage, her arm linked through her mum's. 'You might remember her. I used to play with her granddaughter Abbie.'

Her mum cocked her head slightly as she tried to remember. They stepped into the living room.

'Oh yes, I remember Abbie and she had a brother, didn't she? Ah you were so in love with him; you used to follow him around him everywhere. Your little first crush, now what was his name?'

'Hi, I'm Dominic.' He held out his hand and Lucy's mum looked up and up, into his handsome face, which was beaming a smile. His eyes twinkled.

'That's it, it was Dominic; pleased to meet you.' She shook his hand, fluttering her eyelashes at him. Lucy's face was as purple as the violets in the wedding flowers.

'Hi Lu,' he said to her. She could barely look at him. If she thought he had looked handsome at their fake wedding then that wasn't a patch on this. He was wearing a dark morning suit that made his eyes look darker and bluey grey. His dark blond hair was swept over to the side, apart from a little bit that he could never get to stick down, no matter how hard he tried. He had full lips, which were now uncharacteristically fashioned into a beaming smile showing his even white teeth. He was talking to Grandad and laughing a real hearty laugh.

She hadn't quite realised how well they had begun to get on with each other. She liked that. Her dad hugged her and swung her round. She was so pleased they had come back from Spain for the wedding. Jackson could hear new visitors and came thundering downstairs into the arms of his grandparents.

'Nanny and Grandad, come and see mine and Great-Grandad's train set.' He dragged them off to the garage in the back, one in each hand. Lucy's Grandad walked in and took her breath away.

'Oh, Grandad, you look so handsome.' She wiped a tear from her eye, as did he.

'Look at us, what a pair of softies.' He gave her a cuddle.

The sound of chatter got louder as Jackson led his grandparents back into the house. He was wearing a little morning suit to match Grandad's and Dom's.

'Isn't he just the cutest thing,' said Lucy's mum after she planted a lipstick kiss on her grandson's face.

'Jackson, you need your cravat on. Where is it?' asked Dom.

'In my room,' he answered from the floor where he was sending one of the trains to his nanny and grandad.

'Come on then, we don't want to be late.'

Jackson ran upstairs two at a time and came down with the violet satin cravat.

Lucy was pouring champagne in the kitchen and brought the full glasses in on a tray. As she walked into the living room she froze on the spot, mesmerised by the vision in front of her. Jackson was standing on a chair so he could see in the mirror and Dom was gently helping to put his cravat on for him and talking through the instructions as he did so. Jackson's little hands were mirroring Dom's as they tried to get it right and after a couple of goes they did it. Dom then gave him the comb and, looking at Dom in the mirror, Jackson combed his hair to the side exactly like Dom's.

Hot fat tears sprung to Lucy's eyes as she watched the scene that would remain etched in her heart forever, a loving moment of tenderness between her boy and this man who used to be the bane of her life but who was now . . .? Well she didn't quite know what. Her step-cousin she supposed. That seemed weird. Just before she could look away, she caught Dom's reflection in the mirror and he smiled at her, causing a firework to go off inside her body. She gasped involuntarily. She quickly put the tray down on the table, gulped down a whole glass of the bubbles and ran back round to Dom's house.

Just an hour later and they arrived outside the Signal Box Café where a gold and purple balloon arch had now been ensconced at the entrance.

The wedding car was a vintage Rolls-Royce and had scared them a little when it came to collect the bridesmaids as for a minute – they thought it wasn't going to start. But after a few loud bangs off it went to the applause of some of the neighbours who had popped out to wish them all the best.

Dom was back for when the car arrived and he helped his gran into it.

'You look radiant, Gran,' he said kissing her on the cheek.

'Thank you, darling, and you are as handsome as ever.'

As the journey was only two minutes away, they decided to take the scenic route in order to make the most of the car. They travelled around the whole of the town.

'Can we go to the church first, please?' asked Violet.

'Of course, Gran. Driver, can we just pop to the church first – it's a little further along the high street and left.' The driver followed the instructions and Violet got out of the car and replaced her heels with a pair of flat court shoes. She linked her arm through her grandson's and they made their way over to the place where she visited every week. When she arrived at her destination, she placed a single cream rose on her husband's grave. Dom stood next to her with his arm around her shoulder.

'I just want him to know I haven't forgotten him,' she said dabbing at an errant tear.

Dom squeezed her shoulder. 'He'd be happy for you, Gran. Like I said to you, this is a new love that you can have as well as the old love. It's not a replacement. Your heart is big enough for both.'

She kissed his cheek then wiped her lipstick off him with her thumb.

Abbie and Lucy fussed over Violet when she arrived at the door of the Signal Box Café; Dave was there taking photos as was a friendly man called Joe from the wedding magazine. Dom smiled at Lucy admiringly before he lifted his arm for his gran and led her into the building.

Violet looked proudly at her beautiful bridesmaids and her handsome grandson who was giving her away today. They were stunning. They went inside and headed up the stairs. The bridal music began to play, and the wedding party passed all of the admiring guests.

Grandad stood proudly with his best man Jeffrey. His eyes sparkled as he saw his beautiful bride walking towards him surrounded by their grandchildren and great-grandchild; he couldn't have been happier. He sent a silent kiss up to heaven for his beloved Rose and then welcomed his bride with a delicate kiss on her cheek.

The violets in the bouquet provided a stunning splash of colour and Lucy knew that they looked exquisite, especially so against the background of their pale gold and cream dresses. After the vows there were lots of photos and the bridal party walked down to the river for a few more. Lucy could feel the heat from Dom's body as they were in such close proximity for some of the pictures. She had to try and think of other things to distract herself, as she kept thinking back to that kiss. Every time she looked at him, her eyes were drawn to his lips. She wanted to feel them on hers again, imagine how she would feel after a real kiss if that was the effect he had on her with a fake one. She must snap out of this; it was her grandad's wedding for goodness' sake. She smiled for another photo, laughing to herself that nobody would know what that twinkle in her eye was for.

Lewis the chef had excelled himself with the food; for starters they had seafood salad in a Marie Rose sauce with delicious home-made bread, and butter swirls. The main course was a tender fillet of beef served with fresh vegetables, dauphinoise potatoes and a red wine jus; everything was locally sourced. For dessert they had Eton mess, followed by cheese and biscuits and a slice of wedding cake with coffee or tea. The champagne flowed freely. As they were sitting downstairs now, they were all in tables of four. Dougie and Violet were with Jeffrey and Martha; Lucy was with her mum and dad and Jackson; Dom and Abbie were with their mum and dad with an extra chair on the end for Dave.

After the food came the speeches and Dom stood up first. Lucy made the most of the opportunity to stare at him, to watch his handsome face break into a smile. She imagined herself stroking the crinkles that appeared at the sides of his eyes when he laughed, maybe even kissing them. She mentally slapped her wrists and concentrated on what he was saying.

'I would like to welcome you all here today to celebrate the marriage of my lovely Gran, Violet, and her new husband Dougie.' Violet and Dougie looked at each other with smiling eyes as everybody cheered and tapped their spoons on their glasses. 'Now as you may know I was a little bit unsure about Dougie at first as I wondered if he was leading my gran astray. But since I got to know

Dougie, I've discovered that it was actually the other way round.' He held his hands up as the guests laughed.

'Oi, cheeky,' Violet shouted.

'No, I'm only joking. I'd say it was at least fifty-fifty.' He laughed as he dodged the napkin his gran threw at him. 'Seriously though, I've noticed that Gran has a new lease for life, and I think that each of them have provided the other with the last piece of the puzzle of life.' His eyes sought out Lucy's and they exchanged the briefest of glances, which caused her breath to catch in her throat.

Dom continued, 'As you all know this is their chance of love for the second time around and I think they should seize the day. I wish them all the happiness in the world as they are a wonderful couple and they truly deserve it. So please join me in a toast to the bride and groom.' Everybody stood and joined in the toast.

Dougie stood up and cleared his throat. 'Thank you, Dom, and on behalf of my wife and I . . .' The room erupted with the sound of glasses being tapped with spoons and cheers again. 'I would sincerely like to thank you for making me welcome in your family and in your home. I promise that I will take very good care of your gran as I love her dearly; I never expected that at this stage of my life I would meet and marry such a beautiful lady. I would also like to say a huge thank you to our beautiful granddaughters, Lucy and Abbie, who have made the most stunning bridesmaids today and our great-grandson Jackson for being a handsome pageboy, so I would like to raise a toast to the bridesmaids and pageboy.'

Jeffrey thanked Dougie on behalf of the bridesmaids and then spoke about how he had worked with Dougie years ago and they'd lost touch until they ended up in Sycamore Lodge together.

'He and Violet were like a breath of fresh air in that place and I'm so happy to be here today on this auspicious occasion. Dougie wanted me to say a special thank you to his granddaughter Lucy for all the amazing effort she has put in to making today utterly perfect and as it's the very first wedding here he would like me to raise a toast to the Signal Box Café.' Everybody stood and repeated the toast, including Jackson who toasted with his apple juice and joined in with the spoon tapping.

Whilst the guests were eating and listening to speeches, upstairs was being transformed into the evening venue. The buffet table was set up under the telly screens and smaller chairs and tables were dotted around the room, leaving space for a dance floor. Lydia, a local student who sang at the launch, was singing jazz songs and playing the keyboard. It provided a lovely welcoming atmosphere as the guests drifted upstairs. The DJ was all set up and ready to go for when the disco started. The black window blinds had been pulled down now and the fairy lights in them turned on. The flower arch also had fairy lights threaded in it, as did the decorative garlands around the room. An external staircase from the kitchen to the bar was used to transport the food up so as not to interfere with the wedding party.

Joe from the wedding magazine took his final photo of the evening scene and bade them farewell.

'It's a wonderful venue, Lucy – thanks for letting me take some photos. It's all down to the votes now. Good luck.'

Lucy thanked him and said goodbye.

The first dance was very romantic; they had chosen a golden oldie, 'The Last Waltz' by Engelbert Humperdinck. The room lit up with camera flashes as they glided elegantly around the dance floor. For the next song they were joined by Jeffrey and Martha, then Dave and Abbie. Lucy felt a tap on her shoulder and as she looked straight into Dom's twinkling eyes her heart felt like it would burst out of her chest. He held his hands out to her. They were lovely hands, smooth and tanned a golden colour.

'Dance?' he said.

'Erm,' was all she could manage.

'Aw come on you're not going to leave me hanging, are you?'

She shook her head. 'Of course not, I was just wondering where Jackson was.'

He nodded his head towards the dance floor where Jackson was dancing with her mum. She laughed and took his hand; her body felt on fire where he touched her. He held her close as they swayed around.

'I just wanted to say, I'm sorry for what happened about Jackson.'

'It's fine honestly. I wanted to apologise to you too. It was the panic and the fear talking. I never even thanked you properly for letting us stay. You really didn't have to do that and I truly do appreciate it.'

He smiled at her. 'I enjoyed it a lot. You made my house feel like a home and it's far too quiet without you both there, and Baxter of course.'

'Well you're welcome to come and visit them whenever you want to. My house is never quiet.'

'I might just take you up on that,' he said, enjoying the warmth emanating from her body. She looked even more beautiful than usual today. Although he liked her looking natural too – when she had just got out of the bath and had no make-up on, she was equally stunning. He wanted to dance with her some more but needed to ask his gran to dance now and he could see Dougie heading over to dance with Lucy.

★

The disco was good fun. Dougie and Violet left at about ten to go off to Belvedere Manor for their wedding night. It was a present from Dom, and they were delighted. Jackson was teaching Dom, Lucy, Abbie and Dave some dance moves from pop bands he liked, and they were all giggling as they tried to keep up with him.

Lucy was surprised to see Dom so incredibly relaxed and fun. He had always been so serious before.

The slow dances came on later on and he held his hands out to her. She took his hand once more and a tired Jackson came over and with an arm round both of their waists he swayed along with them. Dom picked him up and they danced in a three. Abbie saw and took a picture of them, Jackson now falling asleep on Dom's shoulder.

At the end of a magical day they said their goodbyes. Dom carried a sleeping Jackson down the stairs. He offered to carry him to Railway Cottage but Lucy insisted she'd be fine so he transferred him gently to her. His eyes flickered but he soon cuddled into the warmth of his mum's body and went off again. Dom walked her over to the house and unlocked the door for her.

'Bye then,' he said and leaned in to her, his lips gently brushing her cheek, close to the corner of her mouth. She wanted to turn her head so his lips would be on hers but she daren't. They looked deep into each other's eyes. The light from the station cast a glow on the sides of their faces, and their eyes twinkled like the fairy lights on the building in front of them.

His face came closer again. Her eyes were drawing him in. Her lips parted and she could feel the warmth of his breath on her face. He lifted his hand to touch her soft hair, her eyes closed and Jackson's eyes pinged open.

'Hi, Dom!' he said, only for them to close again just as quickly.

She released a long breath that she hadn't been aware she'd been holding and they both smiled at each other. Baxter's ears must have pricked up and he started barking loudly and sniffing at the door. They could also hear Maud meowing to tell him to shut up.

'Bye then,' she said in a whisper.

'Bye,' he replied before turning and walking back home.

Chapter 39

'Happy birthday to you,
   Happy birthday to you,
   Happy birthday, dear Jackson,
   Happy birthday to you!'
Jackson's eyes sparkled as he looked at the faces of the people he loved most surrounding him as they sang. Lucy was holding the huge dinosaur cake in front of him and he blew out all nine candles with one puff. Everybody cheered, to his delight. They were upstairs in the Signal Box Café again. They had laid on a little spread for him. He was going bowling later with a few friends to celebrate but this was just a family thing straight after school.

Grandad told him to close his eyes and he giggled as he did as he was told. When he opened them he saw a bike-shaped present, all wrapped up, which Grandad had been hiding in the bar area. He squealed as he ran to it and jumped on it to ride even with the wrapping still on it. 'Don't forget your helmet,' said Violet as she handed it to him.

'Thanks, Gran and Grandad, I love it. I can take turns riding this one day and the scooter off Mummy the next.'

They all turned to the staircase as they heard footsteps and a deep voice asking for the birthday boy.

'Dom,' shouted Jackson, 'I've got a bike and a dinosaur cake – look.' He grabbed Dom's hand and dragged him over to the huge cake.

Lucy's heart went into overdrive when she saw him and she busied herself with a cloth wiping the already spotless table, hoping that nobody would notice her flaming cheeks.

Dom handed Jackson a parcel, which he tore open in double quick time.

'A Liverpool kit,' he cheered and put the top on over what he was wearing.

'There's an envelope in there too,' said Dom.

Jackson retrieved the envelope from the discarded wrapping paper and ripped it open.

'Some tickets to see Liverpool play. Yay,' he shouted, jumping up and down.

'What do you say to Dom?' said Lucy her face still turned away from them all as she scrubbed at an imaginary stubborn mark on the table.

'Thanks, Dom, I've never been to a football match before.'

A smiling Dom ruffled his hair then spoke to Dougie. 'I've got two mates with season tickets as well, so they sold me theirs for this game. I thought me, you and Jackson could go together.'

'That sounds great, son, thank you,' replied Dougie.

'And there's something else.' Dom turned back to Jackson. 'You won't believe this, but you get to meet your favourite player before the game.' Jackson fake collapsed on the floor and made everybody laugh.

After opening more presents from Abbie – a huge remote control dinosaur – and from Rosie – a camera – they extended one of the booths by adding an extra table to it and some of the loose chairs so they were all able to sit together to eat the delicious cake.

'It's so well made it seems such a shame to cut it,' said Lucy, still avoiding Dom's eyes, as she handed him a paper plate. His hands touched hers fleetingly, which sent shock waves through her body. She could almost hear the crackle of electricity. The sudden reaction was felt by both it seemed, as their eyes met just for a second. She quickly looked away and went to get more drinks for everybody.

When she returned to the room, Jackson was sitting on Dom's knee and they were playing a complicated game on his phone. Their heads were close together and bowed down to look at the screen. They were both very animated as the game got more exciting. Lucy was looking at them wistfully and as she looked away, she saw her grandad watching her. He mouthed, *'Are you okay?'* and she nodded.

Jackson's birthdays were always bittersweet for her. On the one hand she cherished the memory of the day her precious boy was born and on the other was the memory of not having the joy of sharing him with the man who helped create him. She'd answered another question about him the other day. Jackson had asked what he did as a job, but he wasn't very impressed when she told him he was a teacher.

'It's nowhere near as good as an astronaut is it, Mum?' he'd said, and then carried on playing with his Lego.

She was collecting all the wrapping paper from the floor, lost in her own thoughts, when she heard someone calling her. 'Lucy . . . Lucy . . . Lu.' It was Dom, he and Jackson were still looking down at the phone. 'Jackson wants to know if he can come for a run with me on a Saturday.'

If only he knew what it did to her when he called her Lu; it was so affectionate and turned her legs to jelly.

'But he'd never be able to keep up,' she replied.

'No, I'll be on my new bike, silly,' added Jackson.

'Oh, I see, well yes – only if you don't mind, Dom.' He took his eye off the screen to smile at her. She could get used to this. His smile was sexy; like a special treat only for her.

Jackson groaned and pulled Dom's face down to look at the screen.

'No, Dom, stop looking at Mummy – you just lost a life.'

'But I like looking at Mummy.' Dom's lips turned upwards at the corners and he winked at her.

She flushed crimson; she had to admit, she liked him looking at her too.

Grandad, Violet and Abbie looked at each other and smiled knowingly.

Chapter 40

'He gets it in the back of the net, and he scores.' Jackson kicked the ball hard and pulled his Liverpool top over his head to run around for a celebration. Except he could hear the ball bouncing down the entry. His shoulders tensed. Realising he'd kicked it over the gate again he pulled his head out of his top and reached up the gate to release the top lock.

Lucy heard him from the kitchen and shouted out the back door, 'Make sure you put that top lock back on, Jackson, as we don't want Baxter getting out again.'

'I will, Mum.'

'I think he must have been going through the bins too, as I keep finding it toppled over or bits of rubbish lying around.'

'Okay, Mum.'

He did as he was told and then his mum called him for his dinner. As he sat eating and swinging his legs his eyes didn't move from the new framed picture, of him with his favourite Liverpool player. It was his prized possession and he'd now decided that that's what he wanted to be when he grew up. It stood next to another picture of him holding hands with Dom dressed as an astronaut; both pictures held such special memories for him and the kids at school no longer picked on him.

Lucy had had an extremely busy but satisfying day. Two new viewings for the Signal Box Café had resulted in bookings and she'd had three appointments with couples who had already booked. She loved showing new people around the place as she absorbed the delight she could see on their faces when they realised they've found their perfect venue. She was still so unbelievably proud of her achievement and that showed in her work. Not many wedding planners had created their own wedding venue. Her job was hard, and she hardly ever had a free moment, but it was also immensely satisfying and as long as she could still manage to work it around Jackson she was happy.

She knew she had grown as a mum too. Whereas before she felt that she had to do everything with Jackson herself, she had now realised that it was good for him to have experiences with other people. He loved spending time with Grandad, Violet, Dom, Abbie and Rosie, and he brought a lot of joy to them as well. Seeing them with him made her heart swell. Especially Dom. Lucy could see that Jackson really looked up to him and had brought out Dom's fun side, which only his mates, or Grandad, in fact most people but her, ever got to see.

Rosie had become a dear friend who loved Jackson too and he adored her. She had taken him to the zoo and the cinema and was always treating him to books, comics and sweets. Lucy felt so grateful; because her job involved a lot of weekend work, she knew she would be lost without her family and close friends.

She finished washing the dinner dishes and helped Jackson finish off the drying.

'I've just noticed your glasses aren't slipping down anymore. I must have tightened them very well this time.' She jokingly flexed her muscles.

Jackson picked up a bowl and placed it on the worktop so he could dry it. He made it look so awkward and Lucy wanted to snatch it off him and dry it in two seconds flat but she knew she had to be patient, as he needed to learn. She remembered standing in the very same spot helping or probably hindering her nana with the washing up.

'No, Mum, it was Dom. He's extraordinarily strong. He tightened them with Grandad's little screwdriver.'

'He's done a good job,' she said, drifting into her imagination where she remembered those strong arms holding her as they danced, then effortlessly picking her tired son up and still holding on to her.

She poured herself a glass of wine and took her daydreams to the living room where she curled up on the couch and recalled every moment with him, from the dancing to the almost-kiss on the doorstep. Just the thought of it sent a ripple of desire through her body.

She was disturbed from her reverie by the sound of her mobile ringing. She saw the name on the screen and a heat rose through her whole body.

'Dom, how are you?'

'I'm good thanks. Are you watching the local news?'

'No, why?' Her voice rose sharply.

'Put it on now. I'm on my way over.'

He hung up and she sat there staring at the phone. He was coming over. She jumped up and looked at her face closely in the mirror. She had looked smart this morning but now her hair was up in a scruffy pony and she had mascara round her eyes. She was torn between putting the news on, as he'd said, and quickly running upstairs to shower, change and put a whole new face of make-up on. She thought she should put the news on first, as he seemed to think it was urgent.

Grabbing a tissue, she dipped it in her glass of water and wiped under her eyes. Sitting there open-mouthed she couldn't quite believe what she was seeing.

The reporter and film crew were in Sycamore Lodge interviewing Mrs King.

'I have had trouble with these particular former residents before, but I never expected them to do something like this – it's totally outrageous,' she said still obviously sucking on the plum in her mouth.

The reporter spoke to the camera as he walked down the corridor. 'Apparently residents of Sycamore Lodge are up in arms over Jeffrey and Martha Peate, a married couple who are not allowed to have a room together. Sadly, Martha has terminal cancer and her only wish is that she is able to cuddle up to her husband at night. Here's Martha and Jeffrey's daughter Mirabelle.' He held the mike to the nervous middle-aged woman's mouth.

'Mirabelle, how do you feel about your mum and dad not being together?'

Mirabelle was a bag of nerves; her hands shook as she held her petition up. Her voice crumbled as she spoke. 'I've started this petition in the local town and we've got hundreds of signatures from people who care. It wouldn't be that much of a hardship to move them in together. We've tried to find other accommodation but there are no places anywhere and we only have a one-bedroomed flat, otherwise we would have had them living with us. They've had to sell their house just to pay for the fees here.' Her tears started to flow thick and fast. 'We sadly don't know how long my mum has left.' She held the tissue to her eyes and said, 'I'm sorry, I can't,' and waved the camera away.

'Thank you, Mirabelle, we do hope you get the outcome you want for your lovely mum and dad.' He walked into one of the bedrooms and Lucy's jaw dropped as she saw a naked couple squeezed into a single bed, thankfully covered up to the armpits by white cotton sheets. The doorbell rang so she paused the TV and ran to let Dom in.

'Have you seen it yet?' He rushed into the house.

'Just paused it.' He stood in the living room doorway and she threw herself back on the couch and pressed play. The camera was zoomed in on a large white placard the couple were holding, on which was daubed in thick black paint, 'Give the Peates a chance,' and then in smaller writing 'for love,' with a red heart painted next to it.

The camera zoomed out and focused on the couple and despite the John Lennon glasses and John and Yoko wigs they were both wearing, there was no denying who the naked pensioners were. Just at that moment Jackson walked in.

'Why are Gran and Grandad on the telly?' He then did a double take. 'And why are they naked?'

The reporter was now talking to Grandad. 'So, Mr Woods, can you let the viewers know exactly what you are hoping to achieve with this protest.'

Grandad leant his head nearer to the mike and spoke into it. 'I wanted to help Jeffrey and Martha, who have become very dear friends of ours. They love each other and are very affectionate. They've been married for over fifty-five years so why should they be apart now at possibly the most important stage of their lives when they need each other the most?

'We are newly-weds and lucky for us we don't have someone telling us that we can't share a bed so we decided to stage this "love-in" and we will not be moved until Sycamore Lodge give the Peates a chance, for love.' They lifted up their placard in unity and made peace signs with their fingers.

The reporter pulled the mike back to himself. 'So, as you can see this is quite an emotive argument and heart-breaking for the Peate family. If you would like to sign the petition we've put it on our website.' He was then interrupted by the rest of the residents who filed into the room and gathered either side of the bed. They were singing along to a ghetto blaster, which was playing the John Lennon song 'Give Peace a Chance', but they replaced 'Peace' with 'the Peates'. Every one of them was naked and holding a placard with the same message on and a lit candle. Three of the pensioners were holding a banner between them and at one point they held it a little too high, revealing something they shouldn't of the short man in the middle. This was pixelated out on later reruns.

Lucy pressed record on her TV as she wanted to keep this forever; she was too stunned at the moment to laugh. Although more than a little embarrassed she also felt immensely proud of her grandad for standing up for what he believed in. She turned the TV off and put her shoes on.

'Come on, Jackson,' she said grabbing his scooter and along with Dom they made their way to the home.

'We've got to try and talk them out of it,' said Dom as they hurried along.

'No, we can't do that. They really believe in this, Dom, and if we try and talk them out of it then we will just undermine what they're trying to do.'

'But it's embarrassing for my gran to be naked on the telly. I must say though of all the things I worried about when Mum and Dad left me to look after her interests, I hadn't ever imagined a scenario like this.'

'Oh don't worry, Dom, at least it's only the local news and most of the locals will be related to one of these naked pensioners.' They looked at each other and laughed; what a crazy, fun pair their grandparents were. They had to stop walking as Lucy was literally bent over double in hysterics and Dom was throwing his head back. He was now laughing at her laughing. They almost calmed down and were able to take another step when they heard Jackson singing and repeating the line over and over again.

'All we are saying, is give the Peates a chance.'

They cracked up again and Lucy just hoped that she didn't wet herself. It was a struggle to make the short journey as every now and then one of them would giggle again and that would set the other one off. When they arrived, Dom took one look around the car park and looked back at Lucy.

'What was that you were saying about the news staying local?'

Lucy threw her hands to her face to cover her open mouth; the car park was full of vans with satellite dishes on them from Sky News to every newspaper imaginable.

There was a flurry of people at the door as reporters and camera operators tried to push their way in. Dom picked up Jackson in a piggyback and grabbed Lucy's hand; he then forced his way through the throng and into the bedroom where all the pensioners were still singing their song and swaying with their candles.

The reporter was still talking to Grandad. 'So, Mr Woods, where did you get the idea to stage this "love-in"?'

'Well I was sitting in a lovely little café boat just along the river there – it's called Serendipity, you really should try it. It's run by a lovely lady called Rosie and her scones are amazing. Anyway, I was sitting there with my grandson Jackson over there.' He pointed and waved to Jackson who had jumped into an armchair in the corner of the room. The camera zoomed in on him; he looked up from the game he was playing on Dom's phone, smiled and waved back. The camera then focused back on Grandad again.

'I had been trying to think how I could help Jeffrey and Martha, when I heard the song playing and remembered when John and Yoko stood up or should I say lay down for what they believed in. Too many people write old people off and that's simply not fair. We still have the same thoughts and feelings that we always had, and we still love and need to feel loved. Keeping this couple apart is a crime in my eyes, a heartless crime.' Everybody cheered.

While the filming had stopped for a bit, Dom used the opportunity to speak to his gran. He found it strange looking into her face with the John Lennon shades and long black wig and he tried hard to forget that she was naked.

'Gran, come on I think you've made your point now; let's get you home.'

'That's the most sensible thing I've heard today, Mr Cavendish. These people are wasting our time and money and making a huge fuss over nothing,' shouted Mrs King from the doorway.

His gran beckoned him closer and whispered in his ear, 'Remember just before I lost Grandad, I wanted to spend every last minute with him? Can you envisage how we would've felt if somebody tried to keep us apart? It's simply too heart-breaking to contemplate.' Although Dom couldn't see her eyes behind the glasses, he could see the tears rolling down her cheeks. She continued, 'This is not a huge fuss about nothing; this means something to each and every one of us here. Imagine how you would feel if Jeffrey and Martha were me and your grandad.' Dom squeezed his gran's hand.

Mrs King continued, 'As a responsible law professional, I think you should be trying to talk some sense into that pair of troublemakers. I had hoped that they would never darken my doors again.'

'You're right,' said Dom 'if you wouldn't mind getting Gran a drink of water, I'll have this all sorted by the time you get back.'

'About bloody time,' she muttered under her breath on the way out.

Lucy followed her as she needed to take Jackson to the toilet.

Lucy arrived back in the room just before Dolores King and wondered why there was such a flurry of activity again. Camera flashes were going off and the reporter was talking to camera again. Mrs King entered the room with the glass of water and stood open-mouthed and slack-jawed as she found that Dominic had not brought the protest to an end and talked some sense into these ridiculous people, but was instead standing there completely butt-naked and carrying one of the spare placards that had been dotted around the place. Everybody in the room had cheered as he appeared from behind the men holding the banner and joined the protest. His gran moved her glasses down her nose and winked at him proudly.

Mrs King shouted, 'Oh really!' and stomped out of the room but not before giving Dom a sneaky quick glance up and down.

Lucy was frozen to the spot. She drew a sharp intake of breath and couldn't take her eyes off him. That handsome face with chiselled cheekbones, his gorgeous broad shoulders, smooth golden skin, a kissable smooth chest, a glimpse of the top of a six-pack and strong legs. She couldn't help but wonder what was behind that placard. The heat began to rise in her again; the memory of the feather-light brush of his warm lips on hers sent shock waves right through her. She licked her lips and eventually managed to close her mouth. He noticed her looking at him.

'Oh well, if you can't beat 'em.' He shrugged his shoulders.

Just then there was a rapping sound on the window. Lucy was the nearest and opened it. It was the manager from the local Indian restaurant.

'I saw the kerfuffle on the news and thought the residents might be hungry so we have supplied some finger food. That way they can eat with one hand and use the other to hold up their banners.'

The residents cheered and the manager climbed in the window followed by two of his staff and they went around the room with serving trays laden with onion bhajis, lamb koftas and lots of other delicious spicy nibbles. The reporter and camera crew enjoyed the food too and there was another resounding cheer when the restaurant staff passed a crate full of bottles of beer through the window. When he'd opened a bottle for everybody in the room, he lifted his up and said loudly, 'Bramblewood Spice restaurant is in full support of this campaign. "Give the Peates a chance!"'

Which everybody repeated and then swigged from their bottles. Jeffrey and Martha who were sharing a placard were thrilled that everyone had gone to so much trouble. The singing started up again. Lucy heard another knock on the window. When she saw it was Greg her lips set in a firm straight line.

'Lucy, I'm sorry but what was I supposed to say to her? I couldn't tell her the truth.'

'You could have told me the truth; you disgust me.'

'Oh, come on don't be like that,' he said. 'Let me in to take a pic. Come on, I'll get shot by my editor if I miss the biggest thing that's ever happened in this town.'

'No way,' she said, and closed the frosted window down with great satisfaction.

'Well put it this way, your secret is now not safe with me,' he shouted through the glass. She ignored him.

A few minutes later she heard another knock on the window and heard Camilla calling her; she opened it and smiled at the happy face that greeted her.

'I couldn't believe it when I saw it on the news.' She laughed. 'Your grandad is fab. Here you go; this is to show that Camilla's Cupcakes supports the love-in.' She handed over a container with a batch of cupcakes she had hurriedly decorated with 'Give the Peates a chance' in black icing with a little sugar red heart on each one and the pensioners cheered again. They were having the time of their lives although some of them were beginning to feel a bit chilly now.

Lucy passed the empty container back to Camilla and thanked her. She could see Greg talking to a contact from one of the more disreputable rags and he looked over to her. She soon forgot about that when she saw the flashing blue lights entering the car park.

'Oh shit, it's the police.' Panic and nausea kicked in. She worried for her grandad. She hurriedly shut the window again. What if he got arrested? She looked over at him and he was having a laugh with Dom, both swigging from their beer bottles.

Young Bill the policeman came in and couldn't keep his face straight. He took a cupcake he was offered and posed for photos for the cameras.

A few of the residents were now wrapped in blankets and the camera crew were packing up when a man they didn't know came into the room. He had a long thin face and a boring suit.

'Hello, everybody, my name is Mr Tidvale and I'm the owner of Sycamore Lodge. Can I ask, where are Mr and

Mrs Peate?' Jeffrey and Martha raised their hands, being careful not to drop their placard.

'Pleased to meet you,' he said, warily shaking their hands. 'I just wanted to let you know that I wasn't aware of your predicament, but I am now and as of today I will ensure that you two will be moved into the same room.'

The residents cheered and Jeffrey and Martha hugged, allowing Lucy to glimpse a little more of Jeffrey's bum than she would have liked, but she was happy for them.

The man continued, 'I have organised a double bed to be delivered in a couple of hours.' He turned to Dougie. 'Thank you for bringing this to my attention. In future I will be providing residents with my contact details and I will be visiting more regularly so that you can speak to me about any concerns you have.'

The camera crew scrambled together again so that the reporter could provide his viewers with the perfect happy ending. Jeffrey and Martha hugged Dougie and Violet, who thankfully were all wearing robes now. Lucy was sneakily watching Dom get dressed, hoping to catch a final glimpse of his chest before he covered it up again. He caught her looking and gave her a cheeky wink.

'I'm surprised you didn't join in, Lu.' He smiled.

'Well I couldn't because I was on window duty, wasn't I? Otherwise you may have missed out on beer and bhajis.'

'Talking of which, how do you fancy coming out for something to eat tonight?'

Her heart stood still. His eyes met hers and before she could answer, a gorgeous young woman entered the room.

'Ah there you are, Dominic. I just saw you on the news. When you recommended this place for my granny, I didn't realise it was quite so exciting here.'

★

'Clarissa, hi,' he replied without raising a smile.

She kissed him on both cheeks.

'As I'm in the area I thought maybe we could catch up, if you're free that is.'

'Lu?' His eyes followed her as she was being led out of the door by a sleepy Jackson. Her mouth was tense as she tried to speak.

'No, you go ahead; I've got to get Jackson back.'

He'd had visions of sitting in her cosy living room, both of them curled up on the couch, Jackson playing trains on the floor; then afterwards when he had gone to bed, he could turn her face towards him and kiss her softly at first and then more passionately. He was brought back to reality by Clarissa's shrill voice asking if he was ready to go for a drink.

Chapter 41

Lucy could hardly stem the flow of tears on the journey home and was grateful that Jackson was preoccupied by his scooter. She had been so close. Dominic Cavendish had just asked her out, and then, of all people, his ex-wife shows up. Did she want to get back with him? Violet had said she hadn't wanted children, which was one of the reasons why they'd split up so maybe she'd changed her mind. She couldn't really blame her. Dom looked so hot today and if this Clarissa had caught a glimpse of him on the news, she was probably kicking herself for letting him go.

'Why did she have to be so attractive too? Why would he even look at me with these mad curls and curves and a crazy family when he could have the very sleek and glossy Clarissa?' she muttered to herself as she walked along.

Jackson scooted ahead and arrived at the door to Railway Cottage before her. He could hear Baxter barking, his tail thudding against the wall in the hallway showing how happy he was to see them. He looked through the letterbox. Maud was sitting on her favourite stair and licking her paws coolly as Baxter jumped around.

'Hi, Baxter; hi, Maud – we're home,' he called through the letterbox.

Lucy was glad to be back. She needed to be tucked away in her little sanctuary again where no one could hurt her.

This little cottage and the Signal Box Café were places that totally relaxed her.

As soon as they got in she let Baxter out of the back door for a wee. She would take him for a longer walk later. Maud had followed him. She liked him a little more now and sometimes they curled up with each other on the living room rug.

Lucy quickly moved around the kitchen and whipped up a carbonara for their dinner. Jackson was starving as usual, so she plated it up as quickly as possible; they had ice cream for pudding.

'Mum, can I play in the garage with Grandad's special train set? I'll be really careful, I promise.'

Knowing that he got lost in his own little world in there she decided to make the most of the peace and quiet and treat herself to some 'me' time. 'Yes okay,' she shouted back to him. 'I'm going to have a nice long soak in the bath then. Can you feed Baxter please.' She ran upstairs and turned on the taps, lit a couple of candles and lined up her favourite scented cleansers and moisturisers. She popped into the bedroom to turn on some tranquil chill-out music and sighed blissfully as she slipped into the relaxing bubbles.

She picked up her phone and flicked through the news channels wondering whether there was any more on the pensioners' love-in. Indeed, there was. Watching it reminded her of laughing about it with Dom and yet she hadn't realised then how much of a starring role Dom would have. She could see herself on the screen every now and then but luckily it was only the back of her head. Ah, a close-up of Jackson waving to Grandad from the chair in the corner. She copied the link and pasted it into a message to send to Jackson. He'd love that.

She toyed with the idea of sending it to Dom. It would be a good excuse to contact him. Her finger hovered over the send button for a few seconds. 'Oh, to hell with it,' she said out loud as with a pounding heart she pressed send. Her stomach flipped at the thought of a reply.

She continued to watch it when Dom appeared on the screen. Her heart fluttered as she was reminded of the contours of his body. She was so proud of him; he didn't mind embarrassing himself, if he believed in something enough, but then why should he feel embarrassed? Just look at that body. She pressed pause and used her phone to take a screenshot. He was just 'wow'.

Lucy was quickly brought back to reality when her phone rang. Panicking as though the caller could see what she was up to, the phone flew out of her hand but luckily she caught it before it landed in the water. She smiled when she saw it was Abbie.

'Lucy, I've just seen the evening news; I can't stop laughing. What are our grandparents like? A naked love-in? I've heard everything now. They are so funny, but bloody hell – good for them. They managed to get what they wanted in the end. Talk about Pensioner Power. I've still got that song going through my head. "All we are saying is give the Peates a chance",' she sang before dissolving into hysterical laughter.

'Where are you?' Lucy asked, her heart thumping still from the near miss with the phone in the water and the fact that she'd been ogling Abbie's brother.

'I'm in Bath, been shooting a gorgeous wedding here for a friend. I can't believe I missed the action over there though.'

'That's weird because I'm in the bath right now.' She laughed. 'Oh, Abbie, it was the funniest thing I've ever seen. Honestly, the look on Mrs King's face surrounded by all these naked pensioners and then she thought Dom was on her side and was going to talk some sense into them, only for him to end up being naked as well.' She laughed but a secret thrill ran through her body at the same time just at the thought of him. 'Then the police arrived, and we panicked but it was just Young Bill visiting his dad after work. I'm sure there are photos of a naked old lady wearing his helmet.' Lucy howled with laughter and Abbie couldn't help but join in.

'I tried to call Dom to wind him up about it but he's not answering his phone or texts. Have you seen him?'

Lucy's stomach flipped; the mention of his name brought back flashbacks to that gorgeous hunky body. He was uncontactable so had probably gone for more than just a drink with Clarissa. Nausea swept through her at the idea of that. 'No, I haven't I'm afraid. Not since earlier when his ex-wife asked him out for a drink at Sycamore Lodge.'

'What? Clarissa?' Abbie shrieked. 'No way! I hope he told her where to go.'

'Not exactly, I think they went out together.'

'Oh my God, wait till I get my hands on him. I can't believe he would be so stupid. What's he thinking?' Abbie sounded furious.

'The thing is . . .' Lucy hesitated. She knew how Abbie felt about Dom going out with her friends, but she really needed to talk to someone about it. 'Well the thing is, just before she came into the room, he'd asked me to go for a drink.'

'And? What did you say?'

'Well that's the thing, before I could answer him, this Clarissa person just burst into the room and asked him out. He gestured to me, but I was far too embarrassed to say yes then so I just told him I had to get Jackson home. Besides . . .' She hesitated again.

'Besides what?'

'Well the thing is I remembered what you said about not wanting him to go out with your friends and you're far too important to me to lose over a silly boy.' She laughed outwardly but tears of sadness filled her eyes.

'Lucy,' replied Abbie tenderly, 'I think that ship has long since sailed, don't you?'

'I don't know what you mean.' She used her foot to turn the tap on for more hot water.

'The way you look at each other, it's obvious you've both fallen head over heels, caught the love bug, are into each other, whichever way you want to say it.'

Lucy felt the flush rise up from her toes right up her body until her cheeks were aflame. 'Don't be silly,' she said, feeling bashful.

'I've never seen him look at anyone the way he looks at you,' Abbie admitted. 'And, Lucy, you're my best friend and always will be. But if you feel you need my blessing to date my brother then you have it, even if it feels a bit icky to me. You're quite obviously perfect for each other. Unlike him and the she-devil.'

Lucy bit her bottom lip and grinned inanely.

'You're smiling like a loon, aren't you?' Abbie laughed. 'I can hear it.'

'How can you hear a smile?' She chuckled.

'I just can. You are though, aren't you?'

'I might be, but anyway while I'm glad I can finally admit I've had a crush on your annoying brother forever, I guess it doesn't matter now because he seems to be back with Clarissa.' Her heart sunk.

'There is no way on earth that I will let that happen. Don't you worry about that. Anyway, I must go. I just want to see if I can catch the news again and show Dave what sort of family he is marrying into. Ooops!'

'What's all this? You're engaged?'

'Not yet but we've talked about it and we're going to go shopping for a ring soon. I'm not supposed to say anything. It's so exciting.'

'Oh congratulations, I'm so happy for you both. I'll see you soon. Love you. Bye.'

'I love you too. Bye.'

Lucy clicked the phone off and put it on the side of the sink. Her heart felt full of joy for Abbie and Dave, but she was sad at the thought of how close she'd come with Dominic only for his horrible but beautiful ex to get in the way.

After another half an hour of blissful soaking, three more hot water top-ups and just her own private thoughts for company, Lucy got out of the bath, put on her pyjamas and fluffy dressing gown and went down to check on Jackson. She put the kettle on to make him a hot chocolate. 'That's odd,' she thought on seeing Baxter's food still in his bowl. Normally he gobbled it up straight away.

'Jackson, it's time for your shower and supper,' she called as she headed down the garden to the garage. 'Is Baxter in there wi . . .' She opened the door to find the room empty, the only sound the buzzing of the train set as it chugged along the track. A flash of panic pulled at each of her nerve endings. 'Jackson, where are you?' She looked under the table, nothing. She walked around the table. It was as if her eyes were playing tricks on her and not letting her see him, but that was ridiculous; he had to be here. He must have gone to his room.

She raced to the house and pounded up the stairs calling his name. The silence was deafening. She flung open the door of every room, opened her window to look outside but there was no sign of him or Baxter. Jackson's phone was on his bedside charging and his coat was still hanging up in the hall. 'Jackson, are you playing hide-and-seek?' she called. 'If you are, then congratulations you've won, and you can have some sweets. Come on, Baxter needs to eat his dinner.'

There was no answer. Normally at this stage she would hear giggling. She grabbed her coat, pushed her feet into her trainers and ran into the garden again. The gate, although closed over was not locked. Adrenaline raced round her body as she ran down the entry. The streetlights glowed yellow against a navy sky. She hammered on her neighbour's door. An old man answered. Lucy's heart was beating in her throat. 'Mr Smith, I'm so sorry to bother you but have you seen my little boy? He's not at home. I was in the bath. He was playing with the trains in Grandad's garage, and now he's gone and so's the dog,' she garbled, nausea overwhelming her.

'I'm sorry, love, I haven't seen him. How long has he been missing for?'

Lucy broke down crying. 'I'm a terrible mum. I d-d-don't know.' She sobbed.

'Now that's not true – your grandad is always telling me what a great mum you are. Would you like to come in for a cup of tea while we think of what to do? In fact, no, let me take you back home just in case he comes back. Maybe he's taken the dog for a walk.'

Lucy allowed him to walk her back to Railway Cottage. She hadn't got her keys, so they went in the back way. The kettle had just boiled so Mr Smith poured the tea and put it in front of Lucy.

'So, when was the last time you saw him?' he asked kindly.

Lucy checked her watch, her hands were trembling. 'About an hour ago, I got in the bath and my friend called.

273

Jackson wanted to play with the train set. I thought he'd be safe.'

'I'm sure he is safe – maybe he's taken the dog out for a walk, popped to the shops or something.'

Lucy shook her head. 'No he wouldn't, not in the dark and not without asking first.' She was adamant about that.

'Okay so first of all call everyone you can think of that he's close to and we'll see if he's gone to one of them.'

Lucy thought that was a good idea and fumbled with her phone. She tried to call her grandad, but it was like she had lost control of her fingers and she kept pressing the wrong numbers.

'Stupid phone,' she screamed and threw it to the floor. She jumped up from the kitchen chair. 'This is wasting time. I need to go out and find him.'

Mr Smith put his hand gently on her arm. 'Let's just try this before you go rushing off on a wild goose chase, because when Jackson turns up, he's going to want his mum here.' He retrieved Lucy's phone and dialled her grandad's number as she paced the floor; she could hear one side of the conversation but felt in a dream-like state as though she were in a bubble.

'Hi, Dougie, no Lucy's fine. It's George from next door. It seems little Jackson and Baxter have gone missing; Lucy is obviously worried, and we just wondered whether you'd seen him? Ah okay. About an hour ago. Okay, see you soon. Bye.' He turned to Lucy. 'Your grandad has just got home and he's on his way round now.'

'Has he got Jackson?' She fired the question at him, clutching on to hope with both hands as though it were a life raft.

The old man's face was filled with sympathy. 'I'm sorry, love, he hasn't seen him but when he gets here, I'm going to call round to a friend of ours who has access to CCTV from the station. Your grandad and I used to work with him.' Lucy nodded at him, a glimmer of optimism in her tear-filled eyes. 'Now can you think of anyone else he might have gone to?'

'Rosie from Serendipity – he loves her, and she loves him. He sometimes pops to see her in the daytime.' Mr Smith handed her the phone and she managed to dial Rosie's number; with a trembling voice she explained the situation. Lucy looked at Mr Smith and shook her head. Mr Smith dialled 999 without hesitation.

Rosie hadn't seen him and was eager to do whatever she could to help. Lucy had declined her offer to come round and sit with her but Rosie had a brainwave.

'Why don't I put it on the community Facebook group?'

'Yes please,' Lucy croaked. 'We need all the help we can get.' Lucy texted her other friends that Jackson knew, and her phone was soon buzzing with replies, but nobody had seen him. Rosie sent a text saying that she had posted on the local page and on the 'pets lost and found' one and would be sure to let her know if anyone commented.

Grandad arrived with Violet. Lucy sobbed into her grandad's chest and he held her tight. Violet busied about the kitchen making tea. Mr Smith told Dougie he was going to check the CCTV. Dougie thanked him.

'The only person I haven't checked with is Dom,' said Lucy. 'Was he home?'

'No, love, I haven't seen him but then Violet and I have only just got back in as we went out with Jeffrey and Martha for a celebratory meal. Maybe he's taken Jackson for a burger or something?'

'Not without telling me, Grandad – I think he's learnt his lesson from last time.'

Her phone buzzed into life. 'It's a text from Rosie. Apparently there's been a sighting of Baxter round by the school.' Lucy threw her coat back on and made for the door.

Her grandad pulled her back gently. 'No, love, you have to stay here. I'll go. Don't worry too much; I'm sure he'll be fine, especially if there has been a sighting. I'm not having you wandering about in the dark though, so I'll go looking for him and you stay home in case he comes back.'

'That's not fair on you, Grandad. I can go. I'll be fine.'

'I'm not having my granddaughter traipsing around country lanes in the night. I'll go and I'll text you when I'm on my way back so you can get the kettle on. Is that a deal?'

'Deal,' she said. 'Hold on.' She rushed into the hall and grabbed Jackson's warm coat. She gave it to her grandad. 'Hurry up and bring him back to me please, Grandad.'

'I will, darling,' he replied and kissed her on the cheek. Realising there was nothing she could do for the time being she flicked through pictures of Jackson on her phone, stroking his beautiful happy face. It was lovely of Grandad to feel protective of her and she knew he was only doing it for the best but ultimately it was her responsibility and she didn't like the idea of other people clearing up her mess. She just felt so helpless. Her phone rang as she was holding it. It was Rosie.

'Fab news, Lucy, there's another comment. The people who live in the house next to the school have found Baxter and he is curled up comfortably in their house awaiting collection. His dog tag had broken off, so they hadn't been able to ring.'

'What about Jackson?' Her voice was high-pitched.

'I'm sorry no but they're out searching for him too.'

'Thank you so much, Rosie. I love you. Grandad is heading that way, so I'll call him now. Baxter knows that walk so well because I often take him to pick Jackson up. I'm going to pop in and see you tomorrow with a huge bottle of wine.'

'Oh, you don't have to do that I'm just glad I could help.'

'Please thank them.'

'I will and don't worry – Jackson will be fine. He's a sensible boy.'

Lucy was called Grandad with the news, and he was glad to receive it.

'I'm right outside that house now, Lucy. I'll be back soon.'

She crept up the stairs to Jackson's bedroom and climbed into his bed; sobbing into the pillow. She wished this nightmare would end.

Violet called her back down as Dougie was back. She opened the door and let him in with a very naughty and bouncy dog who was happy to be home. She dropped to her knees and cuddled him, allowing him to lick her face; his wagging tail thudded against the hall wall noisily. He then rolled onto his back so she could tickle his belly. Maud looked him up and down from her position on the bottom stair as if to say, 'Stop embarrassing yourself.' Grandad kissed the top of Lucy's head.

A police car had just pulled up outside. Two young officers came into the house, and introduced themselves as PC Doyle and PC Carver. They were very patient with Lucy and asked for the details of her son. When they requested a recent photo, she broke down crying. She thought of all the other missing children, some of whom had never come home, and who would forever be remembered by that photo. In the end she gave them the school photo that was on the mantelpiece.

Lucy sent texts to Rosie and Finn and Gracie to update them on the news that Baxter had been found. They were all on the lookout.

The police looked at the CCTV that Mr Smith had got hold of. They saw Baxter bounding out of the entry about an hour and a half ago, and then five minutes later Jackson came flying out too. Lucy's knees were knocking together. Her legs were like jelly. 'Baxter's gone right, which would make sense as it's towards the school, but Jackson's gone left, either to the high street or the river.'

She called Rosie. 'We think he's gone towards the river way; it looks like he was looking for Baxter but went the wrong way.'

As they rewound the tape the policewoman noticed something. 'Wait, stop there. Who's that?' At two o'clock in the morning a hooded figure could be seen creeping into the entry and ten minutes later creeping back out again.

'I've blamed Jackson for leaving the gate open, but it wasn't him, it was this intruder. Who is it and what do they want? It's him, isn't it, Grandad? It's Jackson's dad. This time he's finally come for him.' Dougie grabbed her hand and squeezed.

The police asked her about Jackson's dad, and she gave them as many details as she could. She had no idea where he lived or whether he still worked at the school.

Searching for clues as to who the intruder was, the police managed to pick up a distinctive glow-in-the-dark logo on the backs of his shoes. Their research showed that they were quite expensive and could only be bought in Malta.

Finn had sent a message to say he was going along the river in their boat to see if there was any sign of him along the towpath. Police were stopping people along the high street and showing them the picture of Jackson, but nobody had seen him.

The house rocked with the throbbing sound of a helicopter above. The policeman spoke to her with kindness. 'Don't worry, Lucy, we will find him. We have officers searching everywhere. In the meantime if you can think of anywhere he could possibly be, then do let us know.'

The pain of her nails digging into her skin from fists clenched in anguish forced her to realise that this wasn't a nightmare; it was real life. Instead of pacing the floor she wanted to be out there herself searching for her precious son, but the police assured her she was better off here in case he came home. The policewoman was eagle-eyed, a comforting presence hiding an underlying suspicion, watching her every move, looking out for clues to rule out her involvement in her son's disappearance. She'd watched enough cop shows to know that the parents were often under suspicion. After all she herself suspected his dad.

She had cried all her tears and was now sitting there numb. A sensation of nothingness washed over her. Each limb felt heavy and powerless; she felt paralysed. One of the officers covered her in a blanket as her whole body shook.

Violet was busying herself making tea for everybody, as they waited for news.

Chapter 42

Dominic Cavendish knew when he was being played and he knew that Clarissa was trying to play him right now. After not hearing from her in a couple of years since the divorce, she got back in touch with him recently asking about Sycamore Lodge for her gran. He hadn't recommended it to her but had simply told her that was where his gran was living. Since then she kept ringing him. She was after something; he just didn't know what yet.

He found out when they went for a drink after the love-in. She wanted to get back together with him. He told her that it was out of the question. He could never put up with her whining again; she thought of no one but herself. She'd obviously discovered that there weren't many men who would put up with her, which is why she was coming for him again. Dominic didn't believe in going back and he'd told her so this evening. He suspected she was more interested in his money than him and wasn't prepared to spend any more time being miserable. He saw brighter, happier things in his future; he cursed her for buggering up his attempt at asking Lucy out on a date. That was such bad timing.

Lucy was light years away from Clarissa. She was self-sufficient, creative, strong and funny – everything Clarissa wasn't. Clarissa had been handed everything on a plate and yet still felt she deserved more, whereas Lucy worked hard for everything she had. She had made a wonderful life for her son single-handedly and never expected anything from anybody. They were both beautiful, but Clarissa's beauty was a bit too forced and Lucy's came naturally. He thought about the cute way her nose crinkled when she smiled.

He only stayed for one drink with Clarissa and then wished her luck and happiness in her future, which would be without him.

As much as he wanted to, he didn't feel as though he could go to see Lucy because Jackson had been exhausted, so he decided to go fishing instead, which would help him relax. He gathered all of his fishing stuff together and made his way along the river to the lake. A few of his friends were already settled around there so he cracked open a can of beer, switched off his phone and looked forward to a night of total peace, doing nothing but star gazing and hopefully catching the odd fish.

His thoughts travelled back to Lucy and Jackson again and the time when Baxter stole his fish then dragged Jackson through the mud. That poor kid was filthy, and he ran like the wind to get away from him. He must have thought he was a right miserable git. He couldn't even deny it; that's exactly what he was quite a lot of the time.

A little later on he woke up from a short nap that he'd taken on the camp bed in his fishing tent. He could see his rod pulling and managed to fish out a fairly decent-sized carp. He put it in his net. A child's voice broke the silence: 'Excuse me.'

Dom heard one of his mates asking what was wrong.

'Have you seen a dog? His name's Baxter and he's lost.'

Dom jumped up. 'Jackson,' he called out. 'What are you doing here?'

'Oh, erm we're looking for Baxter.' He shone his Batman torch into Dom's face. Dom shielded his eyes.

'Who are you with?'

Jackson looked around to give himself some thinking time.

'Erm. My friend's dad! Have you seen Baxter?'

'No, I haven't. You look cold and tired, Jackson – here, put this on.' He took off his jumper and put it on the boy. It came to his knees.

'When did he go missing?'

'Ages ago – Mummy always shouts at me for leaving the gate open. I don't think I did but if I did then it's my fault if Baxter gets run over or falls in the river,' he garbled tearfully.

'I'm sure that won't happen. He'll turn up – you wait and see.'

Jackson went to walk off again. Dom stood up and grabbed his hand. 'Your hands are freezing and shaking – here, sit down.' He sat him on his camp bed, wrapped his sleeping bag around him and poured him a cup of hot tea from his flask. 'Now you get yourself warmed up and then we'll find your friend's dad; he'll be worrying about you.' He handed him half a packet of biscuits.

'No, he won't. It's fine. He said I can look for Baxter. I need to find him.' He sobbed.

Their voices were drowned out by the sound of the police helicopter flying a mile or so away, its spotlight shining along the river. Dom had an uneasy sensation in the pit of his stomach and turned his phone on; he had his arm around Jackson and was rubbing him to warm him up. When his phone pinged into life, he could see twenty texts and dozens of missed calls. He dialled Lucy's number and looked into Jackson's face.

'There is no friend's dad is there?'

Jackson shook his head, crying inconsolably now. Lucy's number was engaged so he tried again.

'I'm sorry, I know I promised no more lies but I kept my fingers crossed so I could have an emergency one if I needed it,' he said between sobs. 'Baxter disappeared when I put his dinner in the bowl. I was playing with my trains. When I looked for him, I saw the gate was open. I ran after him as fast as I could but I can't find him.'

Dom pulled him onto his knee and hugged him tightly.

Lucy answered the phone. 'Jackson's missing,' she shrieked.

'He's not,' he said calmly. 'I've got him, Lucy; he's fine.'

Chapter 43

It was gone midnight by the time the police had left; they had sent a car to pick up Jackson and Dom as the lake was closer to the next town along. The welcoming committee of Lucy, Grandad, Violet, Baxter and Maud shed many tears, provided lots of cuddles and many wags of the tail and purrs. Dom had told Jackson that Baxter was fine, but he didn't quite believe it until he saw him with his own eyes.

Lucy's eyes filled with love as she saw her precious son and their beloved pet curled up with each other on the couch. She could hardly tell where one ended and the other began. Grandad and Violet had gone home, and Dom had stayed because Jackson hadn't wanted him to leave his side since they came back. After Jackson had fallen asleep Dom stood up to go.

'I'd better leave you to it,' he said quietly although he was reluctant to leave this cosy house. 'Shall I pop Jackson upstairs for you?'

Lucy was physically and mentally exhausted. 'If you don't mind that would be great, I'll keephim off school tomorrow, he's shattered.. Can I get you a coffee or a wine or anything?' She didn't want him to go.

Dom hadn't expected that. 'A wine sounds good if you're having one,' he replied. He unfurled Jackson from a snoring

Baxter and carried him upstairs. Lucy kissed his head tenderly as he passed.

He took the boy up the stairs and laid him in his bed, took his glasses off, folded them and placed them on his bedside table next to his dinosaur collection.

When he came back into the living room Lucy was sitting on the couch and had put his wine on the coffee table next to hers. Baxter was now in his bed, so Dom sat next to her on the couch.

'I can't thank you enough for finding him, Dom; if anything had happened to him, I wouldn't have been able to carry on.' Her voice cracked as she spoke. 'For the last nine years he has been my whole life. I wouldn't want to be here without him.' She started to weep.

Dom put his wine down and pulled her into his strong arms, the same solid arms that he had carried her son into the house with, had held him for hours until he fell asleep with his dog and had just carried him up to bed. He stroked her curls back from her face tenderly.

'Jackson was telling me the story of how Baxter came into your life, whilst we were in the police car. I can't believe someone just abandoned him.'

'Oh yes, he loves Baxter's story. I used to tell him it every night. One day when Jackson was only two, we heard a noise as we walked past a bush and found a little ball of fluff wriggling round in this old sack. We took him to the vet, and he was so lovely. He checked him over and put him on a drip overnight. We visited the next day and couldn't part with him. We all fell in love with each other. We didn't have any money but Mr Baxter, the vet, didn't charge us a thing. Of course, we never realised how big he was going to grow.'

She yawned. The day had been wrought with every emotion and exhaustion overwhelmed her. Feeling warm and safe in his embrace, she snuggled into his neck, sniffling every now and then. He stroked her hair gently. Her nerve endings were tingling in her head as he stroked and shivers ran down her spine. His neck was so warm and inviting and his skin smelt so good, she wanted to stay there forever. She couldn't help herself but found her lips pressing against the skin of his neck in a gentle kiss. She froze for a second wondering if he'd noticed. He had.

He held her face, his fingers in her hair and his thumbs lightly caressing her cheeks. His grey eyes sparkled with longing.

His eyes found hers and stared deeply into them. They were still full of tears. He was as mesmerised by her as was she with him. He broke the eye contact but only so he could focus on her beautiful mouth.

'What about Clarissa?' she whispered.

'Clarissa who?' he replied. He couldn't resist a moment longer and crushed her lips with his own.

Her hand reached for his perfect cheekbones and she stroked his handsome face, not quite believing she could touch him. His tongue found hers and little tremors of desire coursed through their bodies. They knew this wasn't the right time to go any further so they both enjoyed the moment for what it was, a mixture of relief, longing and desire.

Dom never wanted the kiss to end but he soon realised it would have to when he felt her tears on his cheek.

'Hey, come on, Lu, it's all fine. He's home and safe; you can stop worrying now.' He wiped the tears from one eye with his thumb and kissed away the others. Soft kisses as delicate as a butterfly's wings.

'I know, I'm sorry, it's just that I thought he'd come for him again.' She sniffed and pulled a tissue from the box on the coffee table.

Dom handed her the glass of wine and picked up his.

'Do you want to talk about it, as you can't keep on living in fear of this guy. If he's been violent or abusive then I can help. We could try to get an injunction against him or something?'

'No it's nothing like that and in fact the police had to get in touch with him to make sure he didn't have Jackson and he's on holiday abroad with his wife apparently, so they'd ruled him out of their enquiries pretty much straight away. The thing is, he didn't know I had Jackson and now probably thinks I'm a rubbish mum.'

She took a deep breath and a gulp of wine. Dom sat back and pulled her into his arms with her head resting on his chest.

'Talk to me,' he said softly.

Lucy opened up the dam and let out all the hurt and disappointment that had built up over the last nine years. Her body racked with sobs, shook with anger and cried tears of sadness and joy as the memories of the relationship she'd had with her ex came flooding back.

'I was at college studying business. Jack Archer was a lecturer leading on a few projects in our department. I had such a crush on him. I was so confident then.' She smiled. 'Flirty and full of fun. He offered to tutor me as I struggled a bit with maths and then I'm sure you've heard it all before. It's a cliché as old as the hills but basically one thing led to another. Obviously, we had to keep everything quiet, but I swear if I'd known he was in a relationship then I wouldn't have dreamt of going near him.' She looked into Dom's eyes. He urged her to go on.

'He then got another job at a school, so I thought at last he's not my lecturer anymore, this is our chance to be together, but he stopped contacting me. Then I found out I was pregnant. I was terrified and I thought if I could just let him know then surely he would come back to me and we could get married and live happily ever after as a family. I mean I was nineteen. Everything seemed so black and white then.

'I eventually plucked up the courage and turned up at his school. I waited near his car and that's when I saw him, arm in arm with a woman. He spotted me and the look of horror on his face said it all. Then a teacher came running after them shouting, "Mrs Archer, you've forgotten your handbag." I ran off and threw up in a bush and that's when I realised, I'd created a fairy-tale ending in my head that was just never going to happen.'

Dom cleared his throat. 'So was that the last you saw of him?'

Lucy shifted uncomfortably in her seat; she took a sip of her drink. 'Not quite, no. A few years later when Jackson was about four, we had an open day at the hotel where I worked. They had fair rides and stuff and the local paper was there. They took a picture of Jackson and me with Jaegar Blensar – he was already something of a local celebrity and was playing for Liverpool reserves at the time. Anyway, I didn't think anything of it at the time but because they'd put our names and ages in the article, Jack saw it and put two and two together and one day out of the blue he turned up at the hotel to ask me if Jackson was his.' Lucy's heart was thumping wildly as she remembered the fear she'd felt at that time.

Dom pulled her closer to him as he felt a shiver run through her body. She snuggled into his warmth. 'Did you tell him?'

'No, I denied it, told him he wasn't the only one, even though he had been the only one ever. I knew it would make me look bad, but I didn't care. I didn't want to take the risk of losing Jackson.'

'That's completely understandable.'

'The thing is I confided in my friend there at the time. I was upset and shaking and needed to tell someone. I didn't say his name, I've never told anyone else that, but I did explain he was married. I think that stupid Greg managed to track down the photo of us, and spoken to my so called friend of mine at the hotel, they've obviously spilled the beans and that's why he accused me of being into married men. He's a sneaky little shit.' She stopped and took a deep breath, which she exhaled slowly. 'Just before I came to Bramblewood, I received a letter from Jack. He wanted a DNA test. He was talking about solicitors and everything. I was so scared. I needed to escape and the opportunity to move to Grandad's came at the perfect time. But I've now had to tell the police who he is, and they've contacted him so now he knows for definite that Jackson's his. He's passed his number to me via the police and wants me to get in touch.' She hid her face in her hands to hide her blushes.

'I bet you think I'm a hypocrite, being obsessed with weddings yet having a baby to a married man.'

He pulled her hands away from her face. 'There's nothing hypocritical about you. You didn't know he was married, and you were a young naive girl who was taken advantage of. You have to forgive yourself, Lu; you've been carrying such a burden round for nine, almost ten years. You should be so proud of yourself for all your achievements. I know I am.' They kissed long and slowly, eventually stopping so Lucy could go upstairs and check on Jackson. Dom topped up their wine. When she came back in, Maud was curled up on Dom's lap and he was stroking her.

She sat down next to him.

'Do you mind if I ask you something?'

'No, go ahead.'

'Is he a violent man?'

'Who Jack? No, he's not at all. Why?'

'I was just wondering; I'm trying to see if there's a solution to all this. Jackson is so interested in who his dad is, and I don't think that's going to go away. In fact as he gets older, I think the urge to find his dad will get stronger.'

Lucy didn't like where this conversation was heading.

Dom continued, 'I know his dad has been a real idiot in the past but as he's showing an interest in him, maybe it would be a good idea for them to meet at some point.'

Lucy jumped up and pulled away from him, Maud purred and got down from Dom's knee 'I can't believe you're on his side.'

He tried to calm her. 'No, I'm not at all and if Jackson wasn't interested in his dad then I would say absolutely don't do it, but Jackson is so obsessed with this mystery man that he is making stuff up about him. If I was you, I would have a chat with him and see how he feels about meeting him.'

'No way,' she said. 'I can't believe you would even suggest such a thing.' She put her hands on her hips and began to pace the room.

'Okay,' he said, 'I would just hate for Jackson to get older and say he didn't see his dad because you wouldn't let him.'

She shook her head. 'I know what you're saying but I just can't. You don't understand.'

'I do understand, much more than you realise. It's you who doesn't.'

'What the hell is that supposed to mean?'

'It doesn't matter – come and sit back down.' He patted the seat next to him.;.

'It does matter, tell me.'

He held his head in his hands, 'Look I don't really want to get into all this, maybe I should go.'

He looked defeated.

She placed her hands on either side of his face and kissed him softly on the lips. 'Help me to understand.'

'I just wanted to let you know what I think. You see I've been in Jackson's position.'

Lucy's eyes opened wide; this was news to her.

'I've always known that my dad wasn't my real dad. He met my mum when she was pregnant, they fell in love and he's always been there for me. However, the curiosity got worse the older I got, especially when going through the teenage years, and I would throw it in my dad's face that he wasn't my real dad. I felt I wanted, no needed to know where I came from. Eventually my mum gave in when I was seventeen and I searched for him and eventually found him.'

'What was he like?' Lucy's fingers trailed up and down his arm soothingly.

'I don't know. When I said I found him, I technically mean I found his resting place. He had died two years before.'

'I'm so sorry, Dom.'

'No, it's fine – from what I can gather he was a very ordinary man, nothing special at all. But over the years I'd built him up to superhero status. He knew about me but wasn't bothered. I then realised my other dad – Martin Cavendish – was the real superhero because he chose to look after me and I wouldn't be the man I am now without him.'

'Oh, so we have him to blame do we?' Lucy teased.

'Oi you.' He grabbed her and kissed her.

She giggled. 'I'm sorry, Dom, I never knew any of that. Thank you so much for sharing it with me.'

'I hope it helps. We're not all against you, I promise. Jackson might take one look at his dad and hate him, but you have to let it be his choice. As I said, if he was a violent man, I would never recommend he met him but as he's not, then maybe give him a chance. Anyway, no more talking, come here.' He pulled her into a kiss that made her heart race.

'Let's change the subject. So, what's all this about what your mum said that you used to fawn over Abbie's brother. What was his name again?' He put his finger to his mouth as if in thought. Lucy shrieked and grabbed a cushion to cover her face.

'Oh my God, I can't believe she said that. I think she was talking about a different Abbie with a handsome brother,' she teased.

He tickled her until she giggled.

'Admit it, go on, you fancied me ever since you were seven, didn't you?' She shrieked again, wriggling away from his hands.

'You were so horrible to me and Abbie all the time,' she replied. 'I was hoping you wouldn't recognise me. It's so embarrassing – we used to follow you everywhere.'

'I was hoping you wouldn't recognise me either. I was so mean. Do you remember when I convinced you and Abbie to play hide-and-seek and then ran off with my mates and left you?'

'Yes I do.' She laughed. 'It was in the shed and we stayed there giggling for ages thinking you'd never find us and eventually we realised you'd locked us in and we had to bang on the door and shout until your mum came to let us out.'

'What about when we challenged you girls to a water fight and we gave you tiny little water pistols and then threw buckets of water over you.'

'Yes, luckily it was a swelteringly hot day then, so we dried off quickly.' She laughed. 'We got you back though because we snitched to your mum that you were smoking down by the river.' She laughed at his shocked face.

'So that was you, was it? My mum told me that she had eyes in the back of her head and could see everything.'

'I think that was one of the last times I came to visit. Once I became a teenager I was too interested in spending time with my friends. I couldn't possibly leave them to come away and then of course I had Jackson and my life changed completely.'

'You know why I was so mean to you don't you?'

'Because you were a brat?' she suggested.

'No, because I really liked you, but was too embarrassed to let my friends know.'

'Well that's the biggest surprise of my life; I actually thought you hated me.'

'How could I hate you? I loved you with my little ten-year-old heart.'

He kissed her again and again until they eventually fell asleep in each other's arms, fully clothed on the couch.

The next morning was like a dream come true as she awoke in Dom's embrace. They were snuggled so closely together, and she didn't want to move but the alarm on his phone was going off. She made him a quick coffee and he had to rush off to work. He kissed her passionately on the doorstep before racing back to his house to get ready. Lucy felt slightly self-conscious now that she knew she was on CCTV.

After he'd gone, she went upstairs to bed exhausted. Jackson wouldn't be awake for ages. She drifted off to sleep with thoughts of Dom and their kisses still floating round her head.

Chapter 44

Mid-morning, after she'd cooked a hearty breakfast for herself and Jackson, Lucy had a phone call; Jackson was still incredibly tired so she allowed him to lie on the couch with a DVD. She couldn't quite believe her ears as the woman on the other end of the phone asked her some questions. Her hands were shaking when she hung up. She told Jackson not to move and ran to the paper shop at the station. When she returned with the newspaper, she sat in the kitchen to read it and was too dumbfounded to utter a word.

The local paper had printed a story about a local woman who had a nine-year-old love child to Jaegar Blensar, one of the best football players that Liverpool FC had ever had. The article had a picture of Jaegar posing with a young boy whose face had been pixelated out. She recognised the picture as the one on her dining room table. There was also a picture of a crumpled and rather stained letter written in the young boy's handwriting, entitled: 'The man I most admire'.

Dear Jaegar,

I really liked being with you today and one day I hope to play football just like you do. You are my hero and I hope I can see you again soon.

Also, a man got hit by you, I mean Subbuteo you, but it's okay. I told him you were my dad. I made him promise not to tell anyone.

Love XXXXXXX

The name had been crossed out. She remembered Jackson having to write the letter for school a few weeks ago and he had made a few attempts. She called into him, 'Jackson, do you remember you had to write a letter for school?'

'Yes,' he said lazily.

'Did you write it to the footballer?'

'I did but then I threw it in the bin and wrote it to someone else.'

'Who?'

'I wrote it to Dom instead because he's actually pretty cool.'

'Okay thanks.'

Now she knew who had been sneaking into their garden and going through the bins. It was a reporter, probably Greg after his big story and now he thought he'd got it and she'd nearly lost Jackson and their dog in the process. How did he have the audacity to do that? He was a perfectly good example of gutter press. She would need more proof before she could accuse him. She made herself a cup of tea so she could think of her next step.

She decided to watch the DVD from the CCTV to see if she could recognise him from that. Unfortunately, the images weren't so good and he had remained hooded throughout; then she caught a glimpse of the logo on the back of his shoe, which glowed in the dark, and this gave her an idea.

That morning she had received a text from Greg. He had been texting her a lot lately asking for another chance and practically begging her to see him. He said he couldn't stop thinking about her. She had simply been ignoring them hoping he would go away but this time she answered.

'Hi, Greg, I've been thinking about you too. Do you fancy coming round?'

She received an answer straight away.

'I was hoping you'd see sense. I'm just on my way back from the gym. I can be there in twenty.'

'Looking forward to it, x'

Next, she asked Jackson if he'd like to go to visit Grandad for a little while. He jumped up, wide awake. She ran him round in the car.

'I won't be long,' she shouted on the way out.

When she got back, she had a quick spritz of perfume and plumped up her lips with some balm. Luckily, she was quick as Greg arrived at the door in just eighteen minutes. He was wearing his gym gear but hadn't started his workout yet. He tried to kiss her as soon as he was in the door, but she slowed him down with the promise of some wine.

'You go on up and get ready; I'll bring up the drinks,' she said pressing her finger to his lips.

He kicked off his shoes and sprinted upstairs tearing at the zip of his hoody. She grabbed his shoe and recognised the tell-tale logo on the back of it, taking it into the unlit under-stairs cupboard she was able to confirm that it was glow in the dark.

She shouted up the stairs, 'Greg, where did you get your trainers from? I think Jackson would love a pair of those.'

'You can't buy them over here; I got them on holiday in Malta last year. They're incredibly expensive,' he shouted back; his voice slightly muffled as he was taking his T-shirt off over his head at the time. She took a photo of it for evidence then called to her companion.

★

Greg was startled to say the least when his wife walked into the bedroom and not Lucy. The two women had become quite friendly at the school over the last few weeks and Jane had asked Lucy to let her know if he ever contacted her again, so this morning she did.

That was the first of three things that went wrong for Greg; his wife was not happy and was whacking him with the shoe, screaming at him that he couldn't deny his intentions this time. He eventually came tripping down the stairs still trying to get his clothes back on whilst his wife threw his expensive trainers at him. She was grateful for Dom's business card that Lucy handed to her on their way out.

The second was when the police came to visit him to caution him for trespassing on Lucy's property; the third, when he was called into his editor's office for a warning and a demotion after Lucy had called to speak to his boss and threatened to sue them for unethical journalism and trespassing. She also said she wanted the newspapers that hadn't already been sold to be withdrawn and an apology printed in next week's copy.

Abbie sat open mouthed when Lucy explained the whole story to her over lunch,

'So hold on, let me get this straight, Greg did a search on you, found a picture of you and Jackson in the *Brumstoke News* with Jaeger from years ago and he sees that as evidence that he must be Jackson's dad. What planet is he on?'

'I know, apparently his editor was furious; he had allowed Greg to stand in for him whilst he was on holiday and would never have allowed such a load of tripe to have been printed. He assured me that Greg would be punished with an official warning and he's relieved that the very happily married Jaegar didn't sue them all too.'

'And all because Jackson told him he was his dad.'

'Yes and the fact he's been rooting through our bin for months and found a letter that Jackson was going to send to Jaegar telling him how much he admired him. He threw it away in the end and wrote one to Dom instead. Apparently there had been rumours of Jaegar having a love child and when Greg snooped in my garden he's obviously looked in my window and seen the recent picture of Jackson with Jaegar and the one of Dom in the Astronaut suit and assumed they were the same person. All because he was desperate for a scoop and because I wouldn't sleep with him.'

Abbie shook her head, 'Unbelievable, what a loser.'

'The worst bit was that during his digging around, Greg had spoken to my friend at the hotel. I thought she'd sold me out but apparently he tricked her into giving up the information. She phoned me to apologise but he'd pretended to be the police and she'd had to tell him that the only thing she knew was that Jackson's dad was married.'

Abbie tutted and rolled her eyes..

'I didn't know whether to laugh or cry,' Lucy continued, 'Greg had added two plus two and got nine. The woman on the phone earlier told me that mine and Jackson's identities had been kept secret for now but if I wanted to do a kiss and tell then they could pay me a lot of money and we would be in the nationals. Obviously I declined the offer and told the woman that there was not an ounce of truth in the story.'

'You mean you could have been famous.' Abbie joked.

Lucy laughed, 'I've had my fifteen minutes thanks to your picture of me and Dom, and now I'm happy to stay firmly in the background.'

*

After all the drama Lucy took Jackson to McDonald's for a treat. On the way out of Railway Cottage she saw the *Bramblewood Echo* van stop and a man got out to collect a bundle of the newspapers from the station shop. She almost wanted to high-five herself as empowerment lifted her insides. She had taken control.

Dom's words had begun to sink in and deep down she knew he was right. She couldn't bear the thought of Jack meeting Jackson, but this wasn't about her, it was about her little boy and what was important in his life.

As Jackson sat munching on his McDonald's and swinging his legs, Lucy decided to broach the subject with him.

'So, Jackson, you know how I said you can ask about your dad? Well now I'm ready to talk about it. I'm sorry it's taken me so long.' She chewed nervously on her coffee cup.

'That's okay, Mummy. I understand. You think he's going to take me away, but I'll never leave you.'

'I know you won't, my darling. But if there's anything you'd like to know, just ask.'

Jackson thought for a bit as he chewed his burger. 'How old is he?'

'Thirty four.'

'What colour eyes has he got?'

'Blue. Just like mine and yours.'

He smiled.

'Do I look like him?'

She screwed her eyes up to look at him and to make him laugh.

'Yes, you do a little bit.'

'Can I meet him?' He picked up a handful of fries and chomped them down. Not making eye contact with her.

Her heart leapt out of her chest and back in again, taking her breath away.

'Would you like to?'

She cupped his chin and turned his head to face her. His big blue eyes gazed up into hers. He looked a little embarrassed.

He nodded.

'Okay, honey, that's fine. We can sort that out.' She smiled at him, a smile that hid any fear or concern of what this could do to their relationship.

He smiled shyly back and she knew she was right to let her little boy make the choice of whether to see his dad or not.

When she called Jack later, she was surprised at the depth of emotion in his voice. A huge weight had finally been lifted off her shoulders.

Chapter 45

The man sitting across the table from her was hardly anything like the one she remembered. He'd filled out a lot and his hair was shorter and neater. He also wore glasses now with thick black frames. But when she saw those eyes, she knew it was unmistakably him, clear blue and now looking a little glassy with the emotion of the moment. He was nervously picking at a cardboard beer mat when they walked in; his wife was pretty, with dark curly hair and brown eyes. They both looked nervous. As they approached the table, he jumped up to get them drinks, knocking into the table as he did so.

Jackson was shyer than Lucy had ever seen him, and he kept looking down. Jack's wife Helena couldn't take her eyes off him.

'He's the image of you, Jack,' she said when her husband joined them with the round of drinks.

Jack wiped a tear from his eyes. 'Hi, Jackson,' he said, offering his hand to shake. 'It's so good to meet you. Is that a stegosaurus in your hand there?'

He nodded and shook his dad's hand.

Eventually as they all became a little more relaxed with each other Jackson began to let his guard down slightly and was excited when Jack asked him whether he wanted to play pool.

Grandad, Lucy and Helena made small talk as they watched them play.

'He is sorry for the way he treated you, you know, Lucy, and he's changed a lot. This means so much to him, to both of us. He's such a beautiful boy and Jack has a lot of making up to do.'

'Yes, he said so on the phone. To be honest if I had my way, we wouldn't be here but Jackson is so curious about him so I'm doing it for him.'

'I completely understand, but I'm glad you decided to bring him. Jack made a stupid mistake by misleading you.

'Don't you mean cheating?' Lucy snapped.

'Yes, you're right I don't want to make excuses, but he too was so young at the time. Ironically, we married young because we thought I was pregnant, but it was ovarian cysts, which I had to have removed and then it became impossible for us to get pregnant after that. When Jack told me about your relationship and that he thought Jackson was his, I was heartbroken as you can imagine but we got through it together and hopefully we can all move forward now. We've got such a lot of love to give.'

Lucy didn't quite know what to say. She twisted her bracelet round her wrist. Her face was pink. She suddenly realised how awkward this situation was. She had had an affair with this woman's husband, albeit unknowingly, but even so she felt awful for her. She had been horrified when she found out he was married. Even now she had an unpleasant thought that she were nothing more than a vessel that had produced a child for these people and that made her feel sick to her stomach.

Jackson and his dad came back to the table.

'I won, Mummy,' Jackson said excitedly before gulping his juice down. Lucy looked at Jack and he winked at her; he'd obviously let him win.

Grandad stood up. 'Jackson, why don't we ask Helena to come with us to order the food? And then we can check out the play area outside.'

Helena leapt at the chance. Jack and Lucy told them what they wanted to eat and watched them leave. They could hardly look at each other and sat in awkward silence for a bit. Helena and Grandad both monitored them from the bar before making their way outside with Jackson holding each of their hands.

He looked over at his mum and dad sitting together and smiled. It was something he never thought would happen.

'Lucy.' Jack took off his glasses and rubbed his eyes with the balls of his hands. 'As I said on the phone, I can't even begin to apologise for how I treated you. I was so stupid back then and I've been filled with regret for what I did to you ever since.'

Lucy wondered whether she was dreaming. She had waited so long to hear those words; it was all too surreal. She never would have imagined that one day she'd have been sitting here with Jack and discussing Jackson.

'I don't,' she said, her mind clearer than it had been for the last decade.

'Don't what?'

'I don't regret what you did because I've had the most amazing time with that little boy, and I was lucky enough to call him my very own and I didn't have to share him.'

'You've done an amazing job, Lucy. He's a fantastic kid.'

'I know,' she said. 'As I said to Helena if it was up to me I would keep him to myself forever but he was curious about you and it wouldn't have been fair of me to stop you from seeing each other.'

'I do appreciate it so much and I hope you'll allow me to share the burden with you now.'

'He's not a burden, he's a joy.'

'Sorry yes I didn't mean . . .'

'It's okay, I know what you meant and I'm happy for you to have a relationship but if you ever, ever hurt him you will have me to answer to.'

'I promise you I will never do that. Thank you so much for giving me a chance.'

The others soon returned. They enjoyed a meal together and discussed meeting up again soon. Jack said he would be grateful with whatever arrangements Lucy agreed to.

Chapter 46

Weddings at the Signal Box Café were a regular occurrence now; nearly every weekend was booked for two years solid. Couples were enamoured by such a unique venue and many wedding guests were booking their future nuptials there too after having such a wonderful time.

Lucy had made a real name for herself as a professional wedding planner and was always being approached by people in the business who wanted to be added to her wedding planner album.

Finn and Gracie had enjoyed their son's christening party there too and Lucy had made a special batch of Signal Box scouse for them as part of the buffet, as they had friends coming down from Liverpool.

Lucy was immensely proud of her achievements, especially when she found out that she had won the most unique wedding venue competition from the wedding magazine, which would bring a whole new lot of advertising in for them plus a beautiful engraved silver plaque that would look lovely on the wall.

She hadn't seen Dom for a little while as he'd been away on business and he'd given her and Jackson some space as he knew it would be a complicated process, arranging to meet up with Jack. She was looking forward to seeing him again. She felt different, more self-assured somehow. She had had to make some very grown-up decisions lately and she was pleased with the outcome.

★

Dom had been worried that he'd overstepped the mark when he suggested Jackson be allowed to contact his dad and so was relieved when Lucy had finally done it.

He got back from his business trip at lunchtime so texted Lucy to see where she was. She told him she was upstairs in the Signal Box Café having some peace and quiet, and for him to come over.

Lucy's heart leapt with excitement as she heard Dom coming up the stairs. She had been doing some paperwork in her favourite surroundings, her phone connected to the speaker playing relaxing music. His face lit up when he got to the top of the stairs and saw her sitting in one of the booths. She ran to him and threw herself into his arms, and they kissed hard and fast.

'Oh, wow what a welcome.' He laughed.

'I've missed you,' she said, her head slightly bowed, her eyes looking up into his shyly.

'Me, too,' he said.

She gestured for him to sit opposite her in one of the booths then went to the little bar to prepare some drinks. She came back with a coffee for her and as she sat down the little train came along the track with a bottle of beer in it for him. He laughed as he saw it coming towards him.

'That trick never gets old does it?'

She smiled at him. 'So how was the trip?'

'Not bad, we achieved what we needed to achieve so that was good. I couldn't wait to get back though. Anyway, much more importantly, how's Jackson getting on?'

'He's doing great. Jack and his wife were so grateful and respectful. He apologised profusely for the way he treated me back then but if you think about it he was only twenty-four. We were both stupid kids. They were lovely with Jackson when Grandad and I took him to meet them and Jackson was in his element. I wonder if I should have done it sooner and that makes me feel guilty.'

'You had to go with your gut instinct and there's no point worrying about that now because you can't change the past. You're an amazing mum and Jackson will never forget that.'

'I suppose you're right and I don't regret a thing because Jackson is the best thing that ever happened to me.'

'Ah and here's me thinking that I was the best thing that happened to you.' He laughed.

She noticed his eyes crinkled at the sides. She loved it when they did that. It showed he laughed a lot despite what she'd thought at their first few meetings.

'No,' she replied. 'You're the best thing that happened to *us*.'

He was touched and they leaned across the table toward each other for a kiss, which could finally lead to so much more.

Epilogue

Spring had arrived once more, and the cherry blossom trees were laden with their candyfloss pink petals waiting for the chance to release them.

The Signal Box Café had never looked so spectacular; it was as if it knew that this wedding was more special than any of the others. The bride was radiant in her white fitted dress; sequins delicately sewn into the bodice sparkled like diamonds. Dusky pink roses were entwined through her blonde curls, which fell loosely around her shoulders. As she walked up the aisle towards the flower arch where her future husband stood waiting for her, she felt like she wanted to pinch herself to make sure she wasn't dreaming.

She thought back to the proposal. Dom had taken her away to London for the weekend. They were sitting in elegant chairs in an expensive restaurant. Opulent chandeliers and a harpsichord playing added to the luxuriousness of the place. They had dined on lobster and the finest steaks and were then sipping crystal champagne, looking into each other's eyes.

'Oh no thank you, I couldn't manage another thing,' said Lucy as the waiter offered dessert.

'Let's just have a look, shall we?' suggested Dom winking at her in that sexy way that turned her knees to jelly.

The waiter wheeled over a spectacular silver dessert trolley, which had a crisp white cotton tablecloth concealing the bottom shelf. The top shelf was laden with tempting sweet creations.

'Ooh maybe some chocolate-dipped strawberries to share.' Lucy licked her lips in anticipation. Suddenly the cloth underneath the trolley started moving and Lucy jumped back in her chair grabbing hold of Dom's arm.

'What was that?' She looked from the waiter who was smiling to Dom whose face remained serious.

She soon found out when Jackson appeared from under the trolley giggling.

'Hi, Mum.' He was wearing a little black dicky bow, white shirt and black trousers just like the waiters were.

'Jackson, what are you doing here?' She laughed and hugged him, looking again at Dom for an answer.

'I'm helping Dom with something,' he replied looking up at Dom conspiratorially before handing him a small light blue box.

Dom knelt down on one knee and opened the box to reveal a stunning diamond ring. Lucy's hands flew to her face as a flush of adrenaline tingled around her body. Then her heart melted like a chocolate fountain when Jackson knelt on one knee beside Dom. The other diners oohed and aahed and Grandad and Violet appeared at the table.

'Lucy, I love you so much. You have taught me to never give up on happiness and you have certainly made me happier than I ever thought possible. I've asked for your dad's, your grandad's and Jackson's blessings, so will you marry me?'

Breathless and with tears trickling down her cheeks she looked at the two men in her life kneeling before her, her hands – still partly covering her face – were now trembling.

'Will you marry Dom please, Mummy?' added Jackson wobbling as he tried to balance on his one knee.

'Yes,' said Lucy. Her dream had come true. This man she loved had wanted to include Jackson in his proposal, as he knew how much that would mean to her. She also knew how much Jackson and Dom meant to each other now. They were inseparable. 'I'd love to marry you.'

Dom slipped the ring onto her finger, breathed a huge sigh of relief and pulled her into his arms for a kiss. The other diners applauded, and Jackson jumped up and down, clapping and giggling at them kissing.

It had been a magical moment. Grandad and Violet had taken Jackson out for dinner afterwards and Lucy and Dom had spent the most romantic night of their lives in the hotel.

Passing the guests, her arms linked through her dad's on one side and her grandad's on the other, Lucy was in awe of the special people that were in her life, people she had met since moving into Railway Cottage and who had provided her with such support when opening the Signal Box Café. She was grateful for every single one of them.

Memories flashed through her mind of sitting on a bench in Market Square all those years ago, her nana handing her some coins to throw into the fountain and make a wish. At the age of seven years old she had tossed the coin in the air watching it spin around, heads, tails, heads, tails and so on until it sploshed into the fountain.

'I wish that . . .'

'Oh no,' said her nana softly. 'You mustn't say it out loud or it won't come true.'

Lucy thought her wish instead although her lips moved as the words were being formed in her mind.

'I wish that one day I will marry Dominic Cavendish.'

The memory made her smile. She was wearing her nan's sapphire ring as her something old and borrowed and blue, although she did also have a sexy garter on with a blue ribbon but that would be for Dom's eyes only. She looked shyly into her husband's soft grey eyes, which were watching her in awe as she approached him. He looked so handsome and proud in his morning suit as he stood waiting for her, his best man on one side and his little best man Jackson in his matching suit on the other.

She felt like the most beautiful being on the planet when Dom looked at her. The ice that had formed around her heart when Jack had broken it, had now melted away and been replaced by a fiery passion that burned brightly with her feelings for Dom.

As they took their vows, they couldn't take their eyes off each other, each willing the other not to stumble over the words, each smiling at the promise of a wonderfully happy future together, they held hands throughout.

Abbie and Gracie made beautiful bridesmaids; their dusky pink dresses matched the flowers in Lucy's hair and bouquet and those in the flower arch and garlands that decorated the room.

Abbie followed her friend along the aisle. Her heart sang for two people she loved so much. When she was younger she would pretend that she and Lucy were sisters and from today onwards they would be; she had never seen her brother like this before. He smiled and laughed pretty much all the time now and he looked at Lucy as though she were a goddess and as though it pained him to tear his eyes away from her. She enjoyed the scene in front of her, the bride wearing a beautiful dress. A dazzling veil that was attached to the fresh flowers in her hair draped softly down her back.

★

Dominic Cavendish stood proudly in front of the elegant heart-shaped flower arch, which was entwined with dusky pink roses, gypsophila and greenery. He held on to Jackson's hand and squeezed it as the music started playing the bridal chorus. As his bride appeared, he saw Jackson look at his mummy with total wonderment on his face. She looked like a real princess. He waved to her then looked up at Dom, his eyes shining brightly with excitement. Dom winked at him; his heart bled for this little guy who looked at him with those piercing blue eyes he'd inherited from his mum.

He'd never expected to get married ever again and could quite happily erase his first attempt from his memory banks. He now realised that having reconnected with Lucy that there was in fact plenty of room in his life for hearts and flowers and a little boy who'd melted his heart. This was a special day for Jackson too as this was the day that Dom would sign the adoption papers. When they had discussed the wedding and Lucy had been practising signing her new name, 'Lucy Cavendish' on a notepad, Jackson had asked her a question. They discussed it together and when Dom came home he was so surprised when Jackson asked him if he could adopt him.

'But what about Jack, your real dad?'

'He's just my birth dad. You're my real dad and anyway I've already got his name and now I want yours too.' Dominic hugged the little boy to his chest and tried not to let him see the tears fall from his eyes. 'Mummy checked with Jack and he's fine with it as long as it means I can still see him.'

Lucy had clarified, 'He didn't think he had a right to stop it if it was what you and Jackson wanted.' Tears were cascading down her cheeks too.

Dominic wiped his eyes with the back of his hand. 'I would be honoured to adopt you, son,' he said, ruffling his hair.

That had been the most emotional moment of Dom's life up until now.

Even though he'd seen Lucy in wedding attire before at the photo shoot, nothing could have prepared him for how stunning she looked at this moment. The dress was tasteful and elegant and flattered her amazing curves. Tears sprang to his eyes as he saw her beautiful face. She radiated happiness as if all her dreams had come true at once. He saw her look at Jackson and blow a kiss to him, her smile beaming wider on seeing his face, then she looked at him, deep into his eyes, making his heart do a flip, and neither of them looked away as she came to join him.

Today he was a very happy man.

The cake that stood at the side of the room was another of Camilla's creations. It was made up of three tiers with a trickle of dusky pink roses spilling from the top and gathering at the bottom. On the top stood a little replica of the Signal Box Café, the groom carrying the bride in his arms, and a little boy with glasses cuddling a shaggy dog of indeterminate breed.

As the guests mingled with champagne, Dave the photographer had taken the small bridal party over to the cherry blossom trees along the river. Their arrival was heralded by a trail of golden daffodils that danced delightfully in a gentle gust of wind.

Abbie felt a sense of déjà vu and asked Dave if he would mind if she took some pictures too. The sun was starting to set, the sky a rhapsody of colour, a burst of tangerine streaked with marshmallow pinks and a lilac hue.

As if on cue the blossom petals started to fall, spinning and swirling as they caught on the light breeze, enjoying their moment of glory before softly landing in the bride and groom's hair like nature's confetti.

'And now can we have one of the groom kissing the bride,' requested Abbie.

Lucy flushed slightly with excitement, her cheeks almost the same shade as the dusky pink roses that were entwined in her golden curls.

'Now I can assure you that this will most definitely NOT be the last one,' said Dom as he pulled his beautiful bride into his arms. His hand reached into her hair, his thumb gently stroking her perfectly contoured cheek. Lucy immediately melted into his kiss. After reluctantly pulling apart they made their way back to the Signal Box Café to continue celebrating with their family and friends.

Abbie hung back a little to take a picture of them as they walked away. The sun was setting, casting a beautiful pink and orange glow behind the Signal Box Café. The bride and groom walked towards it hand in hand. The groom had his arm around the little boy's shoulder, pulling him in close, and the bride was holding the lead of a crazy shaggy dog with a dusky pink ribbon around his neck. A light gust of wind sent the pink cherry blossom petals swirling around them as if in a snow globe before settling on the soft carpet of pink. They walked on to start their future as a family.

Acknowledgements

They say it takes a village to raise a child and I must say it takes a whole community of book lovers to make an author. I'll start by saying a huge thank you to my favourite author Milly Johnson and Sara-Jade Virtue as without #TeamMilly which introduced me to the wonderful world of book blogging, I'm certainit would have taken me a whole lot longer to get here. It's an absolute honour that Milly has quoted on my debut novel, it really doesn't get any better than that.

To my gorgeous family whom I love more than anything in the world, Johnna, Jake, Damon and my little editor Lydia who would sit with me every day after school and let me read out what I'd written and correct me occasionally even when I thought she wasn't really listening. I'm so very grateful to all of you for being there for me. I love how proud you all are of me and I'm just as proud of each of you. I hope I've showed you that you can achieve whatever you put your mind to and that dreams can and do come true.

To my first readers and wonderful friends, Kay Davies, my Auntie Margie Morris, Sandra Woods, Katie Nash and Barbara Stone, thank you for the amazing friendship, love and support and the enjoyment of my stories, for encouraging me and giving me the confidence to believe in myself that I really could do this. I wish I could mention all my fantastic friends and family that I feel very blessed to have.

Thanks to Victoria Oundjian for falling in love with Lucy and Dom's story and Olivia and the fabulous team at Orion Dash for all their hard work in bringing my dream to life. Not only did they make everything so easy for me during edits, but I mean what a cover, it literally took my breath away when I saw it. I couldn't have asked for a more beautiful image to represent the old signal box near where I live.

After years of book blogging, I have made so many fabulous author and blogger friends and have literally been having the time of my life at all the fantastic events. It's been so strange to be on the receiving end of the book love and have these wonderful people now supporting me on my writing journey, so I'd like to say a huge thank you to some of the loveliest people I've met in the book world and who were kind enough to help with my blog tour; Linda Hill, Anne Williams, Debbie Johnston, Kim Nash, Vicki Bowles, Lara Marshall, Heidi Swain, Julie Boon, Karen Cocking. Claire Knight, Lynne Shelby, Jo Robertson, Laura Bambrey, Charlene Wedgner, Kirsty Sibley, Dawn Crooks and Kelly Rufus.

I would also like to mention my late friend and mentor Violet Geddes and her husband Dougie for inspiring such wonderful characters. You will never be forgotten.

Finally, I would like to say a huge thank you to the Romantic Novelists' Association which is a wonderfully supportive organisation. Since being a member, I have met so many amazing people and had such fantastic times at conferences and parties and I've learnt a lot too. I need to say a special thank you to my fabulous friends from the London Chapter, the Muses, who have been an incredible source of inspiration to me as well as making me laugh until I scream. I'd just like to finish with words of advice from another author friend Samantha Tonge, 'Never Give Up!'

I hope you enjoy *Wedding Bells at the Signal Box Café*. If you do please tell your friends and maybe leave a review on Amazon. You can find out more about me on my website; annettehannah.com and follow me on twitter @annettehannah and Instagram @Annette.hannah

Thanks for reading

Annette x

Printed in August 2021
by Rotomail Italia S.p.A., Vignate (MI) - Italy